BOMBERS
OF
WORLD WAR II

BOMBERS
OF
WORLD WAR II

Edited by
David Donald

Grange
BOOKS

This edition first published in 1998 for Grange Books
An imprint of Grange Books plc
The Grange
Kingsnorth Industrial Estate
Hoo, nr Rochester
Kent ME3 9ND

This material was previously published in 1990 as part
of the reference set *Airplane*.

ISBN: 1-84013-149-7

Editorial and design by
Brown Packaging Books Ltd
Bradley's Close
74–77 White Lion Street
London N1 9PF

Picture credits
TRH Pictures: 6, 24, 30, 38, 52, 182

Printed in the Czech Republic
60205

Contents

Junkers Ju 88

With the possible exception of the Mosquito, the Ju 88 was the most versatile combat aircraft of all time. Designed as a specialised high-speed bomber, it proved ideally suited to virtually every other kind of combat mission, and more were built than all other Luftwaffe bombers combined.

With the exception of close dogfighting, it is difficult to think of any military duty of the World War II era for which the Ju 88 was not adapted. The original missions were level- and dive-bombing, but to these were added long-range escort, night-fighting, intruding, tank-busting, anti-ship attack, destruction of Allied maritime aircraft, anti-submarine warfare, supply dropping, towing, training, transport, reconnaissance, torpedo dropping, close support, pathfinding and pilotless (missile) attack. Direct developments were the Ju 188 and Ju 388 (the Ju 288 was a completely new design). Today's industry may wistfully note that the number of Ju 88 prototypes and development aircraft exceeded 100, which is about 10 times the total production run of some modern aircraft.

Versatility was the last thing considered at the start of the programme. Indeed, in 1935 the RLM (German air ministry) doubted the practicality of a *Kampfzerstörer* (war destroyer) able to fly bomber, bomber-destroyer and reconnaissance missions. It issued a replacement requirement for a simple *Schnellbomber* (fast bomber) to fly at 500 km/h (311 mph) and carry a bombload of up to 800 kg (1,765 lb). Junkers went flat-out to win, even hiring two designers who had pioneered advanced stressed-skin structures in the USA, despite the fact that the company had already moved on from corru-

gated skin and produced numerous smooth-skinned prototypes. In the first three months of 1936 two proposals were submitted, in the form of the Ju 85 with a twin-finned tail and the Ju 88 with a single rudder well aft of the elevators. Competition came from the Henschel Hs 127 and Messerschmitt Bf 162 (the latter being falsely publicised in 1940 as a major Luftwaffe type, the 'Jaguar') which were eliminated by late 1937 for various reasons.

The Ju 88 V1 (prototype 1) was flown by chief test pilot Kindermann on 21 December 1936 with registration D-AQEN. Flying was based at Dessau but no announcement was made and the type remained unknown to British intelligence, as did the Focke-Wulf Fw 190 in 1939. The Ju 88 V1 crashed at the start of its high-speed testing, but not before it had shown the design to be thoroughly sound with promising performance. The Ju 88 V2 retained DB 600Aa engines with distinctive annular cooling radiators, but the Ju 88 V3 switched to Junkers' own Jumo 211A and had full military equipment

One of the most numerous versions, and the basis for many others, the Ju 88A-4 four-seat bomber introduced the long-span wing and also an induction cooling-duct fairing under the engines; these Ju 88A-4s were pictured with III/LG 1 in mid-1942. Lehrgeschwader 1 (instructional group 1) was based in the Mediterranean.

Stooks of corn in the field below are hard to explain in this picture of the Ju 88 V1 (first prototype) because its flying career extended only from December 1936 until the following Spring! Note the swivelling ciné camera in the position reserved for the upper rear gun and the separate oil coolers under the DB 600s.

Swinging the compass of what is believed to have been the first Ju 88A-1 produced at Bernburg; the date was probably June 1939. Note the tall single-leg main gears with large tyres, three-bladed VDM propellers and short-span wings with ailerons extending to the tips. Colours were black-green and very pale blue.

with a raised cabin roof, dorsal machine-gun, fixed gun firing ahead and internal bomb load of 500 kg (1,102 lb) aimed by a sight in a chin blister. The Ju 88 V4 introduced the familiar four-seat crew compartment with a large 'insect-eye' nose glazed with 20 flat panes and a ventral gondola with an aft-firing MG 15. Last of the pure prototypes was the Ju 88 V5 (D-ATYU) shaped for minimum drag and flown in April 1938. On 9 March 1939 it set a startling world 1000-km (621-mile) circuit record with 2000-kg (4,409-lb) load at 517 km/h (321.25 mph). The Ju 88 was thereby revealed to the world, and incidentally credit for its design was heaped entirely upon chief designer Ernst Zindel; the Americans were not mentioned.

The Ju 88 V6, flown in June 1938, introduced one of the type's distinctive features. Previous prototypes had had American-style twin-oleo main gear units with electric retraction, but the Ju 88 V6 introduced a bold gear with tall single legs in which shocks were absorbed by a *Ringfeder* (ring spring) assembly of high-tensile steel rings with tapered profiles which expanded radially under compressive loads, bounce being prevented by the friction as the rings pushed their way apart. Retraction was hydraulic, the wheels rotating 90° to lie flat in the rear of the nacelles. Thus, though the wheels were made much larger, with low-pressure tyres able to operate from mud and sand at weights double that of the Ju 88 V1, the nacelle became slimmer and drag was reduced. The landing gear later needed patient refinement, but by 1940 was an outstanding piece of engineering.

Later pre-war prototypes introduced large slatted dive brakes under the outer wings and four bomb-carriers under the inner wings, each stressed for an SC500 (500-kg/1,102-lb) bomb but normally limited to SC100 (100-kg/220-lb) weapons when the enlarged pair of internal bays was loaded to its limit of 28 SC50 (50-kg/110-lb) bombs. This total load of 1800 kg (3,968 lb) was impressive enough, but testing at Dessau and Tarnewitz cleared the pre-production Ju 88A-0 for overload missions with four external SC500s, increasing total bomb load to 2400 kg (5,291 lb). At the same time, the Ju 88's capabilities were leading to problems which included wing-spar failure, main-leg failure and other faults caused by overloading. All were cured, but the service-test Erprobungskommando 88 crews had many 'hairy' incidents in the Spring of 1939 whilst testing the Ju 88A-0 batch under operational conditions, and even the production Ju 88A-1 which reached the Luftwaffe in August 1939 had to be flown carefully, with aerobatics prohibited.

The engine of the Ju 88A-1 was the 895-kW (1,200-hp) Jumo 211B-1, one of the classic Junkers series of inverted-Vee 12-cylinder units with direct fuel injection. In several early prototypes and Ju 88A-0s, it drove a four-bladed propeller, but the production standard propellers on almost all subsequent versions had three blades of high

solidity (large chord) which increased further with the introduction of the more powerful Jumo 213 and BMW 801 engines. From the start the blades were fully feathering and fitted with alcohol de-icing. The annular radiators used on all liquid-cooled Ju 88s were particularly neat. Usually the top centre matrix was the oil cooler, and airflow was controlled by annular gills. As in many German aircraft of the period, the engines were hung on two giant Elektron (magnesium alloy) forging beams with lower compression braces, all picking up on four rubber-damped mounts on the firewall at the leading edge. The nacelles were thus unusually long, the Ju 88 becoming universally known as *die Dreifinger* (the three-finger).

Limited fuel capacity

Like almost all Luftwaffe aircraft, the Ju 88 was designed for use in tactical warfare where ranges were moderate. Normal fuel capacity was thus only 1677 litres (369 Imp gal) in tanks between the spars inboard and outboard of the engines, though the capacious bomb bays were plumbed in many versions, including most bombers, for extra tanks bringing the total up to 3575 litres (786.4 Imp gal). The wings had considerable dihedral from the roots and the entire trailing edge was formed by patented 'double-wing' slotted surfaces drooped as flaps for landing. The outer sections also served as ailerons, and like the other control surfaces were fabric-covered. The wing had hot-air de-icing, while in most versions the forward-mounted tailplane had pulsating pneumatic de-icers.

The crew compartment was typically Germanic, and while British propaganda claimed the four men were grouped together to bolster their morale, in fact the arrangement was in many ways cramped and inefficient. The pilot sat high on the left with a stick having a two-pronged aileron wheel, and in dive-bombing he did the sighting through a sight swung down from the roof, the usual angle being 60°. Level bombing was carried out with a sight in the nose by the bomb-aimer low on the right, who in some versions sat higher and doubled as second pilot. Behind on the left was the engineer who manned the upper rear armament, while alongside him on the right was the radio (later also radar) operator who looked after the lower rear gun. The pilot, engineer and lower rear gun position were armoured.

It was clear as early as 1938 that the Ju 88 was potentially a great aircraft, far in advance of the Dornier Do 17 or Heinkel He 111, and plans for production were widespread. Dessau, the HQ, played little part in production, fuselages being assigned to Aschersleben, wings to Halberstadt, tails to Leopoldshall and assembly and test to Bernburg. Other giant plants brought into the programme included Arado at Brandenburg-Neuendorf, Dornier at Wismar, Heinkel at Oranienburg, Henschel at Berlin-Schönefeld and Volkswagen at Wolfsburg. By 1944 many other plants were contributing parts or complete air-

Specification
Junkers Ju 88G-1
Type: three-seat night-fighter
Powerplant: two 1268-kW (1,700-hp) BMW 801D-2 14-cylinder radials
Performance: maximum speed 573 km/h (356 mph) with SN-2 but no upward-firing guns; maximum endurance on internal fuel 4¾ hours; service ceiling 8840 m (29,000 ft)
Weights: empty (typical) 9081 kg (20,020 lb); normal loaded 13095 kg (28,870 lb); overload 14690 kg (32,385 lb)
Dimensions: span 20 m (65 ft 7½ in); length (excluding radar) 14.54 m (47 ft 8½ in), (including SN-2 aerials) 16.5 m (54 ft 1½ in); height 4.85 m (15 ft 11 in); wing area 54.5 m² (586.63 sq ft)
Armament: aircraft illustrated, four 20-mm MG 151 cannon in ventral compartment each with 200 rounds

In the spring of 1944 RAF heavy bombers were being hacked down in droves. The cause was ascribed to concentrations of flak (AAA), and the bombers continued to cruise through the German sky like so many lighthouses, emitting up to three sets of radar signals, whilst so blind underneath that there was not so much as a porthole, let alone a gun. The fact that most of the losses were due to night-fighters emerged gradually, and it was near the end of the war before it was belatedly realised that many of these formated under the bomber and fired upwards in a perfect no-deflection shot. The most formidable night-fighter was almost unknown until, by a fantastic piece of luck, the crew of 4R+UR, a Ju 88G-1 of 7/NJG 2, became hopelessly lost on the night of 12/13 July 1944. They had been looking for minelaying Stirlings and had suffered compass failure. Eventually they homed on a radio beacon which seemed in the right direction, found an airfield and landed. They had brought the vital SN-2 radar and FuG 227 Flensburg to RAF Woodbridge, Suffolk. Unfortunately their aircraft did not have upward-firing guns but just four MG 151 cannon in the ventral box. The Hirschgeweih (stag's antlers) aerials of the SN-2 can be seen on the nose (a very few expert pilots had them on the rear fuselage). Wing dipole aerials received emissions from RAF Monica tail-warning radars and fed them to the Flensburg direction finder. The only things lacking were schräge Musik guns and Naxos for homing on H₂S.

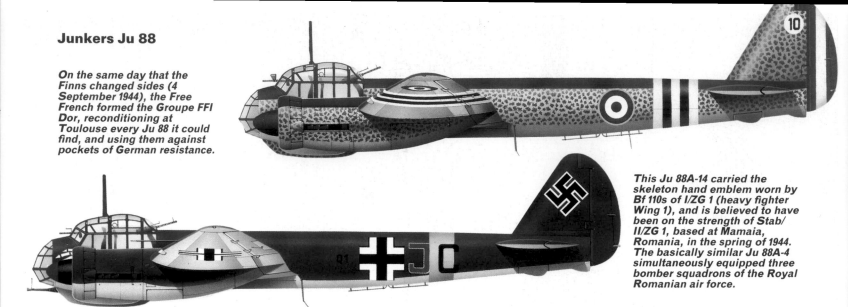

On the same day that the Finns changed sides (4 September 1944), the Free French formed the Groupe FFI Dor, reconditioning at Toulouse every Ju 88 it could find, and using them against pockets of German resistance.

This Ju 88A-14 carried the skeleton hand emblem worn by Bf 110s of I/ZG 1 (heavy fighter Wing 1), and is believed to have been on the strength of Stab/ II/ZG 1, based at Mamaia, Romania, in the spring of 1944. The basically similar Ju 88A-4 simultaneously equipped three bomber squadrons of the Royal Romanian air force.

other glazed-nose Ju 88s served with several satellite air forces including those of Romania and Hungary. In letter sequence the next family is the Ju 88G, though chronologically this did not emerge until mid-1943. By this time the overburdened C-series night-fighters were suffering heavy casualties caused by deterioration in low-speed handling, and a Ju 88R-2 (described later) was modified with the large tail of the Ju 188, becoming the Ju 88 V58. The completely revised armament comprised six MG 151s, two staggered at −3° nose-down angle in the right-hand side of the nose and the other four angled down at −5° in a box under the left-hand side of the belly. A single MG 131 was provided for upper rear defence.

In the production G-series the two right-hand side guns were removed, as they blinded the pilot, and most used the ventral tray plus two upward-firing MG 151s. The long endurance, tremendous performance and wealth of electronic devices made the G-series extremely formidable aircraft which wrought terrible execution on RAF heavies and would have posed a very serious threat had they appeared earlier in the war. As it was, they were available in numbers only from mid-1944, by which time output was falling, and only about 800 could be completed by the final collapse. Final versions had liquid-cooled engines and advanced centimetric radars.

The Ju 88H family was initially ultra-long-range reconnaissance aircraft with the fuselage stretched to 17.647 m (57 ft 3¾ in). The Ju 88H-1 had *Höhentwiel* radar, while the Ju 88H-2 had a devastating battery of six MG 151s for use against aircraft or ships far out in the Atlantic. The Ju 88H-4 was further stretched to 20.38 m (66 ft 10½ in) but found use only as the radar-equipped lower component of the *Führungsmaschine* (guiding machine) long-range pathfinder which had an extra main gear and a *doppelreiter* (overwing-tanked) Fw 190A-8 riding on top as escort!

Only a few dozen were delivered of the various P-series Ju 88s

with anti-tank or anti-bomber guns. Related to these was a test aircraft, the Ju 88N or Ju 88Nbwe, with Professor Dornberger's six-barrel launcher of 21-cm or 28-cm (8.27-in or 11.02-in) rocket shells.

The Ju 88R-1 was a Ju 88C-6b night-fighter powered by BMW 801MA engines, while the Ju 88R-2 had BMW 801Ds. This series was produced in parallel with the C-series from early 1943 until about a year later, when it was replaced by the G-series.

The S-series stemmed from Ju 88 prototype V93 of late 1942, which resulted from the urgent need to make the basic bomber faster, to restore a good chance of returning from a daylight mission. The Ju 88 V93 was powered by BMW 801D engines and given a smooth glazed nose for minimum drag, the underwing carriers being removed. Most production versions had engines giving even greater power at high altitude, and the ventral gondola and most armour was removed to increase performance further. Speed reached about 612 km/h (380 mph) with either the BMW or Jumo engines, still slower than the later G-series night-fighters. Parallel reconnaissance aircraft were of the T-series, not built in quantity.

Not included in the variants list, the *Mistel* missiles were (usually war-weary) Ju 88s rebuilt as pilotless missiles, with the nose replaced by an extremely large warhead, usually a 3800-kg (8,380-lb) hollow-charge device with a long stand-off fuse. The aircraft were flown to their targets by a pilot in a Bf 109 or Fw 190 carried above the Ju 88 on struts with a release system operated from the fighter cockpit. By 1945 Ju 88G-10s and Ju 88H-4s were being turned into *Mistel* aircraft on the assembly line, never flying as ordinary aircraft. Including them in the 355 'fighters' built in 1945, the total Ju 88 production is usually calculated to be 14,780, including 104 prototypes.

Opposite: A Ju 88 crewman strolls from his aircraft after 'another successful mission', according to the propaganda. The yellow spinners denote the Eastern Front.

First of the radar-equipped night-fighter versions, the Ju 88C-6b was powered by 999-kW (1,340-hp) Jumo 211J engines and fitted with FuG 202 Lichtenstein BC radar. The radar receiver aerials were on the wings, and this Ju 88C-6b also has wing dipoles further back for FuG 227 Flensburg which homed-in on RAF tail-warning radars.

The Ju 88P series was uniformly clumsy, sluggish and vulnerable, though the aircraft were well protected against ground fire. This example was a Ju 88P-3, with two BK 3,7 (Flak 38) high-velocity guns of 37-mm calibre housed in a large ventral box, with the guns offset to the left. Similar aircraft were used against bombers.

*Sukhoi's **UTB**, also commonly called **UTB**-2, was a crew trainer based on a simplified and lightened Tu-2 airframe but with much less powerful engines. Roughly 100 of the 500-plus built were assigned to the newly reconstituted Polish air force, one being shown in standard post-war dark green and natural metal finish.*

63 Mainwheel doors
64 Exhaust gill
65 Centre-hinged main bomb bay doors
66 Forward bomb shackle
67 Single 2,205-lb (1000-kg) GP bomb
68 Access panel
69 Starboard mainwheel
70 Mainwheel fork
71 Aft bomb bay bulkhead
72 Radio operator's position
73 Dorsal glazing
74 Dorsal 12.7-mm UBT machine-gun
75 Fuselage construction
76 Control cable shroud
77 Stub aerial
78 Ventral gunner's couch
79 Aft crew entry hatch
80 Ventral gunner's aiming periscope
81 Ammunition tank
82 Beam observation window
83 Ventral glazing
84 Ventral 12.7-mm UBT machine-gun
85 Retractable tailwheel
86 Tailwheel doors
87 Tailwheel retraction mechanisms
88 Aft navigation light
89 Tailplane construction
90 Aerial
91 Starboard tailfin
92 Rudder post
93 Rudder tab
94 Starboard rudder

© Pilot Press Limited

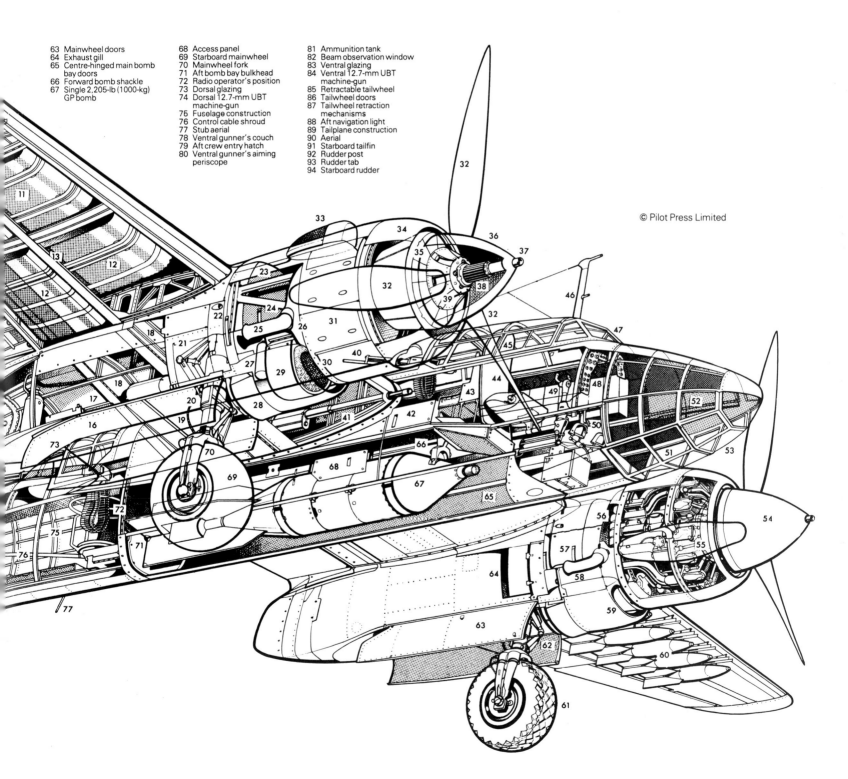

Tupolev Tu-2

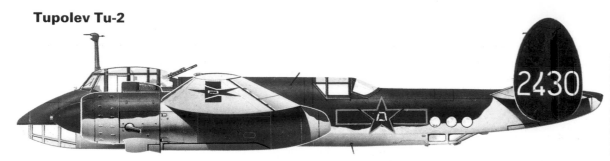

In 1949-50 a number, probably about 100, of regular **Tu-2S** bombers were transferred to China to form the nucleus of the People's Republic's offensive air power. Nearly all these aircraft (at least 75) saw action in the Korean War, though they were not used to great effect and several were shot down.

ASh-82) radial, initially rated at 1104 kW (1,480 hp). Despite the need to produce 1,500 new drawings in most adverse circumstances, the task was done and the aircraft back in the air on 1 November 1941.

Costly delays

Next came the Aircraft 103V production prototype, flown by Vasyakin on 15 December 1941 and as far as possible simplified to ease mass production. Development continued during early 1942 on the Aircraft 103S (*seriinyi*, or series production), the ANT-61, though one questions whether or not the many changes were really worth a delay of two more years before large numbers of aircraft were available. The 1268-kW (1,700-hp) ASh-82FNV was fitted with injection carburettors allowing prolonged negative *g*, the movable guns all became heavy-calibre UBTs, the vertical tails were again made taller, and the lower rear gunner was given three portholes on each side. By this time a major production scheme was being worked out, and in early November 1942 the first three aircraft were sent to the Kalinin Front, where the 3rd Air Army went into raptures and asked for more.

It is generally considered that Aircraft 100716, some way down the line from the first Aircraft 103S (no. 100308, though numbers were far from consecutive) was the first true production machine, the designation Tu-2 being bestowed in January 1943. So brilliantly were the Tu-2s performing that as well as being allowed to use the 'Tu' designation, the designer and his team were released from detention, which made a big difference to the efficiency of the programme. Tupolev was awarded his first Stalin Prize in June 1943. The production Tu-2 had different propellers, no rocket rails, simpler nose glazing, detachable wingtips and many further revisions to the armour and auxiliary systems. The forward-firing cannon were not only retained but often put to good use, and many was the German fighter bounced from astern by a Tu-2, which like most Soviet front-line aircraft spent most of their airborne time at full throttle. Maximum bombload was 3000 kg (6,614 lb), all in the main bay, the largest bomb being the FAB-1000 of 1000-kg (2,205-lb) size.

Many small modifications still crept in, such as slimmer cowlings with 28 small valve-gear blisters, single rear side portholes, and many variations in the engine air inlets, exhaust and oil coolers. Further delays were caused by the stopping of production at GAZ-166 and the concentration of assembly back at GAZ-156, and it was spring 1944 before the Tu-2 was making itself felt against the enemy. Only 1,111 were received by front-line units by the end of the war in Europe, though production continued to 1948 with 2,527 delivered, excluding the mass of variants listed separately.

An early series aircraft, this **Tu-2S** is one of a small number with extended engine air inlet ducts above the cowlings. It also has an early form of engine exhaust system, similar to that on the Lavochkin La-5 fighter and without single projecting pipes on each side. Note the slightly extended chord of the outer ailerons.

The **ANT-63P** carried service designation **Tu-1**, an odd number, because it was a fighter. Based on the ANT-68, it had even more powerful 1454-kW (1,950-hp) AM-43V engines driving four-bladed propellers and despite devastating armament reached 641 km/h (398 mph). It was too late for the war and remained a prototype.

Tupolev Tu-2 variants

ANT-58: original prototype, also called **Samolyet 103, Tu-58** and **FB** (*frontovoi bombardirovshchik*, or frontal bomber); two AM-37 engines, crew of three, speed 635 km/h (395 mph)

ANT-59: improved prototype, also called **Samolyet 103U**, at first with AM-37 engines, later with ASh-82; crew of four and many other changes

ANT-60: simplified production prototype, also called **Samolyet 103V**

ANT-61: initial production model, also called **103S**; UBT movable guns, ASh-82FNV engines, other changes included removal of dive brakes

ANT-61: Tu-2S mainstream production aircraft; total 2,527

ANT-61: Tu-2M modified prototypes with 1417-kW (1,900-hp) ASh-83 engines driving four-bladed paddle propellers (some with welded hollow steel blades)

ANT-62: Tu-2D (*dalnyi*, or long-range) with totally redesigned forward fuselage, long-span outer wings with greatly increased tankage, wide-span tail and other changes; this strategic bomber version had a long nose with much more room for the navigator to sit comfortably ahead of the cockpit, which housed two pilots side-by-side; span 22.06 m (72 ft 4½ in), gross weight 13340 kg (29,409 lb), speed at height 531 km/h (330 mph)

Tu-2/104: first radar-equipped all-weather interceptor in Soviet Union; new forward fuselage, with pilot and radar operator only, and two 23-mm VYa-23 guns in ventral fairings; flown by A. D. Perelyet and engineer L. L. Kerber on 18 July 1944

ANT-63: also called **Tu-2SDB**, two widely differing prototypes for an SDB (fast day bomber), one a two-seater with AM-39 liquid-cooled V-12 engines, the other a three-seater with 1394-kW (1,870-hp) AM-39Fs, with new main gears with single legs attached to the inner ends of the axles and many other changes; speed 645 km/h (401 mph)

Tu-2 Paravan: two aircraft tested with a giant (6-m/20-ft) probe cantilevered ahead of the nose carrying cables attached to the wingtips where cable-cutters were installed; flown successfully into barrage balloon cables September 1944

Tu-2/18/11: prototype possibly fitted with high-lift flaps (no information apart from numerical data showing short take-off and landing)

Tu-2SH: *shturmovik* (armoured attack) version flown 1944; extensive armour and anti-infantry installation of PPSh-300 dispensing 300 grenades; later (1946) aircraft for use against armour had two seats and forward-firing armament of two 20-mm ShVAK, two 37-mm NS-37 and two 45-mm NS-45

Tu-2K: designation from *katapult* for two prototypes in 1944 for tests with ejection seats

Tu-2G: designation from *gruzovoi* (cargo) for several aircraft modified for carrying bulky cargo, such as GAZ-67b scout cars slung externally, and also for parachuting supplies

Tu-2N: one series aircraft used as flying test-bed for imported Rolls-Royce Nene 1 turbojet carried in pod under forward fuselage; kerosene tank in bomb bay, comprehensive instrumentation

ANT-68: Tu-10 second-generation bomber with liquid-cooled engines in airframe same size as Tu-2 but strengthened; prototype with 1380-kW (1,850-hp) AM-39FN-2 engines flown 19 May 1945; small series, believed 50, built post-war with 1491-kW (2,000-hp) AM-42 engines, erroneous designation Tu-4 applied (already chosen for B-29 copy)

Tu-2T: various prototypes for torpedo-bombing, first two modified from 1944 production line carrying 45-36-AN torpedo under each wing root; second aircraft had bomb-bay tanks and range of 3800 km (2,361 miles) with torpedoes

UTB: greatly simplified aircraft designed by team under P. O. Sukhoi as crew trainer, with 522-kW (700-hp) ASh-21 engines in short cowls driving two-bladed propellers; dual side-by-side pilot controls, dual side-by-side navigator stations facing aft and new access catwalk to radio/gunner station (no lower rear position); practice bombs carried externally; at least 500 delivered in 1947, 100 for Poland

ANT-67: long-range bomber derived from Tu-2D but with 1417-kW (1,900-hp) Charomskii ACh-39BF diesel engines, five seats, extended-chord ailerons (standard on all these long-span versions)

ANT-62T: torpedo version of long-span series, first flown 2 January 1947

ANT-63P: Tu-1, the odd number being used because the type was a fighter, a long-range three-seat escort with provision for radar, using airframe of Tu-10 (ANT-68) but with 1454-kW (1,950-hp) AM-43V engines driving four-bladed propellers, no lower rear position and 'solid'

nose with two NS-45 (45-mm) guns, plus two NS-23 in wing roots, twin rear UBT and 1000-kg (2,205-lb) bombload; speed 641 km/h (398 mph) on test from 30 December 1946

Tu-2R, Tu-2F and Tu-6: all designations of dedicated reconnaissance versions, early examples (1943) being conversions; by 1944 standard aircraft was **ANT-64** (Tu-2F) with new long-span airframe as ANT-62 with navigator in nose; at least one rebuilt in 1947 with giant mapping radar

Tu-2RShR: single aircraft with 57-mm RShR gun in lower part of forward fuselage, with large muzzle brake projecting ahead; crew of two, the navigator/radio operator being required to reload the gun

ANT-65: Tu-2DB, a further development of long-range bomber series with advanced version of long-span airframe, 1641-kW (2,200-hp) AM-44TK turbocharged engines and excellent speed of 578 km/h (359 mph) considering gross weight of 16450 kg (36,265 lb)

ANT-69: Tu-8, the ultimate development was this excellent aircraft, last of the long-range bomber variants, but neither Tupolev nor the WS showed interest in view of much larger Tu-4 (B-29); two 1380-kW (1,850-hp) ASh-82FN engines, five seats, 4500-kg (9,921-lb) bomb load, new defensive armament with five new B-20 cannon and rear sighting stations later used on Tu-80 and Tu-85; first flown December 1946

Though it did not come into its own as a bomber until 1944, from 1941 Tu-2s saw action in every Soviet campaign, including operations in Manchuria against the Japanese Kwantung army in 1945.

Tupolev Tu-2

Specification
Tupolev Tu-2S

Type: medium bomber
Powerplant: two 1380-kW (1,850-hp) Shvetsov ASh-82FN 14-cylinder radial piston engines
Performance: maximum speed at full load 550 km/h (342 mph) at medium altitudes; service ceiling 9.5 km (31,170 ft); range with 2500-kg (5,511-lb) bombload, 1400 km (870 miles)
Weights: empty (1943 production) 7474 kg (16,477 lb); maximum loaded 11360 kg (25,044 lb)
Dimensions: span 18.86 m (61 ft 10½ in); length 13.8 m (45 ft 3⅓ in); height 4.55 m (14 ft 11 in); wing area 48.8 m² (525 sq ft)
Armament: two 20-mm ShVAK cannon in wing roots with 100 rounds each, three single 12.7-mm (0.5-in) UBT guns, each with 250 rounds maximum aimed by three aft crew-members; normal maximum bombload 3000-kg (6,614-lb) with provision for 4000 kg (8,818 lb) as overload

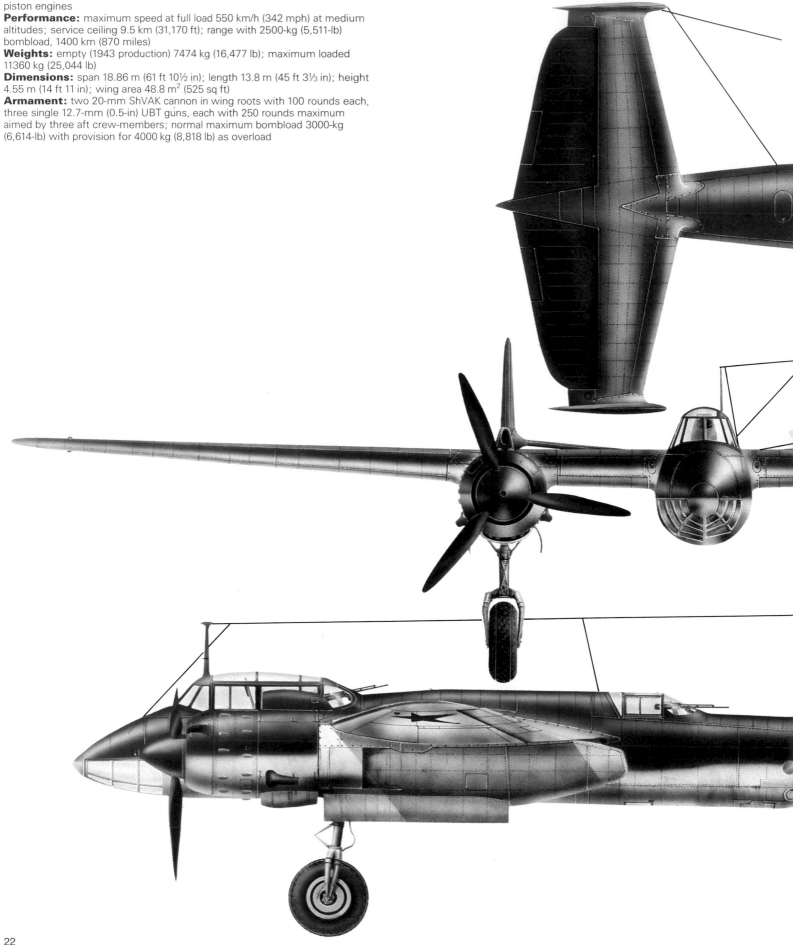

'It handled like a fighter, and with bombs gone it could turn with the best of them.' Praise indeed from a former Tu-2S pilot for an aircraft which proved popular with air and ground crew alike. Effective defensive armament, the ability to absorb a great deal of punishment and a high degree of agility for a medium bomber ensured the type's continued success during World War II. The Tu-2S illustrated incorporates rocker arm blisters on the engine cowlings, enlarged carburettor intakes, and shortened exhausts. Postwar, development continued to exploit the basic design in several forms.

23

Curtiss SB2C Helldiver

For a carrier-based aircraft of its day the Helldiver was a very big machine. Packed with new technology and advanced features it was intended by Curtiss to be a major wartime project. However to those who flew it, the SB2C became known as the 'Son of a Bitch 2nd Class'. Plagued with structural faults and immature design it never succeeded the earlier SBD and while its military career continued through sheer numbers alone, frequent modifications really never overcame its inherent failings.

The Curtiss SB2C, one of the few members of the long and proud series of Curtiss dive-bombers to bear the name Helldiver (officially or unofficially), was intended to be a great war-winner to replace the ancient SBD. Unlike the Douglas product, created by Ed Heinemann working under John K. Northrop, the marvellous new Curtiss had a mighty new two-row engine, an internal weapon bay and a mass of fuel and new equipment all packaged into a tight space. After Pearl Harbor it became the focus of a gigantic nationwide production programme intended to blast the Japanese from the Pacific. The only thing wrong was the aircraft itself. To a man, the US Navy preferred the old SBD, which simply kept on in the forefront of the battle.

The other mass-produced navy Curtiss of World War II was the SO3C Seamew, and it is doubtful if two less-successful aircraft have ever been built in numbers. This experience played a major part in the decline of the once pre-eminent names of Curtiss and Wright in the immediate post-war era, and this was allowed to happen by the US Army and US Navy customers.

In fact the Seamew was designed by a team under the famed chief engineer, Don R. Berlin, while the SB2C was the creation of a newly formed group under Raymond C. Blaylock. As its designation reveals, the SB2C was planned as a scout bomber, for operation from US Navy carriers. The 1938 specification was extremely comprehensive and allowed little room for manoeuvre. The type had to be a

A Curtiss SB2C-3 Helldiver banks hard over a carrier in the Pacific. The aircraft has entered the landing pattern and has its hook down ready for the trap. The aircraft on the deck are Grumman TBF Avengers and F6F Hellcats which fought alongside the Helldiver during the fiercest fighting of the Pacific war.

stressed-skin cantilever monoplane, and the wing had to be raised from the low position in order to allow the accommodation of an internal weapon bay beneath it. This bay did not have to accommodate a torpedo, but it did have to take a 454-kg (1,000-lb) bomb and a wide range of other stores, and be closed by hydraulically-operated bomb doors. There had to be tandem accommodation for a crew of two, a large amount of fuel (various ranges and mission radii were specified) and comprehensive radio and other gear including a hefty camera in the rear cockpit. The structure had to be stressed for dive-bombing, and the aircraft had to be carrier-compatible, with folding wings, catapult hooks and an arrester hook. The specified engine was the Wright R-2600 14-cylinder Cyclone.

Not unnaturally the prototype XSB2C-1 came out looking rather like its rival, the Brewster XSB2A-1 Buccaneer; and, if such a thing were possible, the latter was an even poorer aircraft than the Curtiss. In fact the US Navy had such faith in the Buffalo-based company that it placed a firm order for 200 SB2C-1s before the prototype made its first flight on 18 December 1940. The single prototype, BuNo. 1758, had been ordered on 15 May 1939, and the big production order came on 29 November 1940. Thus, as 1941 dawned Curtiss had a single shiny prototype which occasionally flew, on the strength of which 14,000 workers were being hired for a vast new plant rapidly taking shape at Columbus, Ohio (later NAA and today Rockwell). Plans were already afoot for two further giant production programmes, at Canadian Car & Foundry at Fort William and Fairchild Aircraft at Longueil, Montreal. Curtiss announced that 'The Helldiver is the world's most efficient dive-bomber; it carries twice the bomb load, has double the fire-power, is at least 100 mph faster,

Curtiss SB2C Helldiver

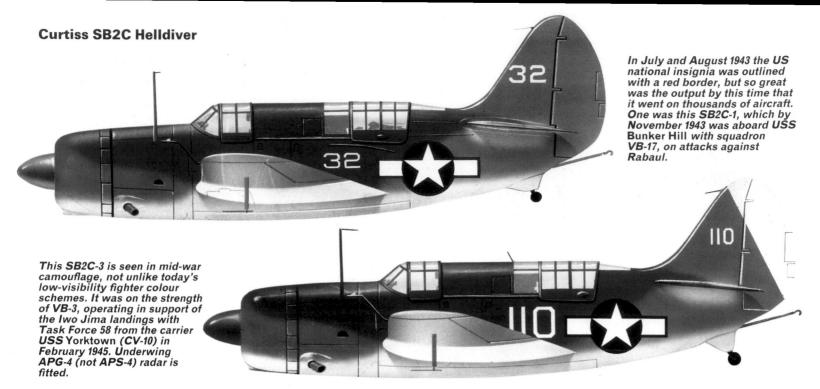

In July and August 1943 the US national insignia was outlined with a red border, but so great was the output by this time that it went on thousands of aircraft. One was this SB2C-1, which by November 1943 was aboard USS Bunker Hill with squadron VB-17, on attacks against Rabaul.

This SB2C-3 is seen in mid-war camouflage, not unlike today's low-visibility fighter colour schemes. It was on the strength of VB-3, operating in support of the Iwo Jima landings with Task Force 58 from the carrier USS Yorktown (CV-10) in February 1945. Underwing APG-4 (not APS-4) radar is fitted.

remains in flight 4½ hours longer and can operate 600 miles further away from its base than any type now in use. We will build 1,000 or more, at the rate of 80 a month.'

Such confidence overlooked the fact that the SB2C was riddled with problems. Some were the normal ones of immaturity, affecting almost all the functioning items and particularly the R-2600-8 engine and 3.66-m (12-ft) Curtiss Electric three-blade propeller. More serious were the deeper faults of the aircraft itself, which resulted in structural weaknesses, generally poor handling, shockingly inadequate stability (especially in yaw and pitch) and unacceptable stall characteristics. Yet the strange thing is that the first prototype looked almost the same as all the production machines. Even the fact that the tail had to be enlarged was not immediately obvious.

Features of the XSB2C-1 included a large wing with all its taper on the trailing edge. On the trailing edge were large flaps split into lower and upper portions, again divided into inboard and outboard sections on the manually folded outer wings. In normal flight the upper flap sections were hydraulically locked to form the upper surface of the wing, the lower part functioning as a normal split flap. For dive-bombing the upper flaps were unlocked by moving the selector lever to a different position, the hydraulic jacks then opening both flaps fully above and below. This held the dive to 354 km/h (220 mph) but buffeted the tail so violently that the pilot feared structural failure (which often did occur, though not necessarily from the buffet). The ailerons, which in most versions had greater chord than the flaps, were unusual in having aluminium skin above and fabric below. In line with the ailerons on the leading edge were large slats which were pulled open by a cable connection to the landing gears, so that at low speeds in the traffic pattern the handling, especially lateral control, was almost acceptable. The US Navy did pass the sluggish ailerons, but in 1944 the British rejected it out of hand, and that was after four years of improvement.

Prototype crash

Unfortunately, BuNo. 1758 crashed quite early, on 8 February 1941, the cause being engine failure on the approach. Like many aircraft of its day the SB2C suffered violent changes in trim with application of flap, dive brakes, gear down or changes in engine power. In the case of this aircraft the forces needed on the stick were at the limit of what most pilots could apply, and very high friction in the control circuits did not help, so it was small wonder that control was lost when the engine cut. But with a gigantic production programme fast taking shape Curtiss simply had to carry on with flight test, so 1758 had to be urgently rebuilt. Almost every part was changed, the fuse-

lage being about 0.305 m (1 ft) longer, the tail areas almost 30 per cent larger and numerous shapes subtly altered. The poor stability led to the expensive addition of an autopilot. Thanks to combat reports from Europe the fuel tanks in the fuselage and inner wings were made of the self-sealing type, local armour was added and the forward-firing armament changed from two 12.7-mm (0.5-in) guns above the cowling to four of these guns in the wings. The rear cockpit was redesigned with improved collapsible decking to improve the field of fire of the observer's single 12.7-mm (0.5-in) gun. Later this gun was replaced by observer armament of twin 7.62-mm (0.3-in) guns, each with no less than 2,000 rounds, with traverse round the mounting ring effected by an hydraulic motor. Wing racks were added for bombs of up to 147-kg (325-lb) depth-bomb size. These and other changes did not all come in at once but most had at least been agreed on paper by the time the prototype resumed flight testing on 20 October 1941.

So enormous was the production scheme that, coming on top of dozens of others throughout North America, it fell seriously behind. Curtiss had agreed to begin deliveries in December 1941, but by this time no production machine was even being assembled. Worse, on 21 December 1941 the sole prototype broke up in the air while on dive-bombing tests, pilot B. T. Hulse managing to escape by parachute. By this time further changes had been demanded, and another 900 Helldivers had been ordered for the US Army Air Force as A-25 Shrikes, with carrier gear deleted, pneumatic tailwheels and

The XSB2C-1 prototype (no. 1758) is seen during flight tests, wearing one of the many pre-war US Navy colour schemes and pre-war national insignia. Design problems were to delay service entry until late 1943.

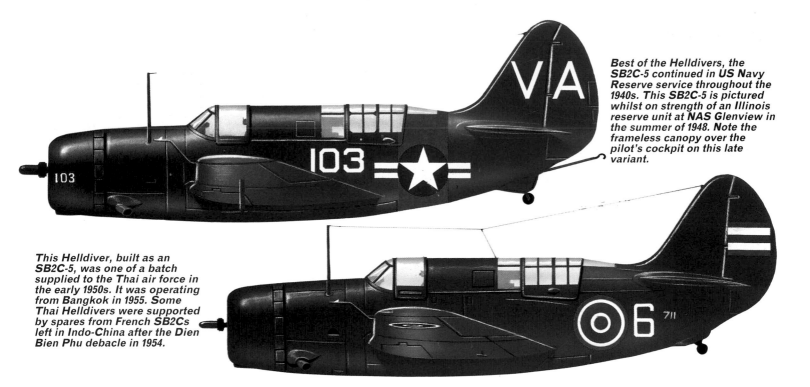

Best of the Helldivers, the SB2C-5 continued in US Navy Reserve service throughout the 1940s. This SB2C-5 is pictured whilst on strength of an Illinois reserve unit at NAS Glenview in the summer of 1948. Note the frameless canopy over the pilot's cockpit on this late variant.

This Helldiver, built as an SB2C-5, was one of a batch supplied to the Thai air force in the early 1950s. It was operating from Bangkok in 1955. Some Thai Helldivers were supported by spares from French SB2Cs left in Indo-China after the Dien Bien Phu debacle in 1954.

many other changes. Everyone worked round the clock to try to speed the programme, and eventually the first SB2C-1 was completed at Port Columbus in June 1942. The US Navy did not fail to notice that 10 days earlier the far better Grumman TBF Avenger had gone into action, though its design was begun almost two years later than the bug-ridden SB2C.

Disappointing results

Urgent testing of the first six production machines revealed that in many respects they were worse than the prototype, the great increase in weight (empty weight rose from 3230 kg/7,122 lb to some 4636 kg/10,220 lb) without change in the engine resulting in an aircraft described at NAS Anacostia as 'extremely sluggish'. But by this time the trickle of production machines was fast building up, and to avoid political scandals some had to be delivered, so US Navy attack squadron VS-9 began to equip with SB2C-1s in December 1942. In fact political scandals had to be accepted; this was wartime, and there seemed to be so many poor or late programmes that the Trumman Committee on the National Defense Program was set up to examine what was going on. This committee finally compiled a damning report on the SB2C, and among other things managed to divert the A-25s to other customers, though many did briefly wear US Army colours.

Subsequently production of the SB2C progressed through the many variants listed separately. Only the original order for 200 applied to the SB2C-1 model, and all of these were retained in the USA for training purposes. The SB2C-1A, which appeared in 1943, was the non-navalised A-25A after transfer to the US Marine Corps,

where many saw action still painted olive-drab. The SB2C-1C introduced several armament improvements, including the option of removing the bomb doors and carrying a torpedo on an external truss, but little use appears to have been made of this. The major SB2C-1C change was to replace the four wing guns by two 20-mm cannon, each with 400 rounds loaded from above the wing. Immediately ahead of the magazines were extra 170-litre (37.4-Imp gal) auxiliary tanks, and at full load the SB2C-1C, the first model to go into action, was inferior in many performance respects to the old SBD, which was far nicer to fly, and safer.

Rabaul strike

The first action was flown by a bomber squadron, VB-17, operating from USS *Bunker Hill*. The SB2Cs flew the second strike mounted on 11 November 1943 against the big Japanese base at Rabaul, New Guinea. They were painted in the sea blue and white scheme then common, though by this time aircraft on the line were being finished in gloss Midnight Blue, usually with a bold white three-figure Modex number on the nose.

A welcome small improvement in performance resulted in the SB2C-3 from fitting the more powerful R-2600-20 engine, its extra power being absorbed by an improved Curtiss Electric propeller with four blades and fitted with root cuffs. Towards the end of the war it became common to omit the spinner, though this was often done at unit level. Certainly by 1944, when the SB2C-3 appeared, the Helldiver was well established in service, and at least was becoming operationally effective, though crashes, inflight break-ups and carrier landing accidents continued at the very top of the 'league

The lone XSB2C-2, no. 00005, was the only Helldiver seaplane. A conversion of the fifth production SB2C-1 with twin Edo floats and a ventral fin, it flew in September 1942 but never led to a combat-ready machine, the 287 planned production SB2C-2s (nos 03862/04148) being cancelled before any had flown.

A line-up of US Army RA-25A Helldivers, either serving as utility hacks and for target towing or abandoned to the elements. Note the crudely overpainted insignia, the camouflaged rudder (possibly a replacement part) and the 'BOX' chalked on the cowlings of several aircraft in the line. Prefix 'R' meant 'Restricted'.

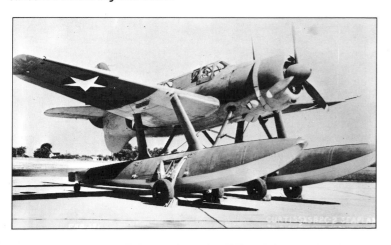

Curtiss SB2C Helldriver

table'. To everyone in the US Navy this aircraft was The Beast, though gradually pilots who became experienced on it came to think this appellation unfair.

Like most wartime programmes, production became a flood after most of the tougher fighting had been done, and the SB2C-4, which did not appear until summer 1944, was the most numerous version of all. From the pilot's viewpoint the chief new feature of this model was that both upper and lower wing flaps were perforated, looking like a sieve. This had virtually no effect on their drag in dive-bombing but did slightly reduce the tremendous tail buffet, which many pilots claimed affected their ability to see the target and aim the dive! Operational effectiveness was considerably increased in this version by strengthening the wing and providing for the carriage of either two drop tanks, two 227-kg (500-lb) bombs or eight 127-mm (5-in) rockets.

End of the line

The final production Helldiver was the SB2C-5, with slightly increasd internal fuel capacity (an extra 132 litres/29 Imp gal). As listed under Variants, most of the Columbus versions had more or less exact counterparts built by the two Canadian companies.

Curtiss was only too keenly aware of the indifferent qualities of the SB2C, and many years after the war the company president, Guy Vaughan, said it was 'one of the biggest of the wartime crosses we had to bear'. Don Berlin left the company in 1942 to join Fisher Body, and Blaylock, possibly working with director of engineering G. A. Page Jr, designed the much better-looking SB3C and corresponding US Army A-40. A single-seater, the SB3C was expected to reach 571 km/h (355 mph) even carrying two torpedoes or a heavy internal bomb load, powered by an R-3350; but the two SB3C prototypes were cancelled.

After the war Helldivers did not vanish overnight. A few continued flying with the US Navy Reserves and with various test units until at least 1947, often being used to tow targets. Others were operated in the attack role by the French Aéronavale, the navies of Italy and Portugal and the air forces of Greece and Thailand. French Helldivers played a significant role in the war in Indo-China, which did not collapse until 1954. One cannot blame the SB2C for that.

JW117 was the Helldiver Mk I used for the ground and air photography sessions at the Aeroplane & Armament Experimental Establishment at Boscombe Down, England, in October 1944. Much of its air evaluation was handled by famed test pilot Lieutenant-Commander E. M. 'Winkle' Brown, RN. His opinion was adverse.

Curtiss SB2C-4 Helldiver cutaway drawing key

1 Curtiss Electric four-bladed constant-speed propeller
2 Spinner
3 Propeller hub mechanism
4 Spinner backplate
5 Propeller reduction gearbox
6 Carburettor intake
7 Intake ducting
8 Warm air filters
9 Engine cowling ring
10 Oil cooler intake
11 Engine cowlings
12 Wright R-2600-20 Cyclone 14 radial engine
13 Cooling air exit louvres
14 Exhaust collector
15 Exhaust pipe fairing
16 Oil cooler
17 Engine accessories
18 Hydraulic pressure accumulator
19 Boarding step
20 Cabin combustion heater
21 Engine oil tank (25 US gal/ 94.6 litre capacity)
22 Engine bearer struts
23 Hydraulic fluid tank
24 Fireproof engine compartment bulkhead
25 Aerial mast
26 Starboard wing fold hinges
27 Wing fold hydraulic jack
28 Gun camera

29 Rocket projectiles (4.5-in/ 11.43-cm)
30 Starboard leading edge slat (open)
31 Slat roller tracks
32 Slat operating cables
33 Starboard navigation light
34 Formation light
35 Starboard aileron
36 Aileron aluminium top skins
37 Aileron control mechanism
38 Starboard dive brake (open position)
39 Windshield
40 Bullet proof internal windscreen
41 Reflector gunsight
42 Instrument panel shroud
43 Cockpit coaming
44 De-icing fluid tank
45 Instrument panel
46 Pilot's pull-out chart board
47 Rudder pedals
48 Control column
49 Cockpit floor level
50 Engine throttle controls
51 Pilot's seat
52 Oxygen bottle
53 Safety harness
54 Armoured seat back
55 Headrest
56 Pilot's sliding cockpit canopy cover

57 Jury strut
58 Wing folded position
59 Fixed bridge section between cockpits
60 Fuel tank filler cap
61 Fuselage fuel tank (110 US gal/416 litre capacity)
62 Fuselage main longeron
63 Handhold
64 Fuselage frame and stringer construction
65 Autopilot controls

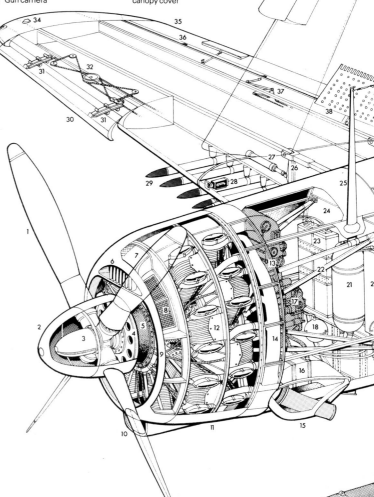

66 Sliding canopy rail
67 Aerial lead-in
68 Radio equipment bay
69 Life raft stowage
70 APG-4 low-level bombing radar
71 Gunner's forward sliding canopy cover
72 Gun mounting ring
73 Gunner's seat
74 Footrests
75 Ammunition boxes
76 Armour plate
77 Wind deflector
78 Twin 0.3-in (7.62-mm) machine-guns
79 Retractable turtle decking
80 Gun rest mounting
81 Folding side panels
82 Upper formation light
83 Fin root fillet
84 Starboard tailplane
85 Deck handling handhold
86 Fabric-covered elevator
87 Remote compass transmitter
88 Tailfin construction
89 Aerial cable
90 Sternpost
91 Rudder construction

92 Fabric skin covering
93 Trim tab
94 Balance tab
95 Elevator trim tab
96 Elevator construction
97 Tailplane construction
98 Tailplane spar root fixing
99 Deck arrester hook
100 Arrester hook damper
101 Tail navigation light
102 Tailwheel leg strut
103 Solid tyre tailwheel
104 Leg fairing
105 Rear fuselage frames
106 Tailplane control cables
107 Lifting bar
108 Gunner's floor level
109 Wing root trailing edge fillet
110 Aft end of bomb bay
111 Rear spar centre section fixing
112 Wing walkway
113 Port upper surface flap dive brake
114 Rear spar hinge joint
115 Split trailing edge flaps
116 Balance tab
117 Aileron hinge control
118 Aileron trim tab
119 Lower surface fabric skinning
120 Wing rib construction
121 Wing tip construction

122 Port navigation light
123 Pitot tube
124 Automatic leading edge slat (opens with undercarriage operation)
125 Slat riblets
126 Slat operating cables
127 Main spar
128 Leading edge nose ribs
129 500-lb (226.8-kg) bomb
130 Rocket projectiles (4.5-in/ 11.43-cm)
131 Drop tank (58 US gal/219.5 litre capacity)
132 Wing fold joint line
133 Main undercarriage leg fairing doors
134 Drag strut
135 Port mainwheel
136 Shock absorber leg strut
137 20-mm wing cannon
138 Cannon barrel fairing
139 Undercarriage leg pivot mounting
140 Wing fold upper spar hinge joint
141 Cannon ammunition box
142 Auxiliary fuel tank (45 US gal/170 litre capacity)
143 Fuel filler cap
144 Centre section fuel tank (105 US gal/397.5 litre capacity)
145 Front spar/fuselage attachment joint
146 Main undercarriage wheel well
147 Retractable catapult strop
148 Approach light
149 Bomb doors (open)
150 Bomb door hydraulic jack
151 Displacement gear jack
152 H-type bomb displacement arm
153 1,000-lb (453.6-kg) bomb

Curtiss SB2C Helldiver variants

XSB2C-1: single prototype (BuNo. 1758) with R-2600-8, several times rebuilt or modified
SB2C-1: first production version; total 200; first block to receive the new 1940 scheme of Assigned Serial Numbers (00001/00200)
SB2C-1A: designation applied to **A-25A**; subsequently used again for 410 ex-USAAF A-25A for US Marine Corps
A-25A Shrike: US Army version of SB2C-1 with various changes; total 900, of which 410 to US Marine Corps, 270 to US Navy and 10 to RAAF
SBF-1: Fairchild-built SB2C-1; total 50
SBW-1: CCF-built SB2C-1; total 38
SBW-1B: CCF-built Lend-Lease aircraft of SB2C-1C standard for the UK; total 28 of which 26 delivered (see next entry)
Helldiver Mk I: Fleet Air Arm SBW-1B, 26 delivered as JW100/125, most to No. 1820 Sqn but rejected for operational use
SB2C-1C: first version with 20-mm wing guns; total 778
XSB2C-2: single aircraft (00005) tested September 1942 with twin Edo floats; intended as reconnaissance bomber
SB2C-3: improved model with 1,900-hp (1417-kW) R-2600-20, four-blade propeller and fitted

from start with APG-4 low-level auto bomb system (also retrofitted to many other versions); total 1,112
SBF-3: Fairchild-built SB2C-3; total 150
SBW-3: CCF-built SB2C-3; total 413
SB2C-3E: SB2C-3 aircraft fitted with APS-4 3-cm radar; over 180
SB2C-4: wing hardpoints for two 500-lb (227-kg) bombs or eight 5-in (127-mm) rockets, perforated wing flap/dive brakes and equipment changes; total 2,045
SB2C-4E: SB2C-4 aircraft fitted with APS-4 radar
SBF-4E: Fairchild-built SB2C-4E; total 100
SBW-4E: CCF-built SB2C-4E; total 270
SB2C-5: improved aircraft with increased internal fuel and other minor changes; total 970 from February 1945 (BuNo. 83128 onwards) and 2,500 cancelled
SBW-5: CCF-built SB2C-5; total 85; 165 cancelled
XSB2C-6: two SB2C-3s (BuNos 18620/18621) completely rebuilt as longer aircraft with increased fuel capacity and 2,100-hp (1566-kW) Pratt & Whitney R-2800-28 Double Wasp engines

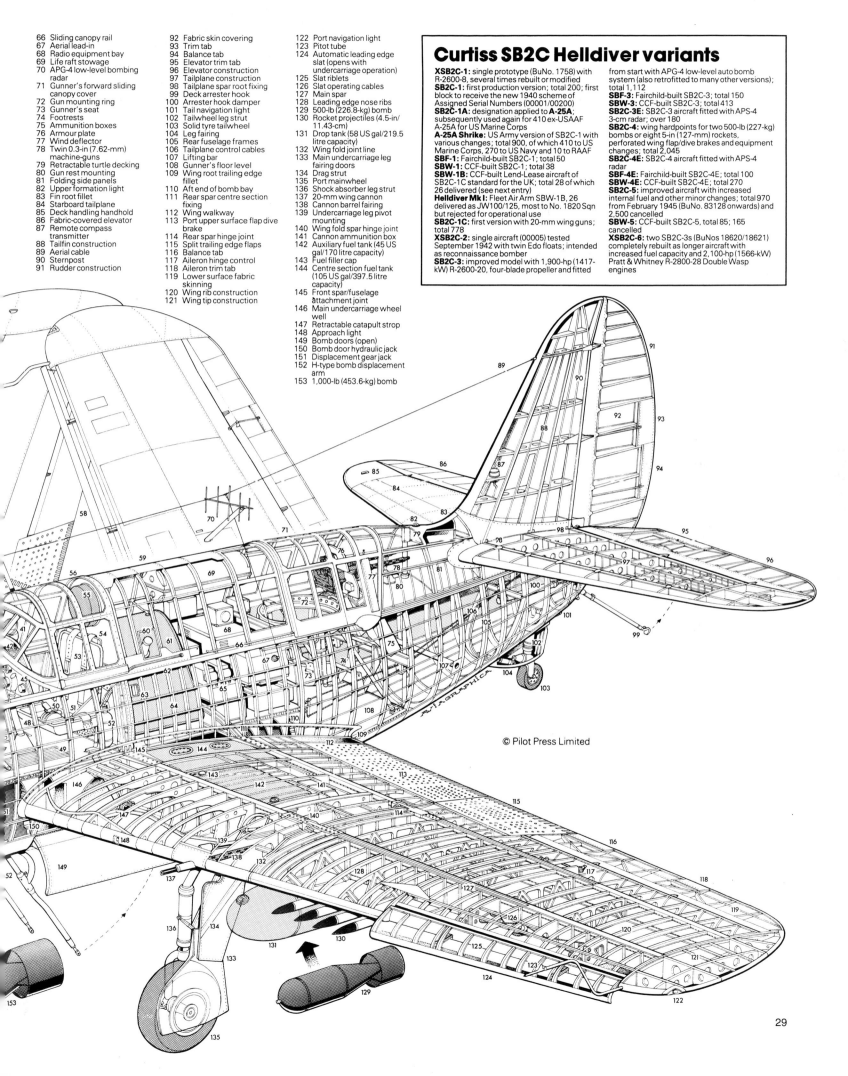

© Pilot Press Limited

29

Boeing B-29 Superfortress

No other aircraft ever combined so many technological advances as the B-29. Designed for a specific strategic task, it later spawned the double-deck Stratocruiser airliner, the KC-97 tanker/transport and laid the foundations for the super-successful Boeing airliner series. It also provided the Soviet Union with the starting block for the entire Tupolev heavy aircraft lineage.

It is probable that a detailed analysis of the Soviet 'Blackjack' swing-wing bomber of the 1980s would unearth design features that can be traced right back to the B-29. And the Boeing B-29 Superfortress was started more than three years before the USA entered World War II, in October 1938. In one of his last acts before he was killed in a crash at Burbank the US Army Air Corps Chief of Staff, General Oscar Westover, had officially established a requirement for a new super-bomber to succeed the Boeing B-17, at a time when the B-17 itself was being denied funds by the Congress. Despite a totally negative reaction from the War Department, procurement chief General Oliver Echols never gave up in his fight to keep the super-bomber alive, and it had the backing of 'Hap' Arnold, Westover's successor. The bomber was to be pressurised to fly

Dave's Dream was built as B-29-40-MO 44-27354, but it is pictured here with Major W. P. Swancutt in command, heading for Bikini Atoll on 1 July 1946, where the modified aircraft dropped the first post-war nuclear weapon. The 509th Composite Group named the aircraft for bombardier Dave Semple, killed in a B-29.

very fast at high altitude: the figures for speed (628 km/h; 390 mph), range (8582 km; 5,333 miles) and military load were staggering.

At the Boeing Airplane Company in Seattle there was, at least, experience of large pressurised aircraft, unlike all other companies, but there seemed no way to reconcile the conflicting factors. For most of 1939 the answer seemed to be to fit Pratt & Whitney's slim sleeve-valve liquid-cooled engines inside the wing, but newly hired George Schairer soon pointed out that as the biggest drag item was the wing, the best course was to make the wing as small as possible and not try to put engines inside it. (Thus began a basic philosophy which saw sharp contrast between the Boeing B-47 and the British V-bombers, and has continued to today's Boeing Models 757 and 767.) How does one pressurise a fuselage containing enormous bomb doors? The answer here was to make the colossal bomb bays unpressurised and link the front and rear pressure cabins by a sealed tunnel. Chief engineer Wellwood Beall was first to crawl through the mock-up tunnel in January 1940.

By March 1940 the demands had increased, including 7258 kg

Boeing B-29 Superfortress

(16,000 lb) of bombs for short-range missions, powered turrets, and far more protection including armour and self-sealing tanks. Weight had already leapt in stages from 21773 to 38556 kg (48,000 to 85,000 lb), and with the fresh demands the design finally rounded out at a daunting 54432 kg (120,000 lb). With just 161.55 m^2 (1,739 sq ft) of wing, the wing loading was going to be 336.9 kg/m^2 (69 lb/sq ft), about double the figure universally taken in 1940 as the desirable limit. Test pilot Eddie Allen was happy that the Boeing Model 345 would be flyable (just) if it had the biggest and most powerful high-lift flaps ever thought of, to reduce take-off and landing speeds to about 257 km/h (160 mph), which was about double the equivalent speed of such familiar machines as the B-17 and Supermarine Spitfire.

Funds from USAAC

As the the BEF was rescued from the beaches at Dunkirk the new bomber was designated the B-29, and in August the US Army Air Corps provided funds for two (later three) prototypes. Work was rushed ahead, but nobody knew how to stop guns and propeller mechanisms from freezing at far over 9145 m (30,000 ft), which Boeing was confident the aircraft could reach. The intense wing loading was all against the designers, but using four monster Wright R-3350 Duplex Cyclones, each with not one but two of General Electric's best turbochargers and driving 5.05-m (16-ft 7-in) Hamilton Standard four-blade propellers, the propulsion was equal to the task.

Behind the nose section were two giant bomb bays, from which an electric sequencing system released bombs alternately from front and rear to preserve the centre of gravity position. Between the two bays was a ring forming the structural heart of the aircraft and integral with the main wing box, the strongest aircraft part built up to that time. On the wing were four monster nacelles, which Schairer showed to have less drag than engines buried in a bigger wing. After four main gears had been studied, a way was found to fold simple two-wheel gears into the inboard nacelles. Fowler flaps were screwed out electrically to add 21 per cent to area of the wing, fighting a wing loading which by September 1940 reached 351.1 kg/m^2 (71.9 lb/sq ft) and climbed to a frightening 396 kg/m^2 (81.1 lb/sq ft) by the time of the first combat mission.

Behind the wing the rear pressure cabin had three sighting stations linked to two upper and two lower turrets, each with twin 12.7-mm (0.5-in) machine-guns. The electric fire control was

One of very few surviving pictures of 'parasiting', this photograph was taken during trials in 1949-51 to see if a bomber really could tow fighters over long ranges. ETB-29A-60 44-62093 was much modified for Project Tom Tom, towing F-84D-1 Thunderjets 48-641 and 48-661. Another B-29 carried the XF-85 Goblin.

Boeing B-29 Superfortress cutaway drawing key

1 Temperature probe
2 Nose glazing
3 Optically flat bomb aiming panel
4 Bombsight
5 Windscreen panels
6 Forward gunsight
7 Bombardier's seat
8 Pilot's instrument console
9 Control column
10 Co-pilot's seat
11 Pilot's seat
12 Side console panel
13 Cockpit heating duct
14 Nose undercarriage leg strut
15 Steering control
16 Twin nosewheels
17 Retraction struts
18 Nosewheel doors
19 Underfloor control cable runs
20 Pilot's back armour
21 Flight engineer's station
22 Forward upper gun turret, four 0.5-in (12.7-mm) machine-guns, 500 rpg
23 Radio operator's station
24 Chart table
25 Navigator's instrument rack
26 Fire extinguisher bottle
27 Forward lower gun turret, two 0.5-in (12.7-mm) machine-guns, 500 rpg
28 Ventral aerial
29 Navigator's seat
30 Hydraulic system servicing point
31 Access ladder
32 Forward cabin rear pressure bulkhead
33 Armoured bulkhead
34 Pressurised tunnel connecting front and rear cabins
35 Astrodome observation hatch
36 Forward bomb racks
37 Bomb hoisting winches
38 Catwalk

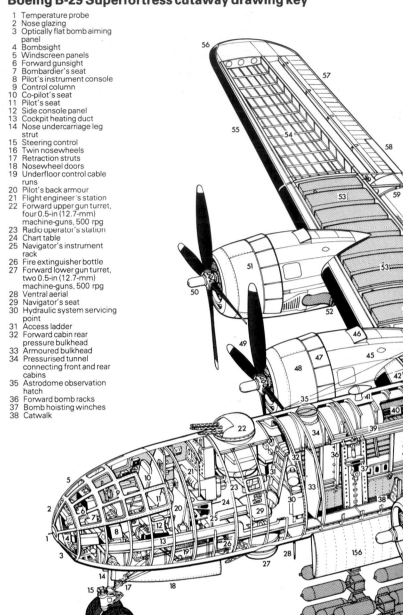

Boeing B-29 variants

XB-29: Boeing Model 345 prototypes (41-002, 41-003 and 41-18335)
YB-29: service-test aircraft with armament (41-36954/36967); total 14
B-29: main production by BW (Boeing Wichita), BA (Bell Airplane) and MO (Martin Omaha); total 1,620 BW, 357 BA and 204 MO
B-29A: span 43.36 m (142 ft 3 in), R-3350-57 or -59 engines, and four-gun forward upper turret; built at Boeing Renton (BN); total 1,119
F-13A: conversions as strategic reconnaissance aircraft with large camera installations and long-range tanks; total 117
RB-29A: redesignation in 1948 of F-13A
TB-29A: conversions as crew trainers
ETB-29A: TB-29A modified for parasite attachments of F-84 jet fighters at wingtips (44-62093)
B-29B: R-3350-51 engines, defensive armament removed except tail turret; built by Bell (BA); total 311
EB-29B: conversion to launch XF-85 Goblin parasite jet from trapeze (44-84111)
B-29D: ex-XB-44, later became B-50
XB-29E: conversion to test different electronic defensive fire-control
B-29F: Arctic conversions of six aircraft
XB-29G: conversion (44-84043) to test experimental turbojets in pod extended below bomb bay
XB-29H: conversion of B-29A for different defensive armament
YB-29J: conversions (six) to test commercial R-3350 powerplants
RB-29J: conversions (two YB-29J) as multi-sensor reconnaissance aircraft; also called **FB-29J**
YKB-29J: conversions (two YB-29J) for tests of Boeing Flying Boom inflight-refuelling system
CB-29K: conversion to military cargo aircraft
B-29L: original designation of B-29MR
KB-29M: major programme of rebuilds as inflight-refuelling tankers (92) with British looped hose method
B-29MR: conversions (74) as receivers to link with inflight-refuelling hose
KB-29P: major programme of conversions (116) as inflight-refuelling tankers with Flying Boom for SAC
YKB-29T: single conversion of KB-29M (45-21734) as triple-point tanker
DB-29: various conversions as drone and target directors
GB-29: conversions to launch the XS-1, X-1, X-2 and X-3 supersonic research aircraft

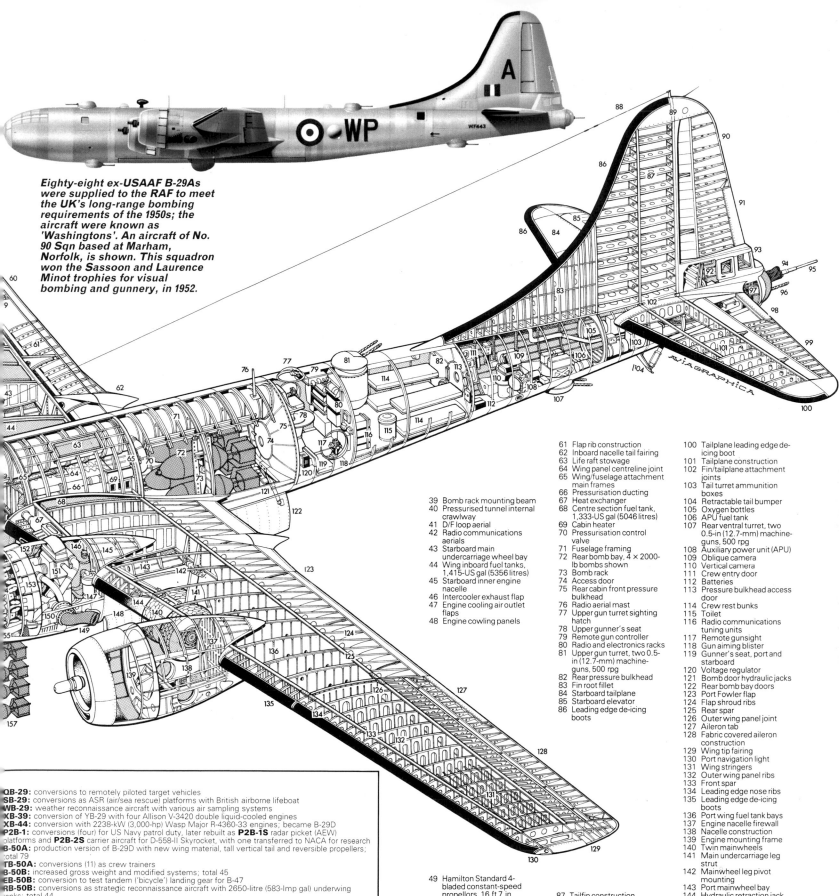

Eighty-eight ex-USAAF B-29As were supplied to the RAF to meet the UK's long-range bombing requirements of the 1950s; the aircraft were known as 'Washingtons'. An aircraft of No. 90 Sqn based at Marham, Norfolk, is shown. This squadron won the Sassoon and Laurence Minot trophies for visual bombing and gunnery, in 1952.

39 Bomb rack mounting beam
40 Pressurised tunnel internal crawlway
41 D/F loop aerial
42 Radio communications aerials
43 Starboard main undercarriage wheel bay
44 Wing inboard fuel tanks, 1,415-US gal (5356 litres)
45 Starboard inner engine nacelle
46 Intercooler exhaust flap
47 Engine cooling air outlet flaps
48 Engine cowling panels

49 Hamilton Standard 4-bladed constant-speed propellors, 16 ft 7 in diameter
50 Propeller hub pitch change mechanism
51 Starboard outer engine nacelle
52 Exhaust stub
53 Wing outboard fuel tanks, 1,320 US gal (4991 litres) maximum internal fuel load 9363-US gal including bomb bay ferry tanks
54 Wing bottom skin stringers
55 Leading edge de-icing boots
56 Starboard navigation light
57 Fabric-covered aileron
58 Aileron tab
59 Flap guide rails
60 Starboard Fowler-type flap

61 Flap rib construction
62 Inboard nacelle tail fairing
63 Life raft stowage
64 Wing panel centreline joint
65 Wing/fuselage attachment main frames
66 Pressurisation ducting
67 Heat exchanger
68 Centre section fuel tank, 1,333-US gal (5046 litres)
69 Cabin heater
70 Pressurisation control valve
71 Fuselage framing
72 Rear bomb bay, 4 × 2000-lb bombs shown
73 Bomb rack
74 Access door
75 Rear cabin front pressure bulkhead
76 Radio aerial mast
77 Upper gun turret sighting hatch
78 Upper gunner's seat
79 Remote gun controller
80 Radio and electronics racks
81 Upper gun turret, two 0.5-in (12.7-mm) machine-guns, 500 rpg
82 Rear pressure bulkhead
83 Fin root fillet
84 Starboard tailplane
85 Starboard elevator
86 Leading edge de-icing boots

87 Tailfin construction
88 HF aerial cable
89 Fin tip fairing
90 Fabric covered rudder construction
91 Rudder tab
92 Pressurised tail gunners compartment
93 Armoured glass window panels
94 Tail gun camera
95 20-mm cannon, 100 rounds
96 Twin 0.5-in (12.7-mm) machine guns, 500 rpg
97 Remotely controlled ball turret
98 Elevator tab
99 Port fabric covered elevator construction

100 Tailplane leading edge de-icing boot
101 Tailplane construction
102 Fin/tailplane attachment joints
103 Tail turret ammunition boxes
104 Retractable tail bumper
105 Oxygen bottles
106 APU fuel tank
107 Rear ventral turret, two 0.5-in (12.7-mm) machine-guns, 500 rpg
108 Auxiliary power unit (APU)
109 Oblique camera
110 Vertical camera
111 Crew entry door
112 Batteries
113 Pressure bulkhead access door
114 Crew rest bunks
115 Toilet
116 Radio communications tuning units
117 Remote gunsight
118 Gun aiming blister
119 Gunner's seat, port and starboard
120 Voltage regulator
121 Bomb door hydraulic jacks
122 Rear bomb bay doors
123 Port Fowler flap
124 Flap shroud ribs
125 Rear spar
126 Outer wing panel joint
127 Aileron tab
128 Fabric covered aileron construction
129 Wing tip fairing
130 Port navigation light
131 Wing stringers
132 Outer wing panel ribs
133 Front spar
134 Leading edge nose ribs
135 Leading edge de-icing boots
136 Port wing fuel tank bays
137 Engine nacelle firewall
138 Nacelle construction
139 Engine mounting frame
140 Twin mainwheels
141 Main undercarriage leg strut
142 Mainwheel leg pivot mounting
143 Port mainwheel bay
144 Hydraulic retraction jack
145 Nacelle tail fairing
146 Self-sealing oil tank, 85 US gal (322 litres)
147 Hydraulic reservoir
148 Mainwheel doors
149 Exhaust stub
150 Exhaust driven turbo-supercharger
151 Intercooler
152 Engine cooling air exit flaps
153 Exhaust collector ring
154 Wright Cyclone R-3350-57A, 18-cylinder, two-row radial engine
155 Engine intake ducting
156 Forward bomb bay doors
157 20 × 500-lb (227 kg) bombs, maximum bomb load 20,000-lb (9072 kg)

QB-29: conversions to remotely piloted target vehicles
SB-29: conversions as ASR (air/sea rescue) platforms with British airborne lifeboat
WB-29: weather reconnaissance aircraft with various air sampling systems
XB-39: conversion of YB-29 with four Allison V-3420 double liquid-cooled engines
XB-44: conversion with 2238-kW (3,000-hp) Wasp Major R-4360-33 engines; became B-29D
P2B-1: conversions (four) for US Navy patrol duty, later rebuilt as P2B-1S radar picket (AEW) platforms and P2B-2S carrier aircraft for D-558-II Skyrocket, with one transferred to NACA for research
B-50A: production version of B-29D with new wing material, tall vertical tail and reversible propellers; total 79
TB-50A: conversions (11) as crew trainers
B-50B: increased gross weight and modified systems; total 45
EB-50B: conversion to test tandem ('bicycle') landing gear for B-47
RB-50B: conversions as strategic reconnaissance aircraft with 2650-litre (583-Imp gal) underwing tanks; total 44
YB-50C: planned prototype of next-generation
B-54: not completed
B-50D: definitive bomber with frameless nose, 2650-litre (583-Imp gal) underwing tanks, new forward upper turret etc; total 222
DB-50D: conversion to launch vehicles in Bell XB-63 Rascal programme
KB-50D: conversion as prototype of later tankers
TB-50D: conversions (11) as unarmed crew trainers
WB-50D: conversions (36) as weather reconnaissance platforms
RB-50E: conversions of RB-50B with new sensors; total 14
RB-50F: conversions (a different 14) with SHORAN navigation radar
RB-50G: conversions (15) with air/ground mapping radar, new navaids and B-50D-type nose
TB-50H: new-build programme of unarmed crew trainers; total 24
WB-50H: weather conversion of TB-50H
KB-50J: major conversion programme for inflight-refuelling tankers with flight refuelling A-12B hose drum unit at wingtips and in rear fuselage, plus extra tankage and new observation stations; rebuilds by Hayes Aircraft which then added 2631-kg (5,800-lb) thrust General Electric J47-23 booster jet pods under the outer wings; conversions of all RB-50E, RB-50F and RB-50G plus seven B-50D aircraft
KB-50K: conversions to KB-50J standard of all TB-50Hs

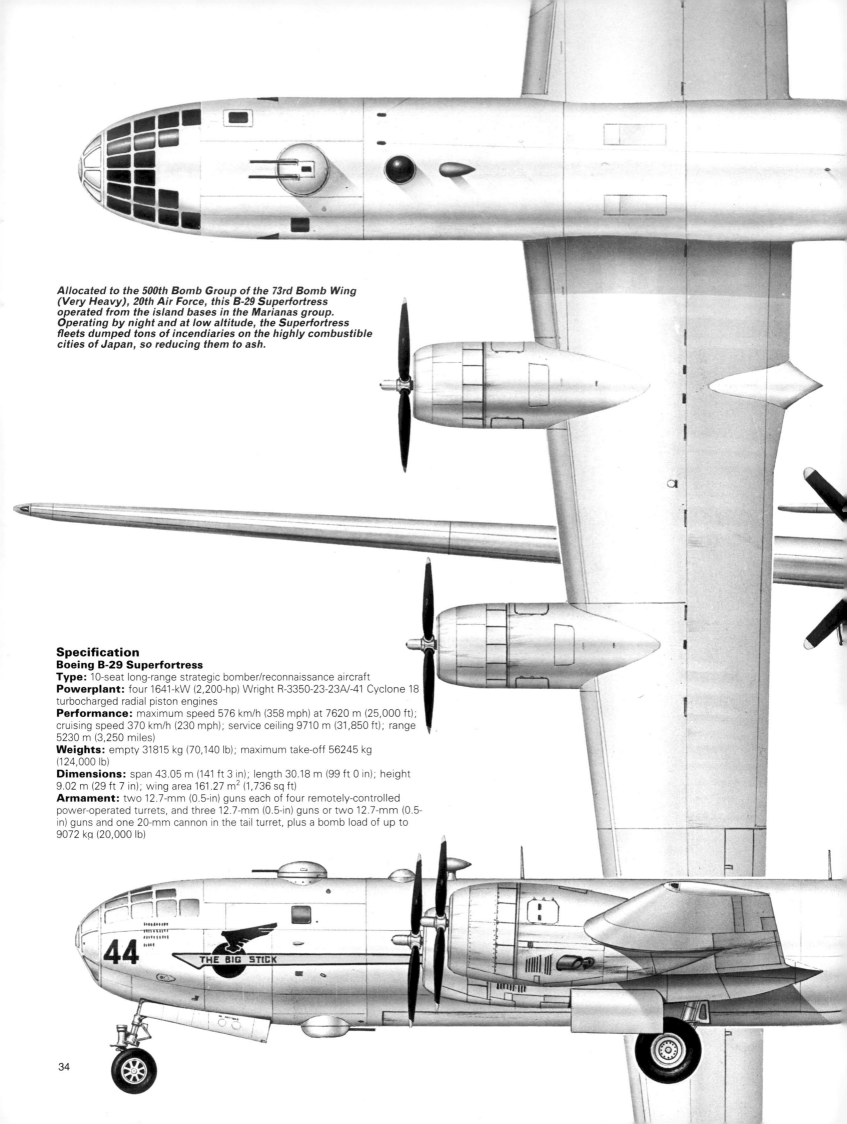

Allocated to the 500th Bomb Group of the 73rd Bomb Wing (Very Heavy), 20th Air Force, this B-29 Superfortress operated from the island bases in the Marianas group. Operating by night and at low altitude, the Superfortress fleets dumped tons of incendiaries on the highly combustible cities of Japan, so reducing them to ash.

Specification
Boeing B-29 Superfortress

Type: 10-seat long-range strategic bomber/reconnaissance aircraft

Powerplant: four 1641-kW (2,200-hp) Wright R-3350-23-23A/-41 Cyclone 18 turbocharged radial piston engines

Performance: maximum speed 576 km/h (358 mph) at 7620 m (25,000 ft); cruising speed 370 km/h (230 mph); service ceiling 9710 m (31,850 ft); range 5230 m (3,250 miles)

Weights: empty 31815 kg (70,140 lb); maximum take-off 56245 kg (124,000 lb)

Dimensions: span 43.05 m (141 ft 3 in); length 30.18 m (99 ft 0 in); height 9.02 m (29 ft 7 in); wing area 161.27 m² (1,736 sq ft)

Armament: two 12.7-mm (0.5-in) guns each of four remotely-controlled power-operated turrets, and three 12.7-mm (0.5-in) guns or two 12.7-mm (0.5-in) guns and one 20-mm cannon in the tail turret, plus a bomb load of up to 9072 kg (20,000 lb)

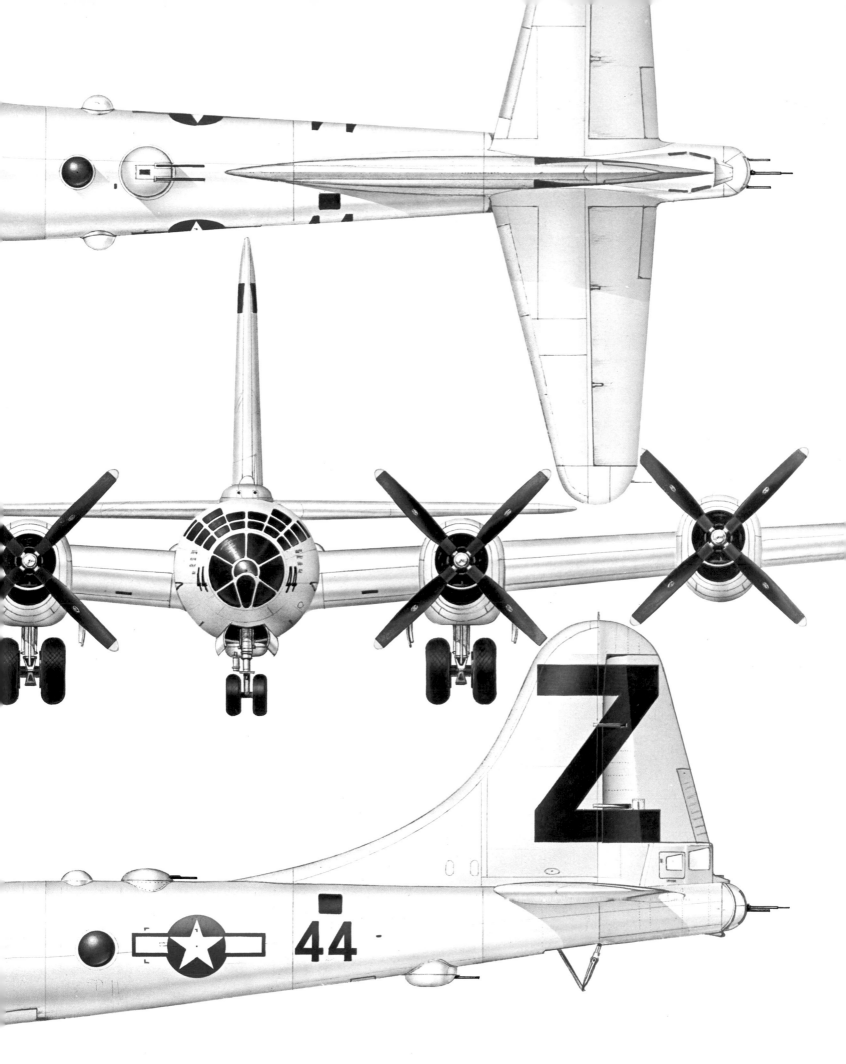

Boeing B-29 Superfortress

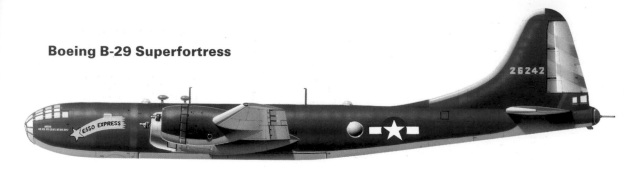

normally set so that the top station controlled either or both of the upper turrets, the side stations the lower rear turret, and the bombardier the forward lower turret, but control could be overridden or switched (because gunners could be knocked out in action). In the extreme tail was another gunner driving a turret with two 12.7-mm (0.5-in) guns and a 20-mm cannon.

In any case, over 2,000 B-29s were to be built before this turret could come into production, because immediately after Pearl Harbor a colossal manufacturing programme was organised, involving vast new plants across the nation. Major parts were made in over 60 new factories, the enormous nacelles, each as big as a P-47, coming from a new Cleveland facility operated by the Fisher Body Division of General Motors. Final assembly was organised at three of the world's largest buildings, Boeing at Wichita, Martin at Omaha and Bell at Marietta (today the same building houses the Lockheed-Georgia Company). Later yet another line was set up at Boeing Renton. All this had been organised before the olive-drab XB-29 (41-002) had even flown, but from the first flight, on 21 September 1942 (initially using three-blade propellers), it was clear that the B-29 was going to be a winner. It could so easily have been what test pilots then called 'a dog'; and one of the firms delegated to build B-29s was convinced Boeing's figures were far too optimistic and that the whole programme was a giant mistake. What made the B-29, by 1942 named Superfortress, now vitally important was that it was obviously going to be the only aircraft with the range to attack Japan.

To say that the good results of ship 41-002 were a relief would be an understatement. Far more money (three billion dollars) had been invested in the B-29 programme long before its wheels left the ground than in any other project in the history of any nation. At the same time the technical snags were severe, and multiplied. Many, such as powerplant fires and runaway propellers, were highly dangerous, and three months into the flight programme the prototypes had logged just 31 of the 180 hours scheduled.

Even when the Superfortresses trickled and then poured off the lines, they were so complex that nobody in uniform fully understood

The very first Superfortress was XB-29 no. 41-002, design of which took place in 1939-40, ready for a first flight on 21 September 1942. Olive-drab and grey, it had three-blade propellers, no defensive turret system and numerous details which were later altered, yet the basic airframe was almost identical to production B-29s.

them. All went to a modification centre at Salina, Kansas, where over 9,900 faults in the first 175, urgently needed for the new 20th Bomb Wing, were bulldozed right by a task force of 600 men in 'The Battle of Kansas'. Sheer manpower and the USA's mighty industrial power forced the obstacles out of the way, and the B-29s not only began racking up the hours but their baffled crews gradually learned how to manage them, how to fly straight and level in a goldfish bowl without continuously using instruments, and above all how to get something faintly resembling the published range with heavy bombloads. Air miles per pound of fuel were improved by exactly 100 per cent between January and March 1944. And the complex systems grew reliable in the ultra-cold of 10060 m (33,000 ft).

On 5 June 1944 the first combat mission was flown from Kharagpur, India, to Bangkok; the worst problem was an unexpected tropical storm. On 15 June the first of the raids on Japan was mounted, from Chengtu (one of many newly bulldozed B-29 strips in China) to the Yawata steel works. The specially created 20th Air Force grew in muscle, and in October 1944 the first B-29s arrived on newly laid runways on the Marianas islands of Tinian, Saipan and Guam, just taken from the enemy. Swiftly the numbers grew as the mighty plants back home poured out B-29s and B-29As with 0.3 m (12 in) more span and the four-gun front turret, while Bell added 311 B-29Bs with all armament stripped except that in the tail, making a considerable difference in reduced weight and complexity. The B-29B was made possible by the patchy fighter opposition, and many Superfortresses were similarly stripped in the field.

Moreover, the commander of the XXI Bomber Command, Major-General Curtis LeMay, boldly decided to bomb Tokyo by night from low level, with a full load of incendiaries. There were many reasons for this, but the chief ones were that it promised much greater bombloads and the elimination of bombing errors attributable to jetstream winds. This policy, totally at variance with the idea of high-altitude day formations, resulted in the greatest firestorms the world has ever seen, and the biggest casualties ever caused by air attack. They were far greater than the 75,000 of Hiroshima, hit by the 20-kiloton 'Little Boy' atom bomb dropped on 6 August 1945 from Colonel Paul Tibbetts' B-29 *Enola Gay,* or the 35,000 of Nagasaki hit by the 20-kiloton 'Fat Man' dropped on 9 August from *Bock's Car.* The war ended five days later.

Many modifications

Only by the incredibly bold decision to go into the biggest multi-company production programme ever organised long before the first flight, did the B-29 manage to make so large a contribution to World War II. By VJ Day more than 2,000 were actually with combat crews, and though 5,000-plus were cancelled days later the manufacturing programme was slowed progressively, and did not close until May 1946, by which time 3,960 B-29s had been built. Hundreds were modified for different tasks, and many were launched on new careers as air/sea rescue aircraft, turbojet test-beds or tankers, which kept them busy for another decade or more. Back in 1942 Boeing had begun to work on the Model 367 transport version with a much larger upper lobe to a 'double bubble' fuselage, the first XC-97 flying on 15 November 1944. Various improved bomber versions were cancelled but the B-29D, with new engines, was continued and

With almost 4,000 examples to draw from, the B-29 was used in the post-war era for countless tasks, some of which may never get on the published record. B-29A-70-BN 44-62260 flew on clandestine missions over Manchuria in the last year of the Korean War.

A feature of the B-29's gun armament was the use of remotely-controlled turrets, periscopically sighted by gunners located within the fuselage. The aircraft illustrated, carrying BTO (bombing through overcast) radar, was based on Tinian for the final heavy raids on Japan in 1945.

became the B-50.

A B-29A (42-093845) was flown with the 28-cylinder Pratt & Whitney R-4360 Wasp Major engine in early 1944 as the XB-44, and the 2238-kW (3,000-hp) engine made such a difference that other changes were made, including a wing made of 75ST aluminium alloy giving much greater strength with 295 kg (650 lb) less weight, and a taller vertical tail. There were many systems changes, and the propellers were made reversible. The new bomber, the B-29D, went into production at Renton in July 1945. Manufacture continued, at a reduced pace, with the changed designation B-50. The first production B-50A finally emerged in June 1947, and Boeing built 79, followed by 45 strengthened B-50Bs (all but one being rebuilt as unarmed RB-50B reconnaissance aircraft with 2650-litre (583-Imp gal) underwing tanks), 222 of the definitive B-50D and finally 24 TB-50H crew trainers.

In the 1950s hundreds of B-29s kept flying, almost all modified for different roles but including 88 ordinary B-29 bombers handed to the RAF and used as the Boeing Washington by Bomber Command's Nos 15, 35, 44, 57, 90, 115, 149 and 207 Squadrons. In the USAF the jet-assisted KB-50J went on tanking until the last pair were struck off charge in Vietnam in 1963. But this is not really the end of the story.

Back in 1943 Josef Stalin began a major campaign to get B-29s. He never succeeded, and work began on a Soviet copy, though smaller and without the complex armament. Then out of the blue, on 29 July 1944, a B-29 made an emergency landing in the Soviet Union near Vladivostok after bombing Japan. Two more arrived later (one of them was the *General H. H. Arnold Special,* the 175th to be built and

picked out on the Wichita line by the USAAF chief of staff, who said "This is the one I want as soon as you can build it; it will complete our first Bomb Group"), and within weeks they were all being carefully taken apart. In an operation without parallel, the Russian technicians studied every part of the B-29 to the extent of preparing their own production drawings, establishing material specifications, manufacturing tolerances and production procedures. The vast Tupolev bureau finally went into production, trying to short-cut some areas by buying tyres and brakes in the USA. These purchases did not succeed, but they did make the US government believe the previously incredible rumours of what the Soviets were doing.

First the Tupolev bureau built much simpler aircraft, the big-bodied Tu-70 and Tu-75 transports, both of which incorporated the complete wing and many other parts of the 'captured' B-29s. The Tu-70 flew on 27 November 1946. On Aviation Day, 3 August 1947, three Soviet copies of the B-29, designated Tu-4 by the VVS (air force), thundered over Moscow. They were followed by over 300 others. Like the B-29 four years earlier, the Tu-4 test programme in 1947-9 was marked by plenty of problems, but the Tu-4 eventually matured and not only comprised the core of a formidable nuclear strike force but, to a far greater extent than the B-29 itself, led to versions of much greater power and capability including the Tu-80 and Tu-85 which represented the all-time pinnacle of piston-engine bomber development to the traditional formula. Very considerable amounts of B-29 technology were carried straight across to the Tu-88 (Tu-16 'Badger') and Tu-95 (Tu-20 'Bear'), and small features can no doubt be distinguished in today's Tu-22M 'Backfire'.

Though three RAF Meteors had been refuelled by a triple-point KB-29 years earlier, this test near Eglin AFB was the first by a triple-point KB-50D, in 1956. Aircraft 48-123, formerly a B-50D-105, was later boosted with underwing jet pods to become a KB-50J. The receiver aircraft were F-100Cs of TAC from Foster AFB.

Externally indistinguishable from the B-29, the Tupolev Tu-4 made its public debut at the 1947 Soviet Aviation Day held at Tushino, Moscow. This photograph of the original aircraft was taken in 1983 at Monino, which was closed to the public shortly afterwards.

Heinkel He 115

*Within a few months of its first flight in 1938, the He 115 had
captured eight world speed records. Its remarkable performance,
for a seaplane of the day, made it an obvious candidate for Hitler's
newly-founded Luftwaffe Seeflieger and a year later the aircraft
went to war as a torpedo bomber. Rapidly overtaken by progress,
perhaps the He 115's greatest claim to fame is that it managed to
serve with Germany, Britain and neutral Sweden.*

World War II was the last conflict in which twin-float seaplanes
played a significant part. Of dozens of types used, the biggest
and most powerful seaplane used in quantity was the Heinkel He 115.
What makes its story even more fascinating is that it saw service not
only with Germany but also with Norway, Sweden, Finland and the
British RAF.

This is despite the fact that the He 115 was, like many con-
temporaries, obsolescent from the start. Though designed as a war-
plane to fly not only patrol but also torpedo and bombing missions,
the 115 was always too slow and ill-defended to have any chance
against fighters. This was far from obvious when the requirement for
a new See-Mehrzweckeflugzeug was issued in July 1935. In early
1938 prototypes of the He 115 proved superior to the rival Ha 140,
and Heinkel was awarded the first of several production contracts.
These were ultimately to total 138 aircraft, of which 76 were built by
Flugzeugbau 'Weser'.

The He 115 V1 made its first flight in August 1937. A conventional
all-metal stressed-skin machine, it had a slim fuselage, mid-mounted

wing with a rectangular centre-section and sharply tapered outer
panels, braced tailplane, twin BMW 132K engines (derived from the
Pratt & Whitney Hornet) each rated at 715 kW (960 hp), and single-
step floats each attached by tandem struts and multiple bracing
wires. The wings had simple slotted flaps, the tailplane was fixed and
there were large trim tabs on all control surfaces. The fuselage was
arranged to accommodate a crew of three. The pilot's cockpit was
above the wing leading edge, covered by a sliding canopy. In the
glazed nose was a seat for the observer who also had a bombsight
and, in an upper cupola, an MG 15 machine-gun. Above the trailing
edge was the cockpit for the radio operator, who also had an MG 15
for upper rear defence. The fuselage beneath the wing was designed
as an internal weapons bay, able to accommodate an 800-kg (1,763-
lb) torpedo or three SC250 1250-kg (550-lb) bombs.

*Displaying the distinctive wing shape of the earlier Heinkel 70, a
Heinkel He 115B taxis in Norwegian waters. Despite a certain amount
of obsolescence, the type proved to be particularly tough, especially
in rough seas, and was also able to sustain a great deal of combat
damage. Water and flight handling were excellent, as was its speed.*

The first prototype flew in August 1938, and to publicise the type was later prepared with a streamlined nosecone and additional fuel for record-breaking. In this configuration it established several float seaplane records for speed with load over various distances on 20 March 1938.

Altogether the He 115 showed itself to be extremely strong, to handle well and to have no significant shortcomings. In March 1938, by which time the 115 had been picked for the Luftwaffe Seeflieger, the prototype was modified with streamlined fairings over the nose and dorsal cockpits and given greater fuel capacity, and used to gain world records for speed with load, covering closed circuits of up to 2000 km (1,242 miles) with payloads up to 2000 kg (4,410 lb) at an average speed of 328 km/h (203 mph). By this time two further prototypes had flown, the V3 being almost representative of the production aircraft. The outer wings had more taper on the leading edge and less on the trailing edge, the nose was lengthened and made more streamlined with a gun cupola on the nose, and the pilot's cockpit was joined to that of the radio operator by a continuous 'greenhouse'. The radio operator was provided with a simple control column and pedals with which it was hoped he could bring the aircraft back should the pilot be incapacitated.

In 1938 two export orders were received: six He 115s for Norway and 12 for Sweden. These were built almost to the same standard as the He 115A-1 which went into production for the Luftwaffe in January 1939. The A-1 closely resembled the V3 prototype, with the addition of underwing racks for two further SC250 bombs. Delivery to the first Küstenfliegerstaffel, 1/KüFlGr 106, began with the outbreak of war, but Heinkel's Marienehe plant terminated production at the 62nd aircraft at the start of 1940. This total comprised 10 pre-production A-0s, 18 export aircraft (called A-2s and differing in radio, guns and other equipment) and 34 A-1 and A-3 seaplanes for the Luftwaffe. The A-3s had improved radio and weapon-release equipment.

All subsequent production was handled by 'Weser' at Einswarden, starting with 10 B-0s with increased fuel capacity. By 1940 the B-1 was in production, with various Rüstsätze (conversion kits) for bombing, minelaying (for example), carrying two 500-kg (1,100-lb) bombs, LMAIII mines or a single monster LMB III of 920-kg (2,028-lb) or photo-reconnaissance. The last 18 B-series were completed as B-2s with reinforced floats fitted with steel skate-like runners for operation from ice or compacted snow. This was often to prove a considerable operational advantage, though pilots had to devise a mild rocking technique, by opening and closing the throttles, to unstick the floats if they were frozen in.

The V1's record-breaking flight led to the first export order from Norway, which purchased six for the Marinens Flyvevaben. Three of these He 115A-2s were successful in escaping to Britain after the invasion, together with one captured German aircraft. They were converted for clandestine operations for the RAF.

Production by 'Weser' was completed with various sub-types of He 115C. This basically resembled the B-series but introduced heavier armament. It had been apparent for some time that two MG 15s was not adequate defensive firepower for a large aircraft with a cruising speed of about 270 km/h (167 mph). In early 1940 the V5 prototype was tested with a 20-mm MG FF cannon aimed by hand from the nose, and one might have thought this, plus a similar cannon aimed by the radio operator, could have provided the answer. What actually happened was that the He 115C-1 went into production with an MG 151/15 fixed under the nose to fire ahead, and two MG 17 machine-guns were added in the engine nacelles firing directly to the rear. The forward-firing gun was a high-velocity weapon with excellent ballistics, but to be effective the big floatplane had to be flown like a fighter. It was virtually useless for defence. As for the aft-firing guns, these could not be aimed at all, and (assuming an attacking fighter knew of their presence) were relatively easy to evade. The C-2 had the ice/snow skids, the C-3 was a specialised minelayer, and the C-4 was an Arctic-equipped torpedo carrier with no forward-firing armament.

Up-gunning in wartime

During their active careers, in 1942, surviving He 115s of all kinds were almost all fitted with the MG 81Z twin machine-gun package in place of the MG 15 in the radio operator's cockpit. This was a neater and very much faster-firing installation which did go some way to improving defensive firepower. Some aircraft, and possibly most, were retrofitted with a powerful MG 151/20 under the nose, in a prominent box which also housed the ammunition. The gun was carried on the left side and caused a noticeable nose-down pull to the left when fired. The original nose MG 15 was retained.

In late 1939, Heinkel stopped production of the He 115, all the tooling being moved to Einswarden for the 'Weser' Flugzeugbau factory. The new production model was the He 115B, incorporating greater structural strength and more fuel. This is a He 115B-1 on pre-delivery trials in early 1940.

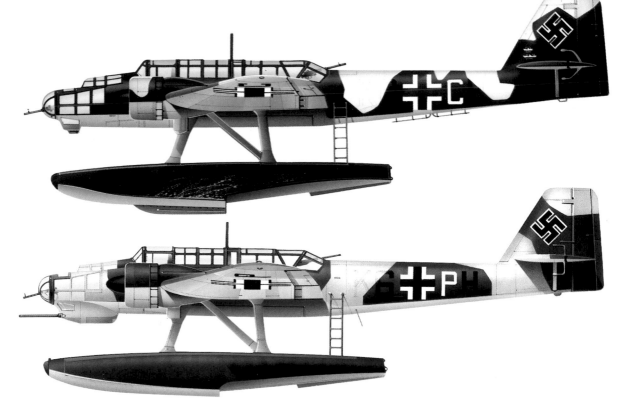

An He 115B-2 of 1./KüFlGr 406, operating in Norway. During winter a white distemper was applied to the normal splinter scheme to camouflage the aircraft in snow conditions. Note the ship kill marks on the fin.

'K6+PH' was an He 115C-1 serving with 1./KüFlGr 406 during 1942, when the unit was involved in attacking convoys taking equipment from Britain to the Soviet Union via the North Cape route.

This He 115C-1 of 3./KüFlGr 106 (code M2) shows the original 15-mm MG 151 cannon installation in the nose. Night minelaying operations were undertaken by the He 115 in British waters, and for this reason they were hastily applied with black paint to mask the light grey undersides, national insignia and white code letter.

There was one attempt to increase flight performance, which had progressively deteriorated as a result of the increased weight of fuel, weapons and equipment of successive versions. In 1939 Heinkel had proposed an improved He 115 fitted with much more powerful engines, and this materialised in 1940 when an ex-Luftwaffe aircraft was returned to Marienehe and considerably modified. The structure was locally strengthened to accept bigger engines and increased gross weights, and two 1194-kW (1,600-hp) BMW 801A 14-cylinder radial engines were installed in installations generally similar to those of the early Do 217E. The fuselage was rearranged for a crew of four, with a 20-mm MG 151 under the left side of the nose, an MG 81 in the nose cupola and MG 81Z twin machine-guns in both the rear dorsal and ventral positions. Maximum speed was increased from about 295 to 380 km/h (183 to 236 mph), despite the increase in weight to 12640 kg (27,865 lb), but only the one aircraft was ever converted. Known as the He 115D-0, it later served with the Küstenfliegerstaffel.

Sturdy build

From the start the He 115 had a good reputation for strength, reliability and all-round capability. They were intensively used by both the Luftwaffe and Norwegian naval air service during the invasion of Norway in April/May 1940. At the end of this conflict one Norwegian aircraft was flown to Finland, where it was repaired and put into active service with the Ilmavoimat, where in 1943 it was joined by two He 115Cs supplied from Germany. Three Norwegian He 115A-2s and a captured B-1 were flown to Scotland, where they received RAF serial numbers BV184-187. All continued flying until there were destroyed or the spares ran out. All were modified, the

The He 115C-1 replaced the B on the production line during 1940, this adding a fixed 15-mm cannon under the nose and rearward-firing MG 17 machine-guns in the rear of the engine nacelle. During 1942-43, the 15-mm cannon was replaced by a 20-mm MG 151 in a bathtub fairing, as seen here.

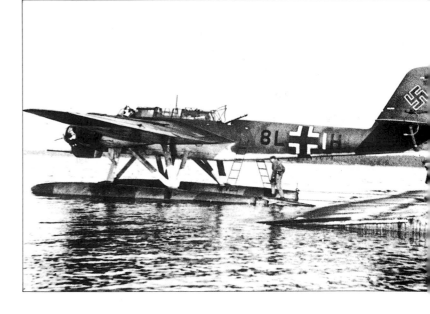

Heinkel He 115

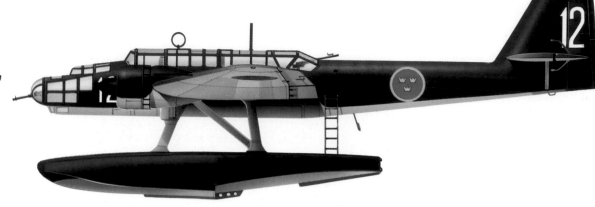

Apart from Norway, the only other export order for the He 115 came from Sweden, which purchased 12 He 115A-2s. These were used for coastal maritime reconnaissance, serving with F2 Roslagens Flygflottilj.

most obvious changes being replacement of the long 'glasshouse' by metal panels and fitting of British armament. Aircraft 185 and 187 were modified for clandestine operations, one startling change being the addition of four Browning machine-guns firing ahead from the leading edge of the wings, plus four more firing to the rear. In October 1941 BV185 was flown round via Gibraltar to Malta, where it enjoyed a charmed life in Luftwaffe markings, making numerous missions to North Africa by night and by day inserting and picking up Allied agents. On one occasion it landed in Tripoli harbour in broad daylight, took on board two agents and returned to Malta. Eventually it was destroyed at Malta by bombing. Meanwhile 187, the former Luftwaffe B-1, flew several long missions between Woodhaven, on the Firth of Tay, and points in Norway. Eventually it was decided that these missions posed too great a risk, mainly from destruction by RAF fighters.

Twilight misions

Luftwaffe He 115s had carried out minelaying operations from the the start of the war, and from 1942 surviving examples were all grouped in northern Norway for operations against Allied convoys. The most important and most successful missions were against the ill-fated convoy PQ17 in July 1942. Eight He 115C-1s of the KüFlGr 406 made torpedo attacks on 2 July, the Staffelkapitän being shot down but rescued, with his crew, by another 115 which alighted on the stormy sea. On 4 July aircraft of KüFlGr 906 disabled one ship, and subsequently aircraft of both units played a part in hunting down and sinking 23 of the 36 vessels that had comprised the convoy. A few 115s lingered on into mid-1944, but they saw little action.

Shortly before the planned invasion of Norway and Denmark, 'Weser' Flugzeugbau received instructions to prepare the aircraft for operations from snow and ice. Additional strengthening to the planing bottom and a steel skid was added, the resultant aircraft being designated He 115B-2, 18 of which were built.

Heinkel He 115B cutaway drawing key

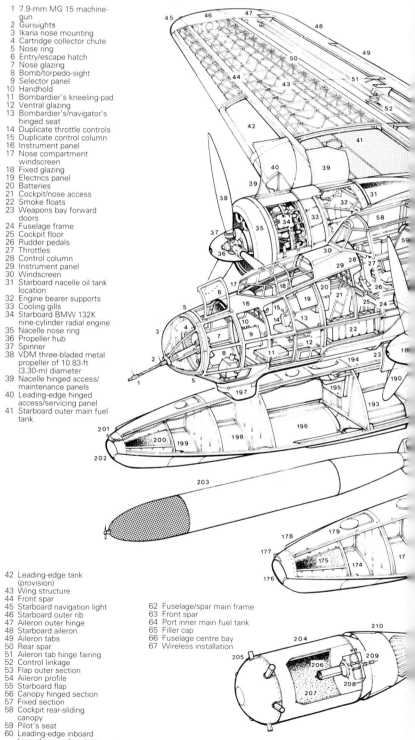

1 7.9-mm MG 15 machine-gun
2 Gunsights
3 Ikaria nose mounting
4 Cartridge collector chute
5 Nose ring
6 Entry/escape hatch
7 Nose glazing
8 Bomb/torpedo-sight
9 Selector panel
10 Handhold
11 Bombardier's kneeling-pad
12 Ventral glazing
13 Bombardier's/navigator's hinged seat
14 Duplicate throttle controls
15 Duplicate control column
16 Instrument panel
17 Nose compartment windscreen
18 Fixed glazing
19 Electrics panel
20 Batteries
21 Cockpit/nose access
22 Smoke floats
23 Weapons bay forward doors
24 Fuselage frame
25 Cockpit floor
26 Rudder pedals
27 Throttles
28 Control column
29 Instrument panel
30 Windscreen
31 Starboard nacelle oil tank location
32 Engine bearer supports
33 Cooling gills
34 Starboard BMW 132K nine-cylinder radial engine
35 Nacelle nose ring
36 Propeller hub
37 Spinner
38 VDM three-bladed metal propeller of 10.83-ft (3.30-m) diameter
39 Nacelle hinged access/maintenance panels
40 Leading-edge hinged access/servicing panel
41 Starboard outer main fuel tank

42 Leading-edge tank (provision)
43 Wing structure
44 Front spar
45 Starboard navigation light
46 Starboard outer rib
47 Aileron outer hinge
48 Starboard aileron
49 Aileron tabs
50 Rear spar
51 Aileron tab hinge fairing
52 Control linkage
53 Flap outer section
54 Aileron profile
55 Starboard flap
56 Canopy hinged section
57 Fixed section
58 Cockpit rear-sliding canopy
59 Pilot's seat
60 Leading-edge inboard hinged access/servicing panel
61 Front spar carry-through

62 Fuselage/spar main frame
63 Front spar
64 Port inner main fuel tank
65 Filler cap
66 Fuselage centre bay
67 Wireless installation

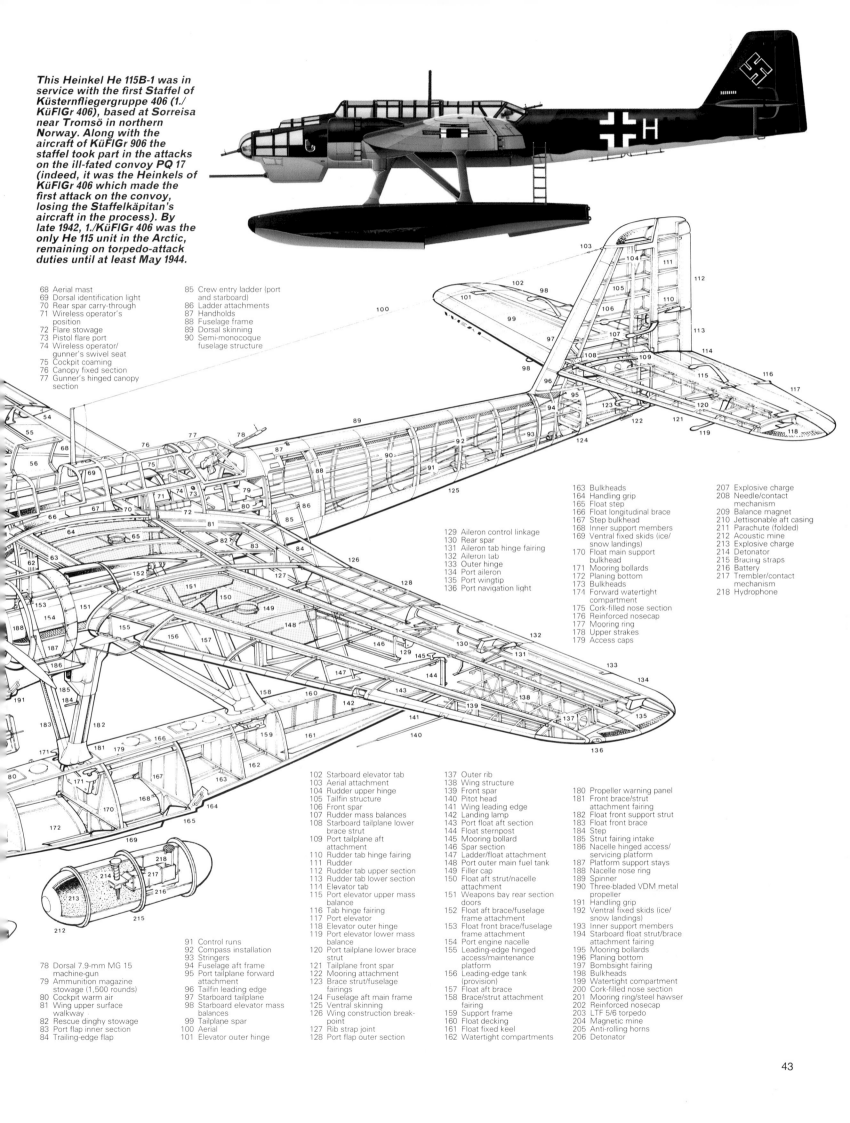

This Heinkel He 115B-1 was in service with the first Staffel of Küstenfliegergruppe 406 (1./KüFlGr 406), based at Sorreisa near Tromsö in northern Norway. Along with the aircraft of KüFlGr 906 the staffel took part in the attacks on the ill-fated convoy PQ 17 (indeed, it was the Heinkels of KüFlGr 406 which made the first attack on the convoy, losing the Staffelkäpitan's aircraft in the process). By late 1942, 1./KüFlGr 406 was the only He 115 unit in the Arctic, remaining on torpedo-attack duties until at least May 1944.

68 Aerial mast
69 Dorsal identification light
70 Rear spar carry-through
71 Wireless operator's position
72 Flare stowage
73 Pistol flare port
74 Wireless operator/gunner's swivel seat
75 Cockpit coaming
76 Canopy fixed section
77 Gunner's hinged canopy section
85 Crew entry ladder (port and starboard)
86 Ladder attachments
87 Handholds
88 Fuselage frame
89 Dorsal skinning
90 Semi-monocoque fuselage structure

78 Dorsal 7.9-mm MG 15 machine-gun
79 Ammunition magazine stowage (1,500 rounds)
80 Cockpit warm air
81 Wing upper surface walkway
82 Rescue dinghy stowage
83 Port flap inner section
84 Trailing-edge flap

91 Control runs
92 Compass installation
93 Stringers
94 Fuselage aft frame
95 Port tailplane forward attachment
96 Tailfin leading edge
97 Starboard tailplane
98 Starboard elevator mass balances
99 Tailplane spar
100 Aerial
101 Elevator outer hinge

129 Aileron control linkage
130 Rear spar
131 Aileron tab hinge fairing
132 Aileron tab
133 Outer hinge
134 Port aileron
135 Port wingtip
136 Port navigation light

102 Starboard elevator tab
103 Aerial attachment
104 Rudder upper hinge
105 Tailfin structure
106 Front spar
107 Rudder mass balances
108 Starboard tailplane lower brace strut
109 Port tailplane aft attachment
110 Rudder tab hinge fairing
111 Rudder
112 Rudder tab upper section
113 Rudder tab lower section
114 Elevator tab
115 Port elevator upper mass balance
116 Tab hinge fairing
117 Port elevator
118 Elevator outer hinge
119 Port elevator lower mass balance
120 Port tailplane lower brace strut
121 Tailplane front spar
122 Mooring attachment
123 Brace strut/fuselage fairings
124 Fuselage aft main frame
125 Ventral skinning
126 Wing construction break-point
127 Rib strap joint
128 Port flap outer section

137 Outer rib
138 Wing structure
139 Front spar
140 Pitot head
141 Wing leading edge
142 Landing lamp
143 Port float aft section
144 Float sternpost
145 Mooring bollard
146 Spar section
147 Ladder/float attachment
148 Port outer main fuel tank
149 Filler cap
150 Float aft strut/nacelle attachment
151 Weapons bay rear section doors
152 Float aft brace/fuselage frame attachment
153 Float front brace/fuselage frame attachment
154 Port engine nacelle
155 Leading-edge hinged access/maintenance platform
156 Leading-edge tank (provision)
157 Float aft brace
158 Brace/strut attachment fairing
159 Support frame
160 Float decking
161 Float fixed keel
162 Watertight compartments

163 Bulkheads
164 Handling grip
165 Float step
166 Float longitudinal brace
167 Step bulkhead
168 Inner support members
169 Ventral fixed skids (ice/snow landings)
170 Float main support bulkhead
171 Mooring bollards
172 Planing bottom
173 Bulkheads
174 Forward watertight compartment
175 Cork-filled nose section
176 Reinforced nosecap
177 Mooring ring
178 Upper strakes
179 Access caps

180 Propeller warning panel
181 Front brace/strut attachment fairing
182 Float front support strut
183 Float front brace
184 Step
185 Strut fairing intake
186 Nacelle hinged access/servicing platform
187 Platform support stays
188 Nacelle nose ring
189 Spinner
190 Three-bladed VDM metal propeller
191 Handling grip
192 Ventral fixed skids (ice/snow landings)
193 Inner support members
194 Starboard float strut/brace attachment fairing
195 Mooring bollards
196 Planing bottom
197 Bombsight fairing
198 Bulkheads
199 Watertight compartment
200 Cork-filled nose section
201 Mooring ring/steel hawser
202 Reinforced nosecap
203 LTF 5/6 torpedo
204 Magnetic mine
205 Anti-rolling horns
206 Detonator

207 Explosive charge
208 Needle/contact mechanism
209 Balance magnet
210 Jettisonable aft casing
211 Parachute (folded)
212 Acoustic mine
213 Explosive charge
214 Detonator
215 Bracing straps
216 Battery
217 Trembler/contact mechanism
218 Hydrophone

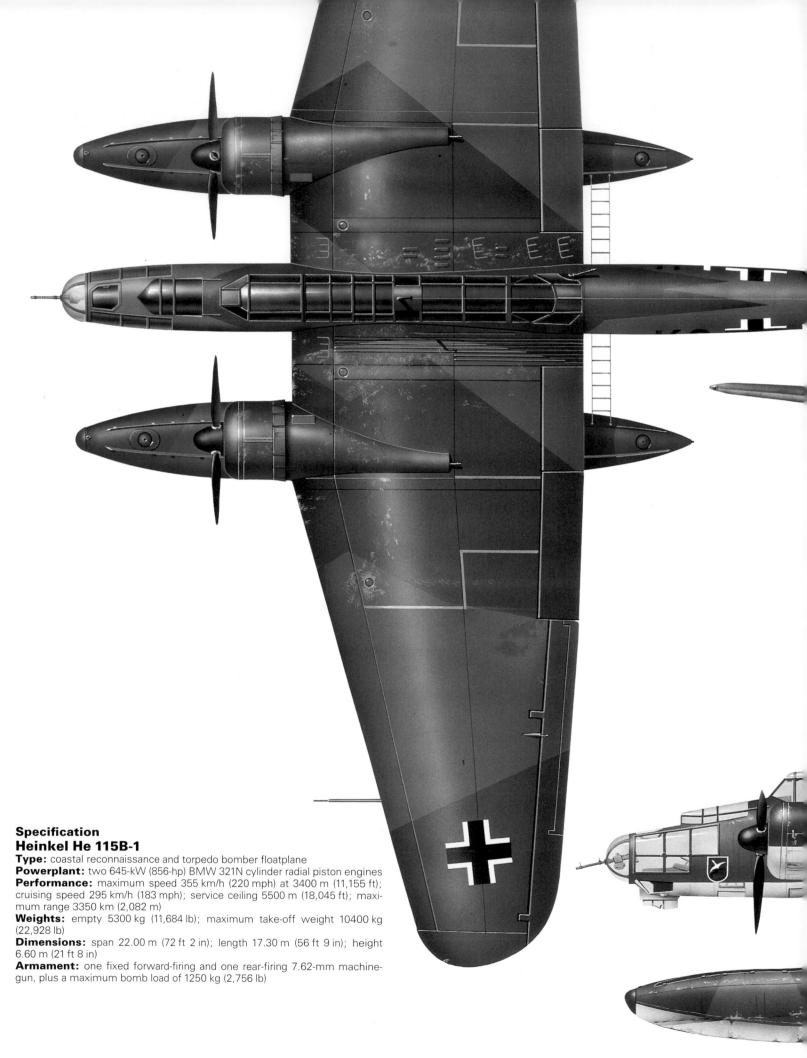

Specification
Heinkel He 115B-1
Type: coastal reconnaissance and torpedo bomber floatplane
Powerplant: two 645-kW (856-hp) BMW 321N cylinder radial piston engines
Performance: maximum speed 355 km/h (220 mph) at 3400 m (11,155 ft); cruising speed 295 km/h (183 mph); service ceiling 5500 m (18,045 ft); maximum range 3350 km (2,082 m)
Weights: empty 5300 kg (11,684 lb); maximum take-off weight 10400 kg (22,928 lb)
Dimensions: span 22.00 m (72 ft 2 in); length 17.30 m (56 ft 9 in); height 6.60 m (21 ft 8 in)
Armament: one fixed forward-firing and one rear-firing 7.62-mm machine-gun, plus a maximum bomb load of 1250 kg (2,756 lb)

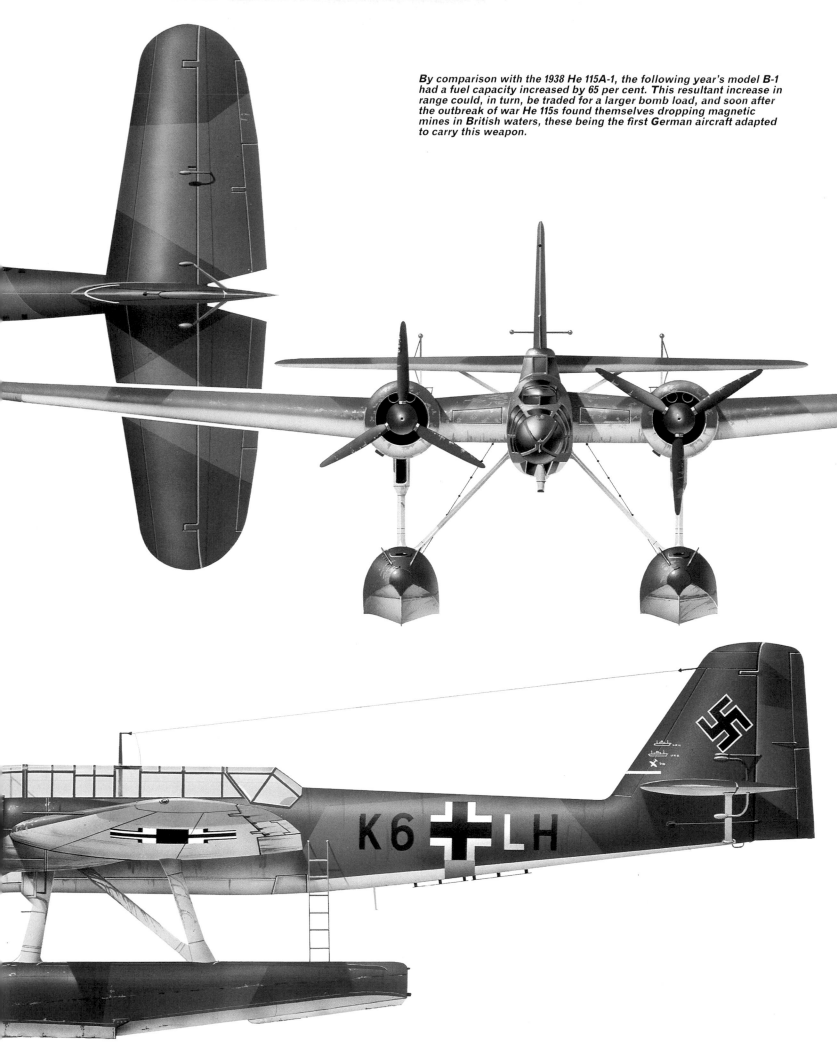

By comparison with the 1938 He 115A-1, the following year's model B-1 had a fuel capacity increased by 65 per cent. This resultant increase in range could, in turn, be traded for a larger bomb load, and soon after the outbreak of war He 115s found themselves dropping magnetic mines in British waters, these being the first German aircraft adapted to carry this weapon.

Fairey Swordfish: Taranto Tinfisher

Archaic in appearance even when it first flew, the venerable Swordfish survived as an anachronism throughout World War II, outlived its replacement and destroyed a greater tonnage of enemy shipping than any other Allied torpedo bomber. It was best known for the courageous attack on the Italian fleet at Taranto.

The origins of the Swordfish lay in the Fairey Aviation Company's privately-sponsored tender to Air Ministry Specification S.9/30, which called for a torpedo-carrying fleet spotter in the early 1930s. The TSR I prototype, powered by a 474-kW (635-hp) Bristol Pegasus IIM nine-cylinder air-cooled radial engine, was flown on 21 March 1933 but was soon shown to be underpowered and directionally unstable, being destroyed after failure to recover from a spin some six months later.

A revised Specification, S.15/33, was drafted and Fairey produced the TSR II with lengthened fuselage, revised tail unit and an uprated Pegasus IIIM3 developing 578 kW (775 hp). Its structure was largely of fabric-covered metal with split-axle wheel landing gear capable of replacement by twin single-step Fairey floats. With a maximum sea-level speed of 235 km/h (146 mph) and first flown on 17 April 1934, this aircraft exceeded the specified performance demands and three prototype development aircraft, named Swordfish, were ordered to meet Specification S.38/34; the third aircraft was completed as a floatplane, making its first flight on 10 November 1934.

The first production order for 86 aircraft was placed in 1935 and initial deliveries were made the following February to No. 823 Squadron, which embarked in HMS *Glorious* later that year, replacing Shark Mk IIs. The standard three-seat production aircraft had a maximum speed of 222 km/h (138 mph) and was easily capable of lifting a standard 457-mm (18-in) 731-kg (1,610-lb) torpedo from the decks of all British carriers with full load, its range in this configuration being 879 km (546 miles).

Further orders continued with Fairey until, by the outbreak of war

in 1939, a total of 689 Swordfish aircraft had been completed or were on order. Mk I floatplanes were serving with Nos 701, 702 and 705 Catapult Flights of the Fleet Air Arm, being embarked in most of the Royal Navy's battleships, battle-cruisers and cruisers in commission, as well as serving with wheel landing gear in 13 squadrons, of which eight were at sea in the carriers HMS *Ark Royal, Argus, Courageous, Eagle, Furious, Glorious* and *Hermes*.

Swordfish were in action from the earliest days of the war and it was a floatplane flown by Lieutenant Commander W.M.L. Brown from HMS *Warspite* during the Battle of Narvik on 13 April 1940 that was used to direct the fire of the battleship's guns, resulting in the destruction of seven German destroyers, one of which was finished off by a bomb from Brown's aircraft; he also sank with bombs the German submarine *U-64* in Herjangsfjord.

In 1940, as production of the Fairey Fulmar fleet fighter increased at Fairey's Hayes factory, responsibility for the Swordfish was taken over entirely by Blackburn Aircraft Limited at Sherburn-in-Elmet, Yorkshire, the first aircraft being completed on 29 December. After 300 Mk Is had been delivered in nine months, Blackburn production switched to the Mk II with strengthened lower wing, with metal skin to permit the carriage of eight rocket projectiles. The provision for interchangeability of wheel and float landing gear was discarded after

A formation of early Swordfish Mk Is in November 1938 from the second and third production batches; these aircraft had provision for interchangeable wheel and float undercarriage. The aircraft shown here were clearly squadron aircraft, although probably not embarked in a carrier (note absence of fuselage chevron).

Originally referred to as the Fairey TSR 2, the prototype Swordfish, K4190, was designed and built to Specification S.15/33 and carried the Fairey works no. F2038 in small characters aft of the service serial number on the rear fuselage.

A Swordfish Mk I, K5972, of the initial Fairey-built production batch in the markings of No. 823 Sqn, embarked in HMS Glorious in 1936. The fin stripes identify the Flight aircraft.

termination of the Mk I production.

Mk Is continued in service throughout 1940, and once again it was Lieutenant Commander Brown who provided excellent spotting services for HMS *Warspite*'s main armament in the 'Action off Calabria' against the Italian fleet on 9 July.

Taranto attack

Later that year, however, the brilliantly-executed attack on the Italian fleet in Taranto harbour on 11 November constituted the pinnacle on which the Swordfish's fame was forever to stand. Following a remarkable feat of low-level reconnaissance by a Maryland crew which disclosed a concentration of Italian naval vessels in the port, it was decided to launch a night strike by the Swordfish of Nos 813, 815, 819 and 824 Squadrons from HMS *Illustrious* (Rear Admiral Lumley Lyster, himself an experienced naval pilot who had served at Taranto during World War I). Led by Lieutenant Commander Kenneth Williamson, the first wave of 12 aircraft (six with torpedoes, four with bombs and two with bombs and flares) was launched 10 minutes before a second wave of nine aircraft (five with torpedoes,

two with bombs and two with bombs and flares) led by Lieutenant Commander John Hale, achieving almost total tactical surprise, the Swordfish crews attacked at low level, sinking the new 35,000-ton battleship *Littorio* at her moorings, and crippling the two older battleships *Conte di Cavour* and *Caio Duilio*, as well as a heavy cruiser and a destroyer. At a single stroke Italy's naval power in the Mediterranean was reduced by a half, at a cost of two Swordfish (Williamson himself being shot down and taken prisoner). A post-script to this attack lay in the fact that the Japanese naval attaché in Rome was recalled to Tokyo and became the architect of the Japanese attack on Pearl Harbor one year later.

Thereafter, and for many months to come, Fleet Air Arm Swordfish, based on Malta, became the scourge of Axis shipping in the Mediterranean, between them sinking more than a million and a half tons of German and Italian ships during 1941-3. Among their other widely varying tasks in that theatre were minelaying, fleet reconnaissance, gunnery spotting, coastal bombing attacks and even agent-dropping. One Swordfish is recorded as having flown 12 mine-laying sorties in a single 24-hour period.

A Swordfish Mk II of the main Blackburn-built production batch. Carrying a smoke float under the starboard wing, this aircraft was typical of the many carrier-based 'Stringbags'.

Fairey Swordfish: Taranto Tinfisher

Super wartime photo of a Swordfish Mk I (P4084) with float undercarriage being launched from a slipway. These aircraft were widely used aboard Royal Navy ships during World War II for reconnaissance and gunnery spotting duties.

The most famous of all Swordfish pilots now joins the story. Lieutenant Commander Eugene Esmonde, a peacetime Imperial Airways pilot from Ireland, and who now commanded a Swordfish squadron aboard HMS *Victorious*, led a torpedo attack by nine aircraft on the German battleship *Bismarck* at large in the Atlantic on 26 May 1941 as she made her way towards Brest. The attack resulted in at least one vital hit, which crippled the vessel's steering mechanism, thereby allowing the British fleet to catch and sink her. Esmonde was awarded the DSO for his part in the operation, and he now joined HMS *Ark Royal* in the Mediterranean; however, when the carrier was torpedoed he managed to fly off all his Swordfish and make for Gibraltar before the ship sank.

By the end of the year Esmonde was stationed in Kent, commanding No. 825 Squadron, deployed to counter any attempt by the German warships *Scharnhorst* and *Gneisenau* to break out of Brest and escape up the English Channel to Germany. On 12 February 1942 the worst British fears were realised when the German ships evaded all patrols and reached the eastern end of the Channel before being spotted. Esmonde's six Swordfish were thus the only aircraft readily available for an initial strike. Flying from Manston, the Swordfish crews missed their fighter rendezvous but pressed home their attack in the face of overwhelming enemy fighter and flak defences. Esmonde, in a Swordfish Mk II (W5984), was himself one of the first to be shot down by a Focke-Wulf Fw 190, followed by all five of his fellow pilots; none of their torpedoes found its mark. Of the 18 crew members only five survived to be rescued from the sea and all received the DSO or CGM. Esmonde was awarded a posthumous Victoria Cross.

Meanwhile efforts had been made to speed a replacement for the now-famous old 'Stringbag' biplane. The Fairey Albacore had been in production for some months but never lived up to its modest expectations (800 were produced, but manufacture stopped in 1943, while that of the Swordfish continued for a further year). The Fairey Barracuda (a Merlin-powered monoplane) for all its grotesque appearance might have had a distinguished career had it not been severely delayed after the abandoning of its original Rolls-Royce Exe engine.

Later Blackfish

As it was, Blackburn continued to produce Swordfish Mk IIs (known locally as 'Blackfish') until 1944, completing the last of 1,080 examples on 22 February that year. Production then switched to the Mk III, which was fitted with a large ASV scanner between the landing gear legs, thereby preventing carriage of the torpedo; when employed on anti-shipping torpedo strikes it was normal practice for one Mk III to assume the search role, while Mk IIs in the strike unit carried bombs and torpedoes. Swordfish were widely used aboard the relatively small escort carriers which were hurriedly introduced for convoy duties, particularly in the North Atlantic in the mid-war years, their normal complement of six Swordfish and six Grumman Martlet fighters being permanently ranged on their steeply pitching decks at the mercy of the elements.

The final version was the Mk IV, retrospectively modified Mk IIs and Mk IIIs with a rudimentary cockpit enclosure, and this version continued in service until the end of the war in Europe. A small number of Swordfish was sent to Canada for operational and training purposes, some serving with No. 1 Naval Air Gunnery School at Yarmouth, Nova Scotia.

The last Mk III (NS204) was completed at Sherburn on 18 August 1944, and it was a Swordfish that flew the Fleet Air Arm's last operational sortie by a biplane on 28 June 1945. By 1967 only six complete Swordfish, of the 2,396 production aircraft built, were known to survive: of these, one (LS326, once registered G-AJVH) has remained in flying condition and still makes frequent visits to air displays throughout Britain with the Royal Navy's Historic Flight, based at RNAS Yeovilton in Somerset.

Fairey Swordfish II cutaway drawing key:

1 Rudder structure
2 Rudder upper hinge
3 Diagonal brace
4 External bracing wires
5 Rudder hinge
6 Elevator control horn
7 Tail navigation light
8 Elevator structure
9 Fixed tab
10 Elevator balance
11 Elevator hinge
12 Starboard tailplane
13 Tailplane struts
14 Lashing down shackle
15 Trestling foot
16 Rear wedge
17 Rudder lower hinge
18 Tailplane adjustment screw
19 Elevator control cable
20 External bracing wires
21 Elevator fixed tab
22 Tailfin structure
23 Bracing wire attachment
24 Aerial stub
25 Bracing wires
26 Port elevator
27 Port tailplane
28 Tailplane support struts
29 Dinghy external release cord
30 Tailwheel oleo shock absorber
31 Non-retractable Dunlop tailwheel
32 Fuselage framework
33 Arrester hook housing
34 Control cable fairleads
35 Dorsal decking
36 Rod aerial
37 Lewis gun stowage trough
38 Aerial
39 Flexible 0.303-in (7.7-mm) Lewis machine gun
40 Fairey high-speed flexible gun mounting
41 Type O-3 compass mounting points
42 Aft cockpit coaming
43 Aft cockpit
44 Lewis drum magazine stowage
45 Radio installation
46 Ballast weights
47 Arrester hook pivot
48 Fuselage lower longeron
49 Arrester hook (part extended)
50 Aileron hinge
51 Fixed tab
52 Starboard upper aileron
53 Rear spar
54 Wing ribs
55 Starboard formation light
56 Starboard navigation light
57 Aileron connect strut
58 Interplane struts
59 Bracing wires
60 Starboard lower aileron
61 Aileron hinge
62 Aileron balance
63 Rear spar
64 Wing ribs
65 Aileron outer hinge
66 Deck-handling/lashing grips
67 Front spar
68 Interplane strut attachments
69 Wing internal diagonal bracing wires
70 Flying wires
71 Wing skinning
72 Additional support wire (fitted when underwing stores carried)
73 Wing fold hinge
74 Inboard interplane struts
75 Stub plane end rib
76 Wing locking handle
77 Stub plane structure
78 Intake slot
79 Side window
80 Catapult spool
81 Drag struts
82 Cockpit sloping floor

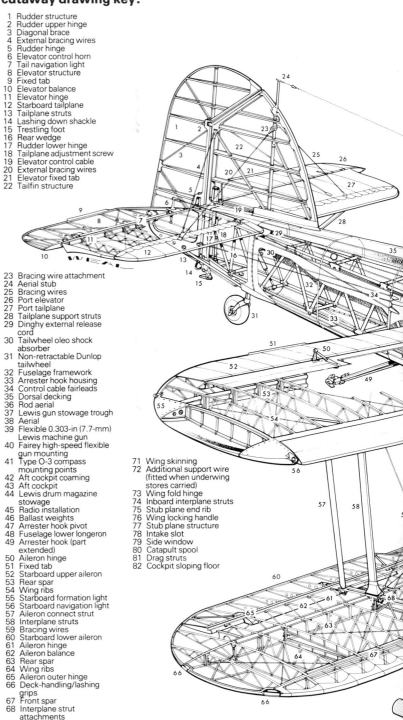

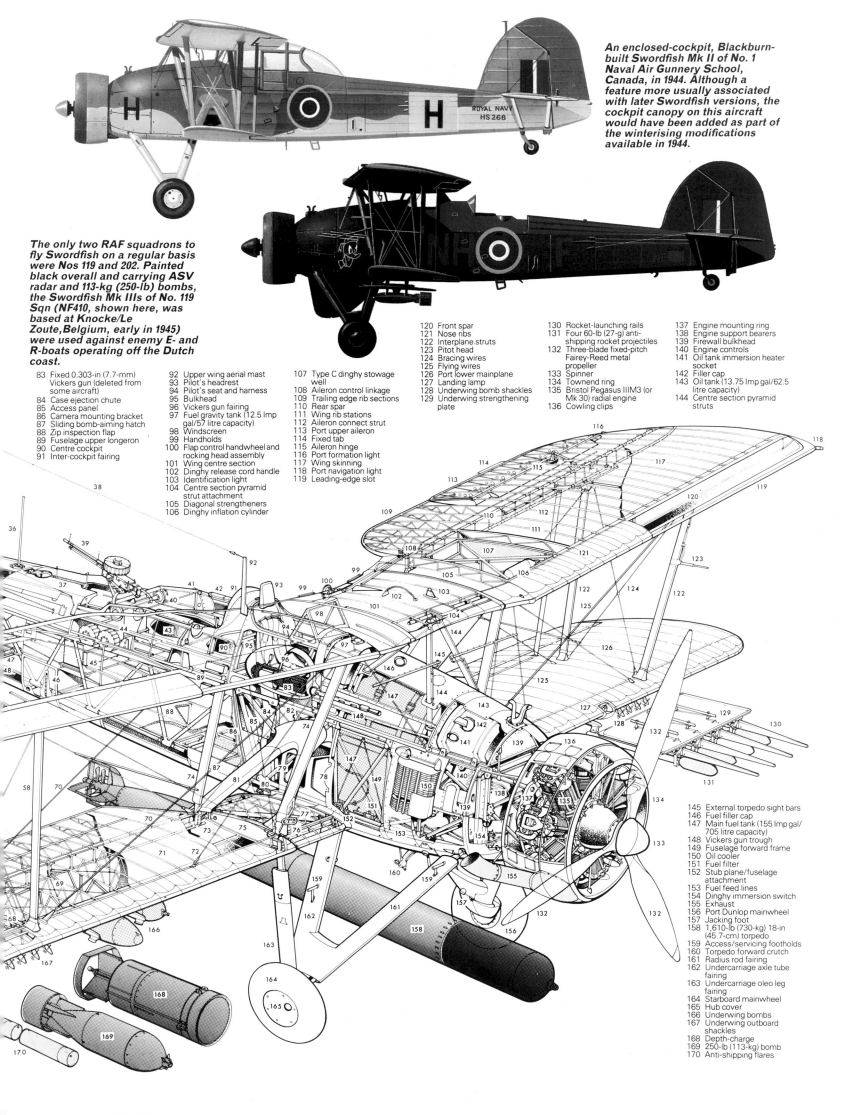

An enclosed-cockpit, Blackburn-built Swordfish Mk II of No. 1 Naval Air Gunnery School, Canada, in 1944. Although a feature more usually associated with later Swordfish versions, the cockpit canopy on this aircraft would have been added as part of the winterising modifications available in 1944.

ROYAL NAVY
HS 268

The only two RAF squadrons to fly Swordfish on a regular basis were Nos 119 and 202. Painted black overall and carrying ASV radar and 113-kg (250-lb) bombs, the Swordfish Mk IIIs of No. 119 Sqn (NF410, shown here, was based at Knocke/Le Zoute, Belgium, early in 1945) were used against enemy E- and R-boats operating off the Dutch coast.

83 Fixed 0.303-in (7.7-mm) Vickers gun (deleted from some aircraft)
84 Case ejection chute
85 Access panel
86 Camera mounting bracket
87 Sliding bomb-aiming hatch
88 Zip inspection flap
89 Fuselage upper longeron
90 Centre cockpit
91 Inter-cockpit fairing

92 Upper wing aerial mast
93 Pilot's headrest
94 Pilot's seat and harness
95 Bulkhead
96 Vickers gun fairing
97 Fuel gravity tank (12.5 Imp gal/57 litre capacity)
98 Windscreen
99 Handholds
100 Flap control handwheel and rocking head assembly
101 Wing centre section
102 Dinghy release cord handle
103 Identification light
104 Centre section pyramid strut attachment
105 Diagonal strengtheners
106 Dinghy inflation cylinder

107 Type C dinghy stowage well
108 Aileron control linkage
109 Trailing edge rib sections
110 Rear spar
111 Wing rib stations
112 Aileron connect strut
113 Port upper aileron
114 Fixed tab
115 Aileron hinge
116 Port formation light
117 Wing skinning
118 Port navigation light
119 Leading-edge slot

120 Front spar
121 Nose ribs
122 Interplane struts
123 Pitot head
124 Bracing wires
125 Flying wires
126 Port lower mainplane
127 Landing lamp
128 Underwing bomb shackles
129 Underwing strengthening plate

130 Rocket-launching rails
131 Four 60-lb (27-g) anti-shipping rocket projectiles
132 Three-blade fixed-pitch Fairey-Reed metal propeller
133 Spinner
134 Townend ring
135 Bristol Pegasus IIIM3 (or Mk 30) radial engine
136 Cowling clips

137 Engine mounting ring
138 Engine support bearers
139 Firewall bulkhead
140 Engine controls
141 Oil tank immersion heater socket
142 Filler cap
143 Oil tank (13.75 Imp gal/62.5 litre capacity)
144 Centre section pyramid struts

145 External torpedo sight bars
146 Fuel filler cap
147 Main fuel tank (155 Imp gal/705 litre capacity)
148 Vickers gun trough
149 Fuselage forward frame
150 Oil cooler
151 Fuel filter
152 Stub plane/fuselage attachment
153 Fuel feed lines
154 Dinghy immersion switch
155 Exhaust
156 Port Dunlop mainwheel
157 Jacking foot
158 1,610-lb (730-kg) 18-in (45.7-cm) torpedo
159 Access/servicing footholds
160 Torpedo forward crutch
161 Radius rod fairing
162 Undercarriage axle tube fairing
163 Undercarriage oleo leg fairing
164 Starboard mainwheel
165 Hub cover
166 Underwing bombs
167 Underwing outboard shackles
168 Depth-charge
169 250-lb (113-kg) bomb
170 Anti-shipping flares

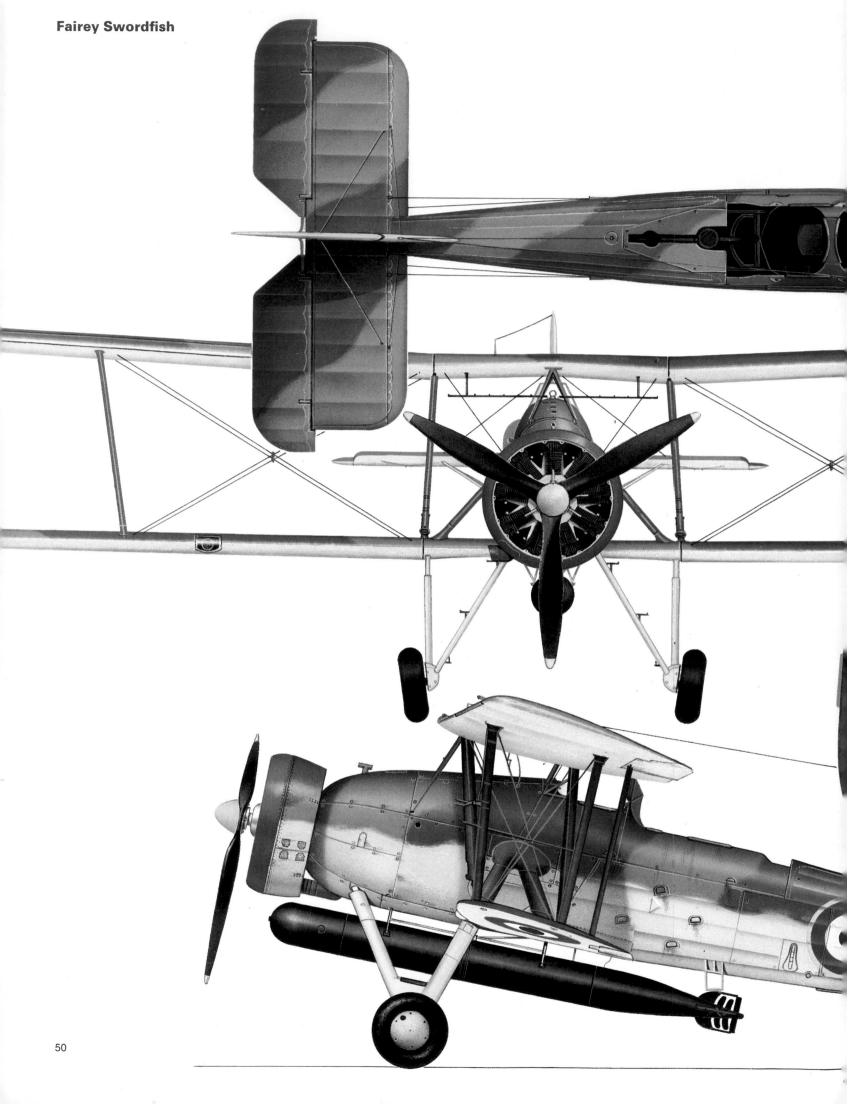

Although fairly anonymous in being bare of serial number, Royal Navy ship and squadron markings, this Swordfish is shown in a colour scheme typical of around 1940-1 (the period of the Battle of Taranto) and is carrying a standard naval 457-mm (18-in) torpedo. The horizontal bar suspended from the top wing centre section, visible in the front view, is the aim-off sight, used for attacks on ships, and the emergency dinghy stowage was located in the top wing immediately outboard of the wing-fold; the rear Lewis gun is shown in the stowed position.

Specification
Fairey Swordfish Mk II
Type: two/three-seat deck-landing or float-equipped torpedo-carrying naval aircraft
Powerplant: one 560-kW (750-hp) Bristol Pegasus 30 radial piston engine
Performance: maximum speed 222 km/h (138 mph); climb to 1525 m (5,000 ft) in 10 minutes 0 seconds; service ceiling 3260 m (10,700 ft); range without weapons 1658 km (1,030 miles), with torpedo 885 km (550 miles)
Weights: empty 2359 kg (5,200 lb); maximum take-off 4196 kg (9,250 lb)
Dimensions: span 13.92 m (45 ft 6 in); length 11.12 m (36 ft 4 in); height 3.93 m (12 ft 10 in); wing area 56.39 m^2 (607 sq ft)
Armament: one fixed forward-firing 7.7-mm (0.303-in) Vickers machine-gun and one flexible 7.7-mm (0.303-in) Vickers 'K' or Browning machine-gun in rear cockpit, plus provision for one 457-mm (18-in) 731-kg (1,610-lb) torpedo, or 681-kg (1,500-lb) mine or bombs under the fuselage, or up to eight 76.2-mm (3-in) 27-kg (60-lb) rockets or four 113-kg (250-lb) bombs under wings

Fairey Swordfish variants

Fairey TSR I: one prototype to Specification S.9/30; Pegasus IIM of 474 kW (635 hp); crashed from spin and destroyed
Fairey TSR II: one prototype (K4190) to Specification S.15/33; Pegasus IIIM3 of 578 kW (775 hp); first flight 17 April 1934
Fairey Swordfish Mk I: to Specification S.38/34, and powered by Pegasus IIIM3 of 515 kW (690 hp) (three prototypes, K5660-K5662, K5662 being completed as floatplane)
Fairey Swordfish Mk I: Fairey production 1935-40, with Pegasus IIIM3; all convertible to floatplanes; K,L and P serials (689 built)
Fairey Swordfish Mk I: Blackburn production 1940-1; aircraft as Fairey-built Mk Is; V serials (300 built)
Fairey Swordfish Mk II: Blackburn production 1941-4, with Pegasus 30 of 560 kW (750 hp); wheel landing gear only and metal-covered lower wings; W, DK, HS, LS, NE and NF serials (1,080 built, some later converted to Swordfish Mk IV with enclosed cockpit)
Fairey Swordfish Mk III: Blackburn production 1944, with Pegasus 30; wheel landing gear only; ASV radar (most aircraft with provision for rocket projectiles); FF, NF, NR and NS serials (327 built, many converted to Swordfish Mk IV with enclosed cockpit)
Fairey Swordfish Mk IV: conversions from Mks II and III with enclosed cockpit

Douglas SBD Dauntless

The Battle of Midway was the turning point of the war in the Pacific and set the seal on Japan's fate. Architect of this victory was the reliable, if unspectacular, Douglas Dauntless, which gave the American carriers the striking power they so desperately needed.

The Douglas SBD Dauntless dive-bomber turned the tide of war at the Battle of Midway on 4 June 1942. To the men involved, the size of their success may not have been immediately evident: their aircraft had a low power-to-weight ratio, burdening it with only fair climbing and manoeuvring characteristics; and their arming systems malfunctioned, at times pitching their centreline-mounted 227-kg (500-lb) bombs uselessly into the sea. Launched from Admiral Chester Nimitz's carrier groups to seek out those of Admiral Isoroku Yamamoto, they were running out of fuel, running out of daylight, and stretched to the limits of range and endurance when they came upon the enemy fleet and attacked. Lieutenant Commander C. Wade McClusky, Commander Max Leslie and the other Dauntless fliers from squadrons VS-5 and VB-3 on USS *Yorktown*, VS-6 and VB-6 on USS *Enterprise*, and VS-8 and VB-8 on USS *Hornet* lost 40 of their 128 dive-bombers swarming down from the late-afternoon sun to strike the *Kaga*, *Akagi*, *Hiryu* and *Soryu*, but when they sent all four Japanese carriers to the bottom of the sea they reversed the trend of the Pacific conflict. Few other aircraft types, perhaps none but the Supermarine Spitfire and Hawker Hurricane, can lay claim to having so altered history as the Dauntless dive-bomber, 5,936 of which were produced before the end of World War II.

The Dauntless owes its origins to the low-wing, two-seat tandem Northrop BT-1 dive-bomber of 1938, and to the superb design work of Jack Northrop and of the mild-tempered but brilliant Edward H. Heinemann. When the El Segundo, California, manufacturer became a division of Douglas Aircraft with Jack Northrop's January 1938 departure, a development of the BT-1, known as the XBT-2, was being tested but seemed to offer only limited potential. Heinemann's design team reworked the sole XBT-2 (BuAer No. 0627), powering it with the 746-kW (1,000-hp) Wright XR-1830-32 engine which would become the world-famous Cyclone, driving a three-bladed propeller. The tail of the aircraft was redesigned following extensive wind tunnel tests, and the XBT-2 was redesigned XSBD-1. Accepted by the US Navy in February 1939, while parallel work was under way on the Curtiss SB2C Helldiver, the SBD was to become the standard by which all other carrierborne dive-bombers ('scout bombers' in the jargon of the time) would be judged.

On 8 April 1939, Douglas received an order for 57 SBD-1 and 87 SBD-2 airplanes. The SBD-1, with the definitive fin and rudder shape for the Dauntless type, was armed with two forward-firing 7.62-mm (0.3-in) guns in the engine cowling and a single 7.62-mm (0.3-in) gun for the radio operator/gunner, who sat with his back to the pilot. Not yet fully cleared for carrier operations, the SBD-1 was earmarked instead for the US Marine Corps and was delivered between April 1939 and June 1940. The SBD-2 model, which differed in having self-sealing rubber-lined metal fuel tanks and two additional 246-litre (65-US gal) tanks in the outer wing panels, went to US Navy squadrons between November 1940 and May 1941.

The fall of France, punctuated by the scream of descending Stukas, impressed the Washington authorities with the value of the dive-bomber (although the US Congress's Truman Committee in 1941 recommended against procuring such aircraft) and a further 174 Dauntlesses were ordered as the SBD-3. The SBD-3 variant had a second 7.62-mm (0.3-in) gun for the rear crewmen, improved armour and electrical system, and bladder-type self-sealing fuel tanks. By now the familiar Dauntless shape was established: the not ungraceful machine had a maximum speed of 406 km/h (252 mph) in level flight, going up to 444 km/h (276 mph) in a dive, a range of 1971 km (1,225 miles) with or 2205 km (1,370 miles) without a bomb-load, and a service ceiling of 8260 m (27,100 ft).

US Marine Corps Dauntlesses were destroyed on the ground during the 7 December 1941 attack on Pearl Harbor. During the Battle of Coral Sea on 7 May 1942, the airwaves were cluttered with radio transmissions and anxious crewmen aboard the USS *Lexington* and *Yorktown* could not tell how the battle was going until a clear voice blasted through: 'Scratch one flat-top! Dixon to carrier. Scratch one flat-top!' Lieutenant Commander Robert E. Dixon, commander of Bombing Two (VB-2), was reporting the sinking of the Japanese carrier *Shoho* with 545 of her crew after a 30-minute battle at the cost of only three US aircraft, a triumph for the SBD-2 and SBD-3 models of the Dauntless, to be exceeded only during the pivotal Midway battle a few weeks later.

In the US Army Air Forces, where it was officially given the name Banshee but still called Dauntless, this aircraft type seemed un-

SBD-1 Dauntless (BuAer No. 1597), the second machine in the initial production run, shows the unexciting markings worn by US Marine Corps aircraft before America's entry into World War II. Fuselage coding '2-MB-1' identifies this craft as belonging to the 2nd Marine Aircraft Wing, apparently at Quantico, Virginia, in about August 1940.

An early production Douglas SBD-3 sporting an overall light grey colour scheme. Sarcastically nicknamed 'Speedy Three', this workhorse was at the forefront of operations in the Pacific until 1942.

Douglas SBD Dauntless

glamorous from the beginning. In January 1941, the USAAF had placed an order for 78 A-24s similar to the US Navy's SBD-3 but for the deletion of carrier landing equipment. In addition, 90 SBD-3s from a US Navy contract were modified to land-based standard and delivered to the USAAF as the SBD-3A (A for Army). Eventually, the USAAF ordered 100 A-24As identical to the SBD-4, and 615 A-24Bs equivalent to the SBD-5 but manufactured at the Douglas plant in Tulsa, Oklahoma.

Although A-24s served with the 27th Bombardment Group at New Guinea and with the 531st Fighter Bomber Squadron at Makin, USAAF pilots found themselves unable to outmanoeuvre aggressive Japanese fighters. Where the rear-seat gunner had been highly effective in the US Navy machine (one US Navy crew actually shot down seven Mitsubishi Zeros in two days) he was less potent aboard the A-24. Casualties were so high that the A-24 was quickly withdrawn from front-line service. Since US Navy pilots at Coral Sea and Midway had demonstrated the ability to handle themselves against the Zero, the US Army's less satisfactory performance with the Dauntless is usually attributed to the inexperience and lesser *esprit de corps* of its flight crews.

Carrier air group

A carrier air group aboard a typical US Navy carrier usually comprised two squadrons of fighters (Grumman F4F Wildcats, or later F6F Hellcats), one of torpedo-bombers (Douglas TBD Devastators, later Grumman TBF Avengers) and two Dauntless squadrons, one in the bombing role and one for the scout mission. These were designated VB and VS squadrons respectively. The scouting mission had been conceived before it was clear that American carriers would have the protection of radar, which they enjoyed from the outset of the conflict while Japanese carriers did not. In practice, there was little distinction and scouting pilots trained and prepared for dive-bombing missions just as their colleagues in the VB squadrons did.

The next model of the Dauntless was the SBD-4, delivered between October 1942 and April 1943. The SBD-4 had improved radio navigation aids, an electric fuel pump, and an improved Hamilton Standard Hydromatic constant speed, full-feathering propeller. A total of 780 was built before production at El Segundo shifted to the SBD-5, powered by an improved R-1820-60 engine delivering 895 kW (1,200 hp); 2,965 examples of this variant were produced between February 1943 and April 1944, one of which became the XSBD-6 with installation of a 1007-kW (1,350-hp) Wright R-1820-66, the 'ultimate' Cyclone. Some 450 SBD-6s were built.

By late in the war, the Dauntless was supplanted in the dive-bomber role by the more advanced Curtiss Sc2C Helldiver, though this troublesome aircraft never won the recognition accorded the Douglas project. The Dauntless was relegated to less glamorous anti-submarine patrol and close air support duties. The SBD also served with no less than 20 US Marine Corps squadrons. Many hundreds of SBDs were retrofitted with Westinghouse ASB radar.

Several ex-USAAF Douglas A-24s were operated by the Mexican air force as late as 1959. Illustrated is an A-24B, which found its way on to the Mexican civil register in 1957.

Identifiable by the deletion of the deck landing hook, the land-based USAAF Douglas A-24s were delivered from the US Navy production line of El Segundo between June and October 1941. Further orders were to follow.

Douglas SBD-3 Dauntless cutaway drawing key

1 Aerial stub
2 Rudder balance
3 Rudder upper hinge
4 Rudder frame
5 Rudder tab
6 Rudder lower hinge
7 Tailfin structure
8 Port elevator
9 Port tailplane
10 Tailfin root fillet
11 Frame
12 Fuselage frame/tailfin pick-up
13 Tailplane spar attachment
14 Tailplane structure
15 Elevator torque tube
16 Tail navigation light
17 Elevator tab hinge fairing
18 Elevator hinge
19 Elevator tab
20 Elevator frame
21 Elevator outer hinge
22 Tailplane forward spar
23 Fixed tailwheel (pneumatic tyre on A-24 versions)
24 Arresting hook uplock
25 Fuselage frame
26 Lift point

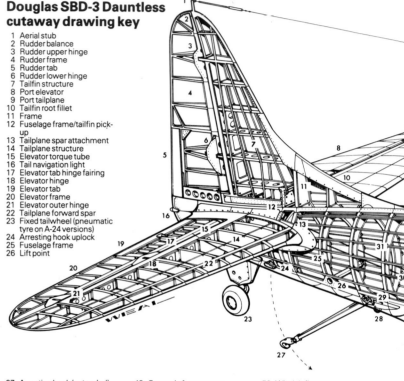

27 Arresting hook (extended)	43 Gunner's face armour	58 Wind deflector
28 Tie-down ring	44 Canopy aft sliding section (open)	59 Armoured centre bulkhead
29 Arresting hook pivot		60 Angled support frame
30 Control cables	45 Gun mounting	61 Gunner's emergency flight controls
31 Fuselage structure	46 Ammunition feed	
32 Bulkhead	47 Canopy aft sliding section (closed)	62 Control direct linkage
33 Section light		63 Hydraulics controls
34 Radio bay	48 Ammunition box	64 Entry hand/foothold
35 Radio bay access door	49 Oxygen cylinder	65 Oxygen rebreather
36 Wingroot fairing frame	50 Oxygen rebreather	66 Map case
37 Stringers	51 Oxygen spare cylinder	67 Pilot's seat and harness
38 Life-raft cylindrical stowage (access door port side)	52 Entry hand/foothold	68 Back armour
	53 Aft cockpit floor	69 Catapult headrest
	54 Radio controls	70 Canopy forward sliding section
39 Dorsal armament stowage	55 Gunner's position	
40 Hinged doors	56 Gun mounting	71 Compass
41 Aerial	57 Canopy fixed centre section	72 Perforated dive flap
42 Twin 0.30-in (7.62-mm) Browning machine-guns		73 Aerial mast

A-24 Dauntless, serial number 42-54543, of France's Goupe de Chasse-Bombardement 1/18 'Vendée', located at Vannes in about November 1944. The ex-USAAF Dauntlesses flown by Free French pilots performed a variety of roles but, like their New Zealand counterparts, were introduced too late in the war to be especially effective as front-line dive-bombers.

74 Aileron tab
75 Port aileron
76 Aileron tab control linkage
77 Port formation light
78 Port navigation light
79 Pitot head
80 Fixed wing slots
81 Wing skinning
82 Underwing ASB radar antenna (retrofit)
83 Port outer wing fuel tank (55 US gal/208 litre capacity)
84 Aileron control rod
85 Telescopic sight
86 Windscreen

87 Armoured inner panel
88 Instrument panel shroud
89 Two 0.50-in (12.7-mm) machine-guns
90 Control column
91 Switch panel
92 Instrument panel
93 Case ejection chute
94 Ammunition box
95 Engine bearer upper attachment
96 Armoured deflection plate
97 Machine-gun barrel shrouds
98 Engine bearers
99 Oil tank

100 Exhaust slot
101 Oil cooler
102 Cooling gills
103 Exhaust manifold
104 Engine cowling ring
105 Machine-gun troughs
106 Carburettor air intake duct
107 Wright R-1820-52 Cyclone radial engine
108 Three-blade propeller
109 Spinner
110 Propeller hub
111 Port mainwheel
112 Oil cooler intake
113 Exhaust outlet
114 Engine bearers

115 Bomb displacement crutch (in-flight position)
116 Hydraulics vent
117 Case ejection chute outlet
118 Engine bearer lower attachment
119 Starboard mainwheel well
120 Wingroot walkway
121 Starboard/inner wing fuel tank (75 US gal/284 litre capacity)
122 Centre-section dive flap (lower)
123 Wing outer section attachment plate fairing
124 Starboard outer wing fuel

tank (55 US gal/208 litre capacity)
125 Mainwheel leg pivot
126 Mainwheel leg door actuation
127 Wing nose ribs
128 Multi-spar wing structure
129 Wing ribs
130 Stiffeners
131 Perforated dive flaps
132 Aileron inner hinge
133 Starboard aileron frame
134 Aileron outer hinge
135 Starboard navigation light
136 Starboard formation light
137 Wingtip structure

138 Fixed wing slots
139 Wing leading-edge
140 Underwing radar antenna (retrofit)
141 Underwing stores pylon
142 100-lb (45.4-kg) bomb
143 Mainwheel leg door
144 Starboard mainwheel
145 Mainwheel axle
146 Mainwheel leg
147 Bomb displacement crutch
148 500-lb (226.8-kg) bomb
149 Aluminium drop tank (58 US gal/219.5 litre capacity
150 Underwing shackles/fuel line

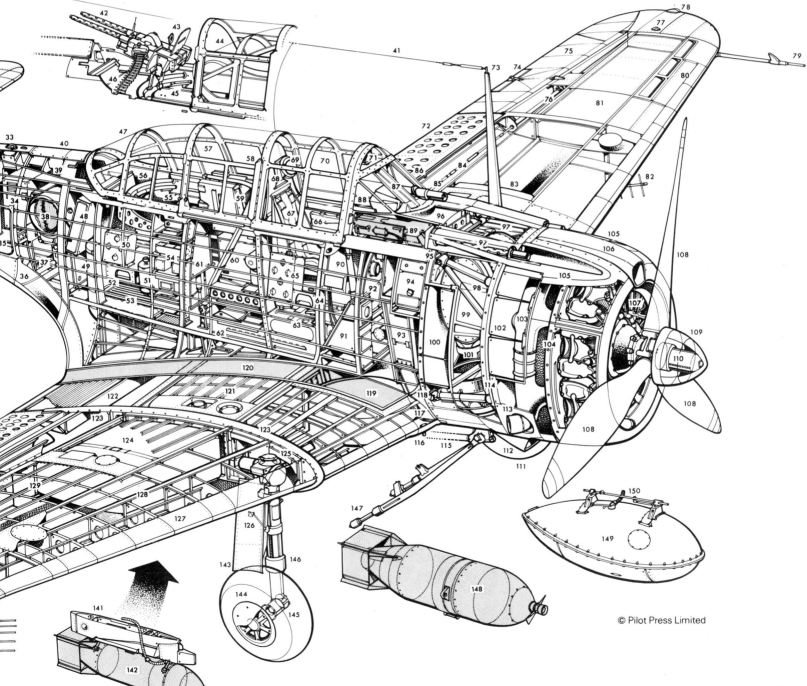

© Pilot Press Limited

Douglas SBD Dauntless

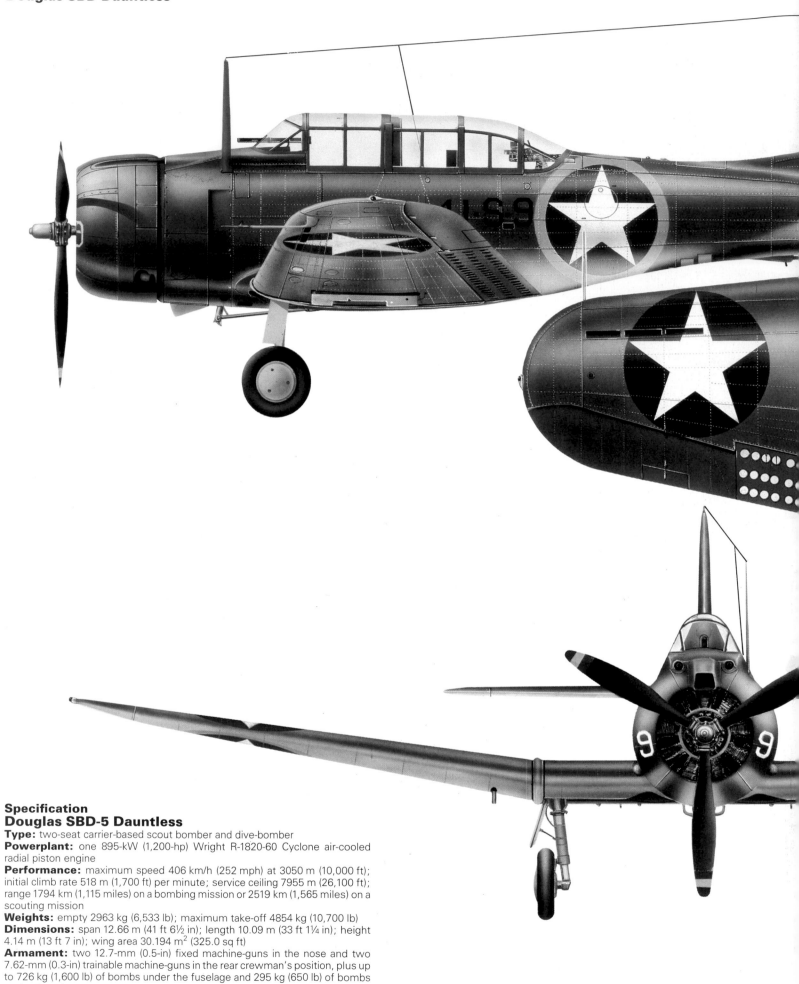

Specification
Douglas SBD-5 Dauntless

Type: two-seat carrier-based scout bomber and dive-bomber

Powerplant: one 895-kW (1,200-hp) Wright R-1820-60 Cyclone air-cooled radial piston engine

Performance: maximum speed 406 km/h (252 mph) at 3050 m (10,000 ft); initial climb rate 518 m (1,700 ft) per minute; service ceiling 7955 m (26,100 ft); range 1794 km (1,115 miles) on a bombing mission or 2519 km (1,565 miles) on a scouting mission

Weights: empty 2963 kg (6,533 lb); maximum take-off 4854 kg (10,700 lb)

Dimensions: span 12.66 m (41 ft 6½ in); length 10.09 m (33 ft 1¼ in); height 4.14 m (13 ft 7 in); wing area 30.194 m² (325.0 sq ft)

Armament: two 12.7-mm (0.5-in) fixed machine-guns in the nose and two 7.62-mm (0.3-in) trainable machine-guns in the rear crewman's position, plus up to 726 kg (1,600 lb) of bombs under the fuselage and 295 kg (650 lb) of bombs under the wings

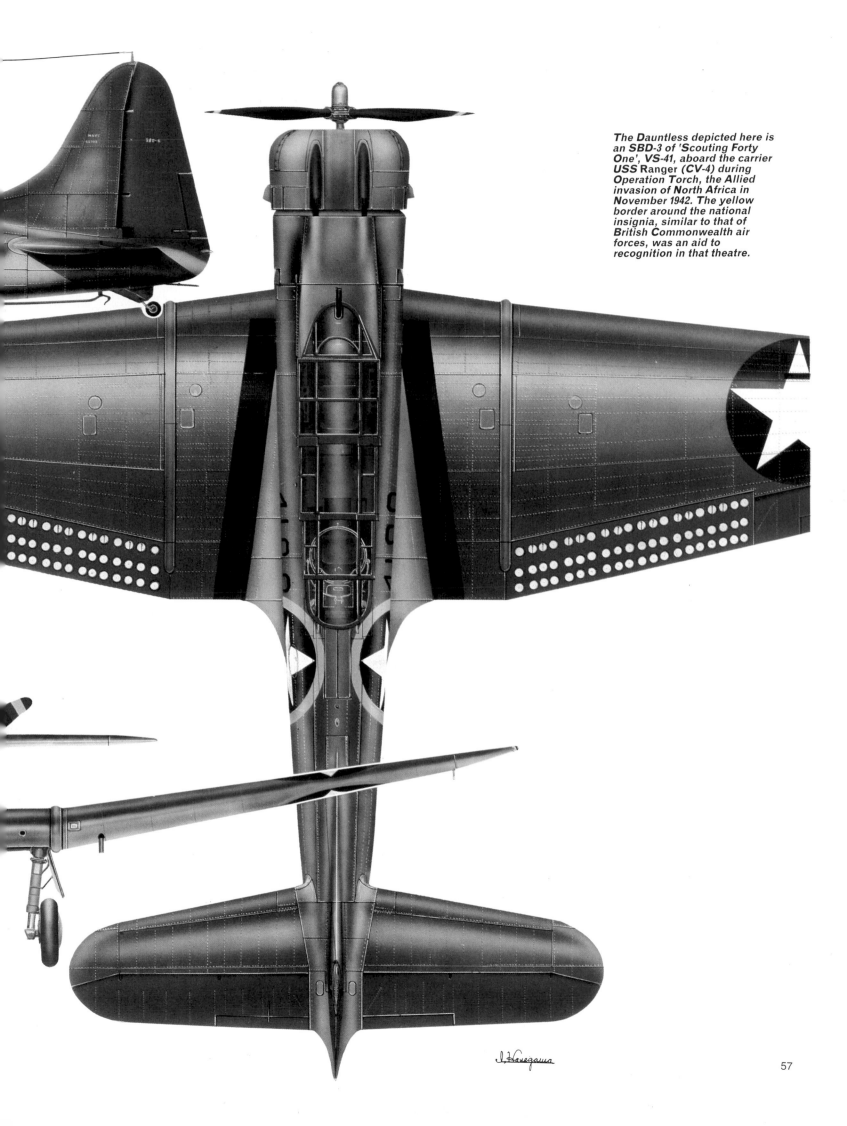

The Dauntless depicted here is an *SBD-3* of 'Scouting Forty One', *VS-41*, aboard the carrier *USS* Ranger (*CV-4*) during Operation Torch, the Allied invasion of North Africa in November 1942. The yellow border around the national insignia, similar to that of British Commonwealth air forces, was an aid to recognition in that theatre.

Airbrakes extended, this Dauntless is in classic dive-bomber pose. Early SBDs could carry a 545-kg (1,200-lb) bomb load but by the end of the war and the coming of the SBD-5 model this had increased.

The UK obtained nine SBD-5 aircraft and named them Dauntless DB.Mk I. A machine which had been a top performer in 1940 was, by the time British test pilots flew it in 1944, regarded as underpowered and slow. British pilots also found the Dauntless fatiguing, noisy and draughty. There was never to be general agreement about the type's vulnerability to fighters, the Pacific war indicating that it was not unduly vulnerable, RAF test pilots being persuaded that it was. The British machines were evaluated extensively but it was too late for the Dauntless to have an operational career in British service.

Foreign users

In July 1943, No. 25 Squadron of the Royal New Zealand Air Force received 18 SBD-3s from US Marine Corps inventory. Later to receive 27 SBD-4s and 23 SBD-5s, the RNZAF squadron fought at Bougainville. Another foreign user of the Dauntless was France, which equipped two units of the Free French Navy, Flottille 3B and

Flottille 4B, with A-24s and SBD-3s at Agadir, Morocco in the autumn of 1944. Dauntlesses went into operation in metropolitan France against retreating German forces and fought in dwindling numbers until VE-Day. Though production of the type ended on 22 July 1944, French SBDs were used at the fighter school at Meknes as aerobatic trainers until 1953.

In American service, where the A-24 was redesignated F-24 in 1947, an unpiloted QF-24A drone and its QF-24B controller aircraft (both rebuilds with 1948 serial numbers) kept the Dauntless type in service until 1950.

The pilot of an SBD-6 Dauntless found himself sitting high up front in a machine of all-metal construction with fabric-covered control surfaces. His cantilever, low-mounted wing had a rectangular centre section with outer panels tapering in chord and thickness to detachable wing tips. The 'Swiss cheese' pierced flaps and dive-brakes, above and below the trailing edge of the outer wings and below the trailing edge only of the centre section beneath the fuselage, together with the 'multi-cellular' construction of the wing itself, were hallmarks of the design's indebtedness to Jack Northrop. The oval

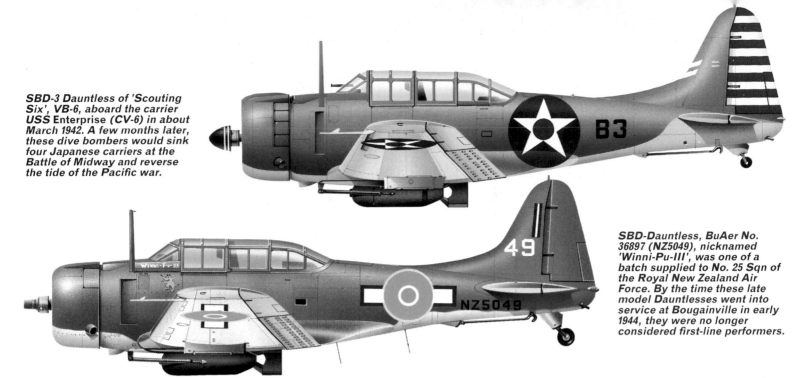

SBD-3 Dauntless of 'Scouting Six', VB-6, aboard the carrier USS Enterprise (CV-6) in about March 1942. A few months later, these dive bombers would sink four Japanese carriers at the Battle of Midway and reverse the tide of the Pacific war.

SBD-Dauntless, BuAer No. 36897 (NZ5049), nicknamed 'Winni-Pu-III', was one of a batch supplied to No. 25 Sqn of the Royal New Zealand Air Force. By the time these late model Dauntlesses went into service at Bougainville in early 1944, they were no longer considered first-line performers.

duralumin monocoque fuselage was built in four sections, and the crew was housed beneath a continuous transparent canopy with a bullet-proof windshield and armour plate. A swinging bomb cradle with a maximum capacity of 454 kg (1,000 lb) was centred beneath the fuselage and a bomb rack was mounted under each outer-wing section.

Flying the Dauntless, pilots found it a forgiving machine of few vices, although it had a troublesome tendency to stall in tight turns. On dive-bombing missions, the pilot approached his target at 4570 to 6095 m (15,000 to 20,000 ft), took position almost directly overhead, pulled up the nose, and deployed upper and lower dive flaps. He then 'rolled in', the Dauntless accelerating less rapidly than might be expected while plummetting at over 70°. Using the Mk VIII reflector sight which, from the SBD-5 model on, had replaced the earlier extended telescope, which had a tendency to fog over in a dive as a result of temperature changes, the pilot aimed his bomb load literally by pointing his aircraft at the target. His bomb release was a red button marked 'B' on the top of the stick and he could drop his ordnance singly or in salvo. US Navy legend has it that pilots were prone to 'target fascination', which could lull them into failing to pull out of the dive in time. With its bomb load gone, the Dauntless pulled out quite handily, with an easy motion on the stick. The

A formation of Douglas SBD-5s of VMS-3, US Marine Corps, high over the Atlantic. The dark grey and off-white colour scheme was adopted for Atlantic theatre operations in early 1944.

machine generally handled well in normal flight and the pilot's visibility was excellent, both when level and when descending for a tricky landing on a carrier deck. Few aircraft were tougher or more reliable, the Dauntless often coming home with severe battle damage.

A few A-24B Dauntlesses found their way, post-war, into the hands of the Mexican air force, which was apparently the last user of this type, employing it until 1959. Today, a beautifully preserved Dauntless is in the US Marine Corps Museum at Quantico, Virginia, and the sole remaining flyable machine is with the Confederate Air Force at Harlingen, Texas.

Douglas SBD Dauntless variants

XSBD-1: conversion of Northrop XBT-2, Bureau of Aeronautics number (BuAer No.) 0627; total 1
SBD-1: initial production version, BuAer Nos 1596/1631 and 1735/1755; total 57
SBD-1P: eight conversions to reconnaissance role
SBD-2: improved armour, self-sealing tanks, BuAer Nos 2102/2188; total 87
SBD-2P: 14 conversions to reconnaissance role
SBD-3: improved production version; BuAer Nos 4518/4691, 03185/03384 and 06492/06701; total 584
SBD-3A: aircraft from US Navy contract diverted to USAAF as A-24
SBD-3P: 43 conversions to reconnaissance role and 24-V
SBD-4: production aircraft, improved propeller and electrical systems, BuAer Nos 06702/06991 and 10317/10806; total 780
SBD-5: production aircraft, R-1820-60 engine, BuAer Nos 10807/10956, 10957/11066, 28059/28829, 28831/29213, 35922/36421, 36433/36932 and 54050/54599; total 2,965
SBD-5A: aircraft from USAAF contract,

originally intended for US Army as A-24B but delivered to US Navy, BuAer Nos 09693/09752; total 60
XSBD-6: prototype for SBD-6, BuAer No. 28830; total 1
SBD-6: final production version, R-1820-66, one converted from SBD-5 (BuAer No. 35950); other, BuAer Nos 54600/55049; total 450
A-24: originally designated SBD-3A, delivered to USAAF, serial numbers 41-15746/15823 and 42-6682/6771; total 168
A-24A: USAAF version of SBD-4, serials 42-6772/6831 and 42-60772/60881; total 170
A-24B: USAAF version of SBD-5, serials 42-54285/54899; total 615
RA-24A: redesignation after 1942, to indicate obsolescence
RA-24B: redesignation after 1942, to indicate obsolescence
F-24A: redesignation after 1947
F-24B: redesignation after 1947
QF-24A: rebuilt as target drone, serial 48-44; total 1
QF-24B: rebuilt as drone controller aircraft, serial 48-45; total 1

SBD-5 or Dauntless Mk I (JS997) of the Royal Navy at RAE Farnborough in about October 1944 for very belated flight tests comparing it with the Curtiss Helldiver and Vultee Vengeance. Why RAF and Royal Navy pilots were testing the Dauntless at this late stage in the war is unclear. They found it pleasant to fly but not breathtaking in performance, and it never saw combat wearing British roundels.

Lockheed Hudson family

The introduction of the small Lockheed airliners in the mid-1930s pulled the company back from the brink of penury, and set the Burbank-based manufacturer on the road to recovery. When war came, the shortage of patrol bombers and fast transports immediately became apparent and Lockheed grasped the opportunity with both hands.

By 1932 the Lockheed company was on the brink of financial disaster, with the federal receiver valuing the company's assets at a mere $129,961 and putting it up for sale. While founder Allan Loughead sought cash to buy his old concern, broker and banker Robert Ellsworth Gross snapped up the almost defunct aviation company for a fabled $40,000. Like many other entrepreneurs, Gross knew little of the intimate aspects of aeronautical engineering, but possessed a sound business mind and a growing fascination with the new wave of commercial air transports that daily plied the US domestic air space. With well measured consideration Gross predicted that the company's future lay not in the production of mailplanes, or even in the military field, but in the development of fast and relatively small commuter and feederliner aircraft with an eventual eye to challenging the dominance of the new Boeing and Douglas aircraft. Gross brought with him Hall Hibbard, a young Massachusetts Institute of Technology aeronautical engineer, who, with Lloyd Stearman, started to work on various designs that might be able to gain an entry into a difficult and demanding market, but it was Gross who steered the project on to the lines of a small, all-metal, twin-engine commercial transport. The design team was joined by George Prudden and James Gerschler, and later by C. L. 'Kelly' Johnson, who gave an early display of his brilliance by solving the wind-tunnel asymmetry problems of the new Lockheed design, now known as the Model L-10.

Roll-out for the Lockheed Model L-10 Electra took place on 23 February 1934. It was a beautiful little twin-engine aircraft, resplendent in glistening polished natural aluminium. Power came from two 336-kW (450-hp) Pratt & Whitney R-985-SB radials, cabin and crew seats numbered 12, empty weight was 2928 kg (6,454 lb), and the gross weight was 4672 kg (10,300 lb). Tests gave a maximum speed of 325 km/h (202 mph), and a spanking maximum continuous cruising speed of 306 km/h (190 mph). After exhaustive tests the protoype L-10 Electra was flown by Marshall Headle to Mines Field, Los Angeles, for FAA certification which was granted a few weeks later. On the return to Burbank a heart-stopping incident took place. Up to the time of the L-10's first flight Lockheed had gone into debt for $139,404 for its development, and as its priceless prototype, newly certificated, made its approach all attempts by the crew to lower one of the main wheels ended in stubborn failure: only a skilfully-handled one-wheel landing at nearby Union Air Terminal by pilot Headle, with minimal damage to the Electra, prevented a major lay-off of the work force and the renewal of financial straits. There the matter rested. Sales of the Model L-10 Electra rocketed, with examples going to Mid-Continent Airlines, Northwest Airlines, Northeast Airlines, Cia Nacional Cubana, Pan American Airways, Panair do Brasil, Braniff Airways, National Airlines, British Airways,

Lockheed A-29 in US Army Air Force colours of early 1942. Initially all 800 A-29 and A-29A aircraft were allocated to the RAF under Lend-Lease, but with the crisis taking place in the Pacific and the Far East a large number were repossessed and pressed into service with the USAAF: some were used as crew trainers, and others as bombers and maritime patrol aircraft, one being the first USAAF aircraft to sink a U-boat in World War II.

Delta Air Lines, Eastern Air Lines, Chicago and Southern, LAV (Venezuela), LOT (Poland), LARES (Romania), AEROPUT (Yugoslavia), LAN-Chile, and to a host of private buyers including Amelia Earhart.

An L-10 Electra was the seventh Lockheed aircraft successfully to fly the Atlantic Ocean when Dick Merill and John Lambie flew NR16055 on a round-trip to London to collect photos of King George VI's coronation in 1937. Also that year, somewhere in the Pacific ocean wastes between Lae, New Guinea and Howland Island, aviatrix Amelia Earhart and her navigator disappeared for ever during a record attempt in their L-10 Electra. A total of 149 L-10s was built and delivered between 29 June 1934 and 18 July 1941, and many saw military service in the RCAF and Argentine navy, and with the US Army, US Navy and US Coast Guard designated as C-36, C-37, R20 and R30 sub-types.

Bigger and better

The interim Model L-12 Electra Junior was taken into the air for the first time by Marshall Headle at 1212 on 27 June 1936, exactly on the scheduled time. By now business was booming, with Lockheed getting $2 million worth of orders in the previous year. Price-tagged at $40,000 the Model L-12, with six-seat capacity, was aimed

The ultimate military development of Lockheeds's twin family was the PV-2 Harpoon, which featured underwing racks for rockets and five 12.7-mm (0.5-in) machine-guns in the nose.

squarely at the business and commuter markets, and in fact was a scaled-down version of its predecessor with two Pratt & Whitney R-985-SB radials. Grossing 3924 kg (8,650 lb), the Electra Junior's top speed was 362 km/h (225 mph) and service ceiling 6800 m (22,300 ft). Its performance and handling qualities exceeded those of the majority of contemporary fighters, and it became another good seller. Several records fell to the Model L-12, including a new route average of 388 km/h (210 mph) by test pilot E. C. McLead, despite four fuel stops, from Amsterdam to India on a delivery flight of a L-12 for the Maharaja of Jodhpur. A total of 130 Model L-12s was built before work stopped in mid-1942.

Incorporating many of the latest aviation developments, the larger and more powerful Lockheed Model L-14 Super Electra took to the air for the first time on 29 June 1937. New features on this 14-seat aircraft included use of 24SRT duralumin, high-speed aerofoil (NACA 23018 and 23009 at root and tip respectively), single main spar, and high wing loading, massive Lockheed-Fowler flaps, and two of the latest Wright Cyclone engines, the GR-1820-G3B. With an empty weight of 4854 kg (10,700 lb) and a gross of 7938 kg (17,500

A Dutch KLM Model 14 Super Electra over Rotterdam shows the distinctive lines that were to be carried over into the Hudson progeny. Featuring all-metal construction, Fowler flaps and two 611-kW (820-hp) Wright GR-1820-G3B radials, the Model 14 first flew on 29 July 1937, and was later sold to a number of commercial concerns. In such an aircraft Howard Hughes made his great round-the-world record bid.

Lockheed Model 18 Lodestar, one of 625 sold, showing the raised tailplane designed to eliminate turbulence. Flown by Marshall Headle on 2 February 1940, the Model 18 served with a number of airlines, including Mid Continent (which ordered three at $90,000 apiece before the first had been built), Régie Air Afrique and Netherlands East Indies.

lb), the new L-14 had a top speed of 414 km/h (257 mph): its cruising speed was some 48 km/h (30 mph) faster than that of any other commercial transport in the United States and, at a cruise speed of 381 km/h (237 mph), the Super Electra cut the West Coast-New York flight time of the Douglas DC-3 by four hours. Such was the reputation of the company that even before roll-out over 30 L-14s were on the order book, and the aircraft itself was soon to justify all expectations. Millionaire Howard Hughes purchased a Model L-14, and increased tankage from the normal 3438 to 6980 litres (644 to 1,844 US gal) for a round-the-world record attempt. Departing from New York on 10 July 1938, Hughes and his crew flew via Paris, Moscow, Yakutsk, Fairbanks and Minneapolis to land at Floyd Bennett Field after a 23670-km (14,709-mile) flight achieved within the time of three days, 17 hours, 14 minutes and 10 seconds. The 112 Model L-14s are remembered today as the progenitors of what was to be one of Lockheed's most successful warplanes. Licence production of the L-14 in Japan amounted to 64 by Tachikawa and 55 by Kawasaki.

Enter the Hudson

To the United States in April 1938 came the British Purchasing Commission in search of good-quality American aircraft to bolster the strength of the Royal Air Force in its preparation for an inevitable war: the mission had $25 million with which to acquire its finds. At that time Lockheed engaged only 2,000 workers, and had eschewed the design of military types in favour of the commercial market. But in 10 days of frantic labour the concern had cobbled together something that might whet the appetites of the commission: this was nothing other than a mockup of a Model L-14 provided with bombbay, bomb-aimer's panel and nose glazing, and provision for various armaments. The British, with a need for a medium-range maritime patrol bomber for North Sea operations with RAF Coastal Command, were impressed. At the invitation of Sir Henry Self, the contracts director at the Air Ministry in London, Courtlandt Gross (brother of Robert Gross) travelled to the UK with Carl Squier, C. L. Johnson, Robert Proctor and R. A. van Hake for consultations. The initial order for 175 Model B14s, now known as the Hudson, was signed on 23 June 1938, with provision of up to a maximum of 250 by December 1939: it was the largest military order gained by a US company to date. The first Hudson Mk I bomber took to the air on 10 December 1938, with the company, now numbering a work force of

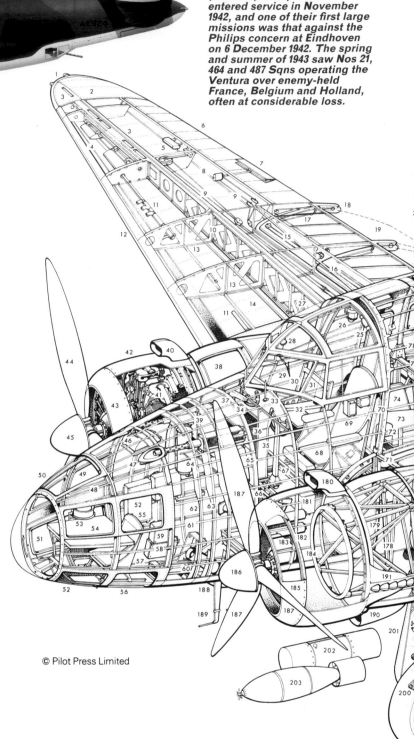

© Pilot Press Limited

Lockheed PV-2 Harpoon in US Naval Reserve markings, with upper twin Colt 12.7-mm (0.5-in) machine-guns in the nose. The first of 69 delivered in 1944 went into service in March, with squadrons seeing action over the Kuriles. Production was eventually dropped in favour of the superlative P2V Neptune.

Wartime-vintage Lockheed Venturas were converted in many instances to luxury executive-type aircraft in the years of peace. This smart twin, N5390N, is a Howard Aero Super Ventura.

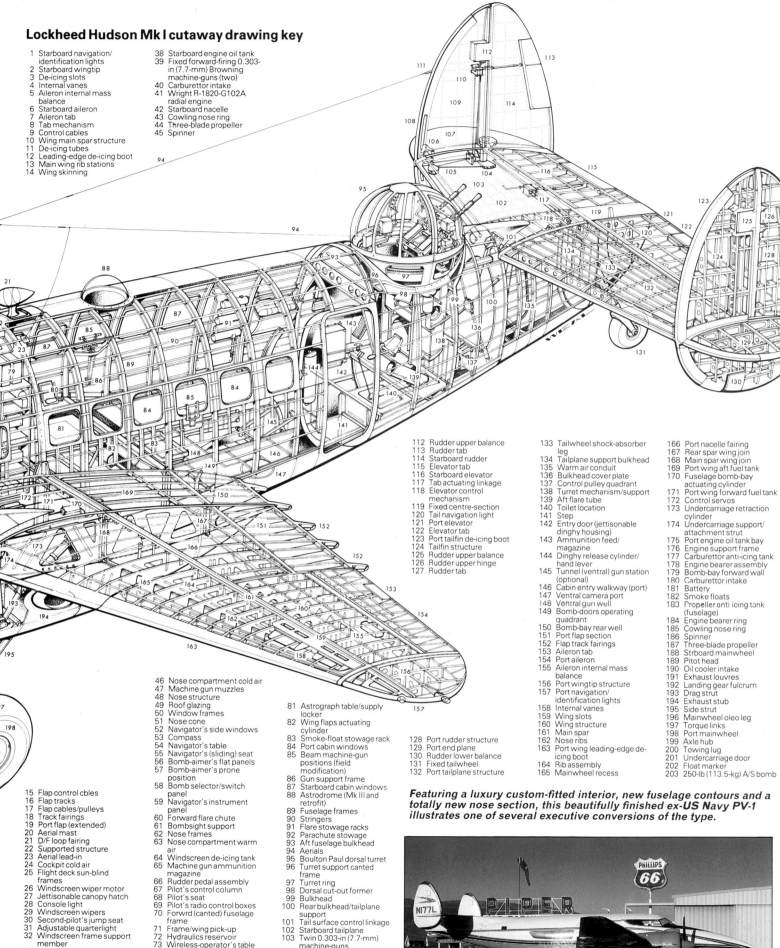

Lockheed Hudson Mk I cutaway drawing key

1 Starboard navigation/ identification lights
2 Starboard wingtip
3 De-icing slots
4 Internal vanes
5 Aileron internal mass balance
6 Starboard aileron
7 Aileron tab
8 Tab mechanism
9 Control cables
10 Wing main spar structure
11 De-icing tubes
12 Leading-edge de-icing boot
13 Main wing rib stations
14 Wing skinning

15 Flap control cbles
16 Flap tracks
17 Flap cables/pulleys
18 Track fairings
19 Port flap (extended)
20 Aerial mast
21 D/F loop fairing
22 Supported structure
23 Aerial lead-in
24 Cockpit cold air
25 Flight deck sun-blind frames
26 Windscreen wiper motor
27 Jettisonable canopy hatch
28 Console light
29 Windscreen wipers
30 Second-pilot's jump seat
31 Adjustable quarterlight
32 Windscreen frame support member
33 External gunsight
34 Second-pilot's (back-up) control column (cantilevered)
35 Central instrument console
36 Starboard nose compartment entry tunnel
37 Bulkhead

38 Starboard engine oil tank
39 Fixed forward-firing 0.303-in (7.7-mm) Browning machine-guns (two)
40 Carburettor intake
41 Wright R-1820-G102A radial engine
42 Starboard nacelle
43 Cowling nose ring
44 Three-blade propeller
45 Spinner

46 Nose compartment cold air
47 Machine gun muzzles
48 Nose structure
49 Roof glazing
50 Window frames
51 Nose cone
52 Navigator's side windows
53 Compass
54 Navigator's table
55 Navigator's (sliding) seat
56 Bomb-aimer's flat panels
57 Bomb-aimer's prone position
58 Bomb selector/switch panel
59 Navigator's instrument panel
60 Forward flare chute
61 Bombsight support
62 Nose frames
63 Nose compartment warm air
64 Windscreen de-icing tank
65 Machine gun ammunition magazine
66 Rudder pedal assembly
67 Pilot's control column
68 Pilot's seat
69 Pilot's radio control boxes
70 Forwrd (canted) fuselage frame
71 Frame/wing pick-up
72 Hydraulics reservoir
73 Wireless-operator's table
74 Wireless-operator's seat
75 Transmitter
76 Receiver
77 Main spar centre-section carry-through
78 Spar/frame attachment
79 Wireless bay racks
80 Cabin cold air

81 Astrograph table/supply locker
82 Wing flaps actuating cylinder
83 Smoke-float stowage rack
84 Port cabin windows
85 Beam machine-gun positions (field modification)
86 Gun support frame
87 Starboard cabin windows
88 Astrodome (Mk III and retrofit)
89 Fuselage frames
90 Stringers
91 Flare stowage racks
92 Parachute stowage
93 Aft fuselage bulkhead
94 Aerials
95 Boulton Paul dorsal turret
96 Turret support canted frame
97 Turret ring
98 Dorsal cut-out former
99 Bulkhead
100 Rear bulkhead/tailplane support
101 Tail surface control linkage
102 Starboard tailplane
103 Twin 0.303-in (7.7-mm) machine-guns
104 Rudder control quadrant
105 Cable linkage
106 De-icing tube
107 Starboard end plane
108 Tailfin de-icing boot
109 Tailfin skinning
110 Rudder tab actuator
111 Aerial attachment

112 Rudder upper balance
113 Rudder tab
114 Starboard rudder
115 Elevator tab
116 Starboard elevator
117 Tab actuating linkage
118 Elevator control mechanism
119 Fixed centre-section
120 Tail navigation light
121 Port elevator
122 Elevator tab
123 Port tailfin de-icing boot
124 Tailfin structure
125 Rudder upper balance
126 Rudder upper hinge
127 Rudder tab

128 Port rudder structure
129 Port end plane
130 Rudder lower balance
131 Fixed tailwheel
132 Port tailplane structure

133 Tailwheel shock-absorber leg
134 Tailplane support bulkhead
135 Warm air conduit
136 Bulkhead cover plate
137 Control pulley quadrant
138 Turret mechanism/support
139 Aft flare tube
140 Toilet location
141 Step
142 Entry door (jettisonable dinghy housing)
143 Ammunition feed/ magazine
144 Dinghy release cylinder/ hand lever
145 Tunnel (ventral) gun station (optional)
146 Cabin entry walkway (port)
147 Ventral camera port
148 Ventral gun well
149 Bomb-doors operating quadrant
150 Bomb-bay rear well
151 Port flap section
152 Flap track fairings
153 Aileron tab
154 Port aileron
155 Aileron internal mass balance
156 Port wingtip structure
157 Port navigation/ identification lights
158 Internal vanes
159 Wing slots
160 Wing structure
161 Main spar
162 Nose ribs
163 Port wing leading-edge de-icing boot
164 Rib assembly
165 Mainwheel recess

166 Port nacelle fairing
167 Rear spar wing join
168 Main spar wing join
169 Port wing aft fuel tank
170 Fuselage bomb-bay actuating cylinder
171 Port wing forward fuel tank
172 Control servos
173 Undercarriage retraction cylinder
174 Undercarriage support/ attachment strut
175 Port engine oil tank bay
176 Engine support frame
177 Carburettor anti-icing tank
178 Engine bearer assembly
179 Bomb-bay forward wall
180 Carburettor intake
181 Battery
182 Smoke floats
183 Propeller anti icing tank (fuselage)
184 Engine bearer ring
185 Cowling nose ring
186 Spinner
187 Three-blade propeller
188 Strboard mainwheel
189 Pitot head
190 Oil cooler intake
191 Exhaust louvres
192 Landing gear fulcrum
193 Drag strut
194 Exhaust stub
195 Side strut
196 Mainwheel oleo leg
197 Torque links
198 Port mainwheel
199 Axle hub
200 Towing lug
201 Undercarriage door
202 Float marker
203 250-lb (113.5-kg) A/S bomb

Featuring a luxury custom-fitted interior, new fuselage contours and a totally new nose section, this beautifully finished ex-US Navy PV-1 illustrates one of several executive conversions of the type.

The Lockheed XC-35 was built to a US Army Air Corps contract of 1936, to investigate high-altitude flight. Modified from a Model 12, its circular-section fuselage was stressed up to 0.69 bars (10 psi) pressure differential. It was the first aircraft to feature a pressure cabin and engine-driven turbo-superchargers, and flew for the first time on 7 May 1937.

7,000, hard at work to fill the orders which rose in value with additional orders for P-38s and B-34s to an impressive $65 million.

Arriving by sea, the first Hudson Mk Is reached the UK on 15 February 1939. The type was powered by two 820-kW (1,100-hp) Wright GR-1820-G102A Cyclones with two-speed Hamilton propellers. For reconnaissance duties the Hudson Mk I carried an F.24 camera, assorted flares and a bombload of up to 499 kg (1,100 lb) comprising either four 114-kg (250-lb) GP, SAP or AS, or 10 50-kg (110-lb) anti-submarine bombs; an overload of 12 51-kg (112-lb) Mk VIIc AS bombs could be carried, but in this event the bomb doors could not be fully closed. Modified with extra items at the Lockheed-Vega subsidiary at Speke (Liverpool), the first Hudson Mk Is and Mk IIs (the latter differing in the installation of Hamilton Standard Type 611A-12/3E50-253 constant-speed propellers) were delivered to Wing Commander E. A. Hodgson's No. 224 Squadron at Leuchars, Scotland, in August 1939. Although less manoeuvrable than the lighter Avro Anson, the Hudson was considered by the squadron to be eminently suitable for its patrols over the North Sea as far as Norway, the Skaggerak and the German Bight. Cruising at 610 m (2,000 ft) at 306 km/h (190 mph), a fuel consumption of 323 litres (71 Imp Gal) per hour gave the Hudson an endurance of over six hours with 20 per cent reserves and a 917-km (570-mile) radius of action. Armament was light initially, and the twin 7.7-mm (0.303-in) nose guns, beam guns and the Boulton Paul Type 'C' Mk II turret were retrofitted during the autumn of 1939 and the spring of 1940.

With the outbreak of war the Hudsons of RAF Coastal Command were among the first RAF aircraft to go into action, and the first combat with a German aircraft was recorded on 4 September 1939, when No. 224 Squadron's T-Tommy (N7214), captained by Flying Officer H. D. Green, engaged a Dornier Do 18 over the Dogger Bank. In addition to No. 224 Squadron, Nos 206, 269, 233, 320 and 220 Squadrons were equipped with Hudsons during 1939-40. Much

A pair of Hudsons from No. 269 Sqn, RAF Coastal Command, on a typical low-level patrol from their base at Wick in Scotland. For much of the war the squadron flew from Iceland and Greenland on U-boat patrol.

action was seen off Norway during the *Altmark* incident and the subsequent German invasion of Scandinavia, and over the Channel during the Dunkirk evacuations, in addition to patrol work over the western approaches and the North Sea. During 1941 RAF and RCAF Hudsons, operating from the UK, Iceland and Newfoundland, conducted a difficult war against the U-Boat menace: on 27 August 1941 a Hudson of No. 269 Squadron from Kaldadarnes forced the crew of the *U-570* to surrender after repeated attacks. Use of the Hudson was not limited to the RAF and RCAF, and in early 1942 US Army A-28s and A-29s, and US Navy PBO-1s did much work along the eastern seaboard of the United States, while in the Far East those of Nos 1 and 8 Squadrons, RAAF fought well against great odds during the Japanese invasions of Malaya, Java and Burma. Six primary marks of Hudson, engaged in maritime and transport work, emanated from Lockheed's 2,941 examples made up to June 1943 when production ceased, seeing service on all Anglo-American war fronts.

The Model 18 progeny

A direct development of the L-14 series, the Lockheed L-18 Lodestar first flew on 21 September 1939: the fuselage had been stretched by 1.68 m (5 ft 6 in), and to minimise tail flutter the elevator was raised slightly. By the end of 1940 some 54 of the 17-seat Model 18s had been sold to such varied customers as Mid Continent (first to buy the $90,000 aircraft), Régie Air Afrique and the Netherlands East Indies, BOAC and South African Airways. During World War II the Model 18 series was adopted by the US Army and the US Navy as a transport: US Army versions included the C-56 (in models up to C-56E), C-57 and C-57B, C-59, C-60 and C-60A, C-66 and C-111, all of which featured differences either in engines, seating or ancillary equipment. Naval versions included the R5O (in models up to R5O-6), while the RAF used Lodestar Mks I, IA and II models.

In response to a request from the British, Vega Aircraft Corporation developed a military version of the Model L-18 series which was

After World War II many Venturas remained in service around the world. This former GR.Mk V of the Royal Canadian Air Force was replaced by a Lancaster MR.Mk 10, but went on into the 1950s as a target tug at Sea Island, Vancouver. The orange/black livery was called 'Oxydol special' after a popular brand of soap powder.

By far the most important of the post-war users of the Ventura was the South African Air Force, which gathered its own survivors (including this GR.Mk V) and many former B-34s and PV-1s to serve as ocean patrol and medium bomber aircraft until Shackletons arrived in 1958. No. 6472 served with No. 17 Sqn.

employed by the RAF as the Ventura, by the US Army Air Force as the B-34 and B-37, and by the US Navy as the PV-1 patrol bomber. All were powered by two 1492-kW (2,000-hp) Pratt & Whitney R-2800-31 radials, with the exception of the RAF's Ventura Mk I which had Pratt & Whitney R-2800-S1A4G engines, and the few B-37s which featured Wright R-2600-13s. The first Ventura Mk I flew on 31 July 1941 and, together with the up-rated Mk II and Mk IIA versions, entered service with No. 2 (Bomber) Group in November 1942. On daylight missions over France and the Low Countries the Ventura fared badly against the dangerous Focke-Wulf Fw 190As of

the Luftwaffe, and losses to flak and enemy fighters were consistently high. During the summer of 1943 the type was withdrawn from No. 2 Group, its place being taken by North American Mitchells and Douglas Boston Mk IIIA bombers. The B-34s of the USAAF saw little action, while the B-37 (Ventura Mk III) saw none at all. In the Solomons and South Pacific area Ventura Mk IVs and GR.Mk Vs of the RNZAF saw considerable action against the Japanese bastions at Kavieng and Rabaul, and proved their worth. The last-mentioned

Above: A Lockheed PV-1 Ventura seen on Bougainville in the Solomons during January 1944. The Ventura was widely used for coastal patrols in the Pacific campaign. This was equivalent to the RAF's Ventura GR.Mk V. Approximately 1,600 had been delivered to the US Navy by May 1944, with a further 875 shared between the RAF and USAAF.

Venturas of the Royal New Zealand Air Force featured prominently in the campaigns in the south-west Pacific, in the Solomons and against the Japanese bastions at Rabaul and Kavieng. These PV-1s, three of 388 procured under Lend-Lease, flew as the Ventura GR.Mk V with the RNZAF in the Solomons during 1943-44. The nearest aircraft is NZ4534, coded ZX-D. They are demonstrating single-engine flight.

Lockheed twin-engine variants

Lockheed Model L-10 Electra: all-metal, twin-engine 10-seat L-10 introduced into commercial service in 1934; 149 aircraft built; **Lockheed Model L-10A** had two 298-kW (400-hp) Pratt & Whitney R-985 Wasp Juniors, **Lockheed Model L-10B** two 313-kW (420-hp) Wright Whirlwinds, **Model L-10C** two 336-kW (450-hp) Wasp SC1s, and **Model L-10E** two 336-kW (450 hp) Pratt & Whitney R-1340 engines; in service with US Army, US Navy and US Coast Guard as the **C-36/C-37, R2O** and **R3O** respectively
Lockheed Model L-12 Electra Junior: introduced in 1936 with six-seat capacity for business use, with two Pratt & Whitney R-985-SB Wasp Juniors as the **Model L-12A**; 130 built; service with the US Navy as **JO-1** and **JO-2** sub-types, and with the US Army as the **C-40, C-40A** and ex-civil **UC-40D**; military nose-wheel trainers (one each) as the **XJO-3** (US Navy) and **C-40B** (US Army); eight out of 13 **Model 212** military trainers delivered to Royal Netherlands Indies Air Division in Java in 1942; other variants were the **Model L-12B** with 328-kW (440-hp) Wright R-975-E3d radials, and the **Model 12-25** with 336-kW (450-hp) Wasp Junior SB3 radials
Lockheed Model L-14 Super Electra: introduced in 1937 with 12-seat capacity for commercial use, with two 559-kW (750-hp) Pratt & Whitney Hornets **(Model L-14H)** or various models of Wright Cyclones **(Model L-14W)** and **Model L-14N,** the latter only for private owners); typical late-production L-14 had 14-seat configuration with two Wright GR-1820-G3B engines; became the progenitor of the military Hudson, A-28, A-29 and PBO-1 series; impressed Model L-14Ws were designated **C-111,** while Japanese production produced the **Army Type LO Transport**
Lockheed Model 14B Hudson Mk I: general-purpose patrol bomber with two 745-kW (1,000-hp) Wright GR-1820-G102A engines with two-speed Hamilton-Standard propellers; in service with RAF Coastal Command in mid-1939
Lockheed Model 414 Hudson Mk II: as Mk I but with Hamilton Standard 611A-12/3 constant-speed propellers; standard armament included twin 7.7-mm (0.303-in) forward-firing machine-guns, two beam guns and twin-gunned Boulton Paul Type 'C' Mk II dorsal turret; pilot and fuel tank armour
Lockheed Model 414 Hudson Mk III: two Wright GR-1820-G205A Cyclones each rated at 895-kW (1,200-hp) and Hamilton-Standard hydromatic propellers defined this prolific version which introduced a ventral gun position; **Hudson Mk IIIA** (US Army designation A-29) powered by two 895-kW

(1,200-hp) Wright R-1820-87 Cyclones, and designated the **PBO-1** by US Navy; the **A-29A** had a convertible troop-transport interior, and the **A-29B** was a photographic-survey version; the **AT-18** and **AT-18A** were gunnery and navigation trainers respectively
Lockheed Model 414 Hudson Mk IV: two Pratt & Whitney R-1820-SC3G Twin Wasp engines; primarily for RAAF service, but a few to the RAF; no ventral gun position; US Army designation was **A-28** (two R-1830-45s), becoming **Hudson Mk IVA** in RAAF service
Lockheed Model 414 Hudson Mk V: two Pratt & Whitney R-1830-SC34G engines with Hamilton Type 6227A-0 propellers, and the ventral gun position
Lockheed Model 414 Hudson Mk VI: two Pratt & Whitney R-1830-67s; US Army designation **A-28A**
Lockheed Model L-18 Lodestar: direct development of the Model L-14, with crew of three and 14 passengers; powerplant comprised Pratt & Whitney S1E-3G Hornets, or Pratt & Whitney SC-3G Twin Wasps, or S4C-4G Twin Wasps, or Wright GR-1820-G102As, or GR-1820-202As or GR-1820-G205As; naval transport versions designated **R5O-1, R5O-4, R5O-5** and **R5O-6**; US Army versions were the **C-56, C-57, C-59, C-60** and **C-66**; RAF versions were the **Lodestar Mks I, IA and II**
Kawasaki Ki-56 (Army Type 1 Transport): the Japanese produced the Lockheed L-14WG3 under licence, and with refinements; two 708-kW (950-hp) Army 99 (Nakajima Ha-25) engines; in service with the JAAF in 1940; 121 built
Lockheed B-34 (Model 37): military patrol bomber developed from the Model 18 series to RAF specification, and designated the **Ventura Mk I** in RAF service **(Model 37-21);** two Pratt & Whitney R-2800-S1A4G engines rated at 1379-kW (1,850-hp); the **Ventura Mk II (Model 37-27)** was powered by two R-2800-31 engines; RAF also used the **Ventura Mk IIA (Model 37-127)** and **Ventura GR.Mk V**; US Army designations were **B-34** and **B-37**, with definitive maritime version, the **PV-1 (Model 237)** (alias Ventura GR.Mk V), serving in the US Navy
Lockheed PV-2 Harpoon (Model 15): development of US Navy's PV-1, with completely redesigned airframe; two 1492-kW (2,000-hp) Pratt & Whitney R-2800-31 engines; produced or converted in additional **PV-2C, PV-2D** and **PV-2T** sub-types
Lockheed PV-3 Harpoon: designation of 27 Ventura Mk IIs retained by US Navy

Lockheed Hudson family

marks were known in the US Navy as PV-1s, of which 1,800 were built. Carrying a crew of four or five, the PV-1 weighed in at 9161 kg (20,197 lb) empty and 14097 kg (31,077 lb) gross, and was capable of a maximum speed of 502 km/h (312 mph) at 4205 m (13,800 ft). Armament consisted of two forward-firing 12.7-mm (0.5-in) guns, two more guns of the same calibre in a Martin CE250 dorsal turret, and two 7.62-mm (0.3-in) guns in the ventral position; up to four 454-kg (1,000-lb) bombs could be stowed internally, with another two under the wings, while an alternative was a single Model 13 Mk II torpedo. US Navy PV-1s operated from Aleutian bases during 1943-45 in all weathers on anti-shipping strikes and attacks on the Japanese bases at Paramushiro and Shimushu, and fought off frequent aggressive attacks by the Mitsubishi A6M3 Reisens of the 13th Koku Kantai (Air Fleet) which defended the area. The PV-1 more than compensated for the relatively poor showing by the Ventura in Europe, and performed useful service in all sectors of the Pacific.

The final version of this long and successful series of the Lockheed twins that had started the little Model L-10 in 1934 was the PV-2 Harpoon maritime patrol bomber. In this model the fuselage and tail unit were redesigned, and the wing span increased from 19.96 m (65 ft 6 in) to 22.86 m (75 ft). The first flight of the PV-2 took place on 3 December 1943, the first aircraft being delivered to US Navy squadrons in March 1944 for action from Aleutian bases. Wing flexing problems added to production difficulties, but the PV-2 saw out the war and continued to serve in naval reserve wings for many years afterwards.

Specification
Lockheed PV-2 Harpoon

Type: four/five-seat patrol bomber
Powerplant: two 1491-kW (2,000-hp) Pratt & Whitney R-2800-31 Double Wasp 18-cylinder radials
Performance: maximum speed (clean) 454 km/h (282 mph) at medium altitude; service ceiling 7285 m (23,900 ft); range (with outer-wing tanks available, after curing major sealing problem) 2880 km (1,790 miles)
Weights: empty 9538 kg (21,028 lb); maximum 16330 kg (36,000 lb)
Dimensions: span 22.84 m (74 ft 11 in); length 15.86 m (52 ft 0½ in); height 3.63 m (11 ft 10 in); wing area 63.77 m² (686 sq ft)
Armament: internal day for bombload of 1814 kg (4,000 lb), plus underwing racks for two 454-kg (1,000-lb) bombs, depth charges or other stores, or (as illustrated) eight HVAR (high-velocity aircraft rockets) in addition to drop tanks

This Lockheed PV-2 Harpoon served at the end of World War II with US Navy squadron VPB-142 in the Marianas Islands. It was one of the original and most common variant with a forward-firing armament of five guns, two high in the nose and three below; later the number was increased to eight. In fact, hardly any of the PV-2 was identical with the corresponding parts of any PV-1, the unchanged portions being confined to small portions of the fuselage, inboard wing ribs and the cowlings (but not the nacelles). Another item common to some PV-1s was the type of Martin dorsal turret, but the lower rear guns were changed to the same 12.7-mm (0.5-in) calibre as used elsewhere.

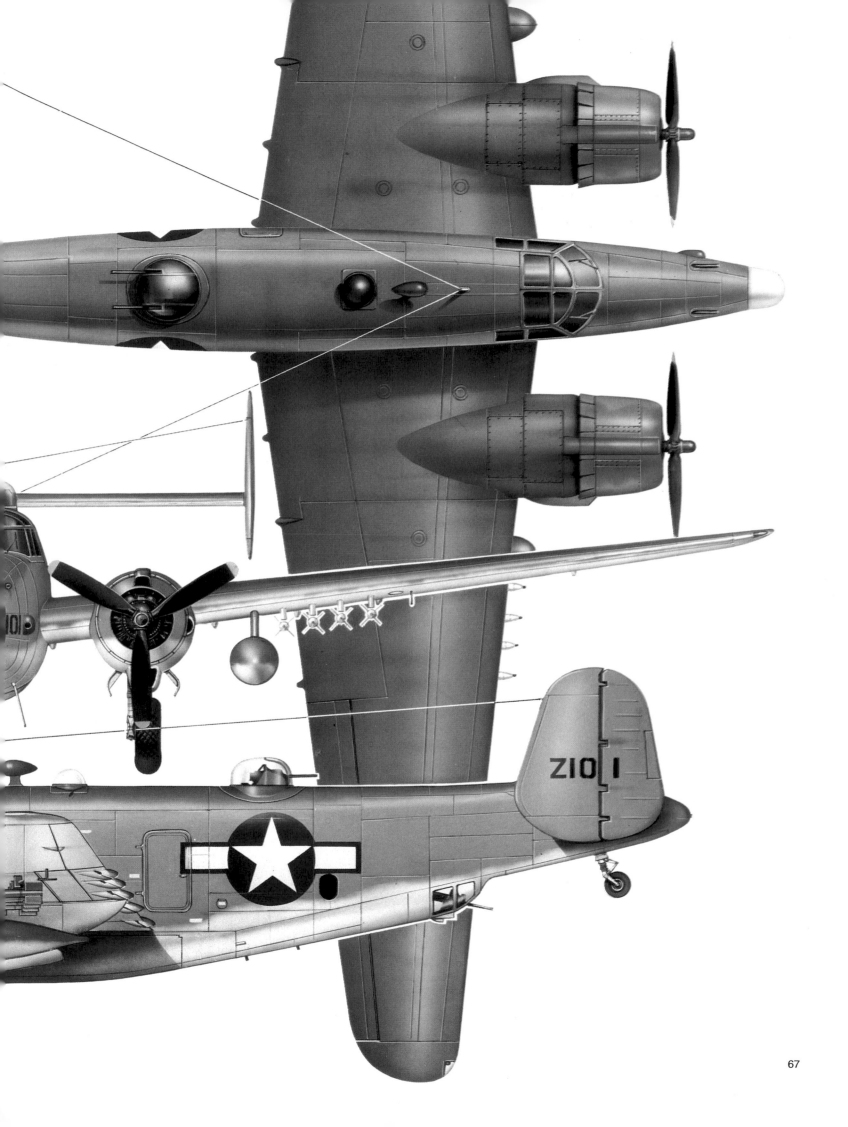

Avro Lancaster: Belligerent Bomber

The backbone of the RAF's bombing effort, the Lancaster came to represent the might of bombing power in World War II. A classic case of turning a sow's ear into a silk purse, the Lancaster emerged from the unpopular Manchester to become the best all-round bomber of the war, with a combat record to prove it.

The Lancaster, Britain's greatest bomber of World War II and by far the most important instrument of 'Bertie' Harris's policy of mass night attacks on German cities, came about solely through the outstanding structural design of the staff of A.V. Roe Ltd, at Chadderton, Manchester, on a quite different bomber of 1936. Air Ministry Specification P.13/36 called for a new tactical medium bomber more powerful than the Vickers Wellington and Armstrong Whitworth Whitley, able to carry a heavy load of bombs or two torpedoes, or a heavy overload of fuel. It was to have a small wing, and to use catapulting to take-off at maximum weight. Two very powerful engines were suggested, rather than four of the 597/746-kW (800/1,000-hp) size then becoming available.

One of the many designs submitted was the Avro 679 Manchester. Powered by two 1306-kW (1,750-hp) Rolls-Royce Vultures, it was a neat mid-wing monoplane of modern stressed-skin construction. Avro had never built an airframe of this type, nor anything remotely approaching the Type 679 in weight and power. It first flew on 25 July 1939 from Ringway (now Manchester Airport) and though it suffered from directional instability (a third fin being added) and severe lack of power by the engines, it had some fine qualities. It was improved by adding to the outer wings to increase span from 24.43 m (80 ft 2 in) to 27.46 m (90 ft 1 in), whereupon it became delightful to fly. Unquestionably it was the best of all the new British bombers in overall design, for it was simple, easy to make and a welcome relief to the ground crews by comparison with the tricky and inaccessible machines from other factories. In November 1940 No. 207 Sqn of Bomber Command was equipped with the Man-

chester I, but suffered terribly from poor engine performance and shocking engine reliability. One unit, No. 97 Sqn, was grounded so often that it was nicknamed 'the 97th Foot'.

Something had to be done quickly. Manchesters were pouring off the lines at Avro and at Metropolitan-Vickers. Rolls-Royce managed to test the Vulture at over 1492 kW (2,000 hp), but knew it could not spare the effort needed to make the engine reliable. Avro began studies of the Manchester II with two Napier Sabres or, better still, two Bristol Centaurus radials; but the dynamic boss of Rolls-Royce, E.H. (later Lord) Hives, was not having that. He went to the Air Ministry and outlined a scheme for a Manchester III with four Merlins. The Merlin X had just been designed for the Beaufighter in the form of a self-contained unit that could be bolted on and coupled up without the need for any design effort by Avro beyond increasing yet again the span of the outer wings. Avro said it could do this, and under chief designer Roy Chadwick the Manchester III was created in three weeks in late 1940. A Manchester (BT308) was taken off the production line and completed with the longer outer wings and four underslung engines. It was flown by Capt. H.A. 'Sam' Brown at Ringway on 9 January 1941.

By this time the four-engined machine, the Type 683, had been renamed Lancaster I. In parallel Chadwick schemed a high-wing transport version, the Type 685 York, but little effort was allowed to be spared for the York for two years. Meanwhile another Manchester (DG595) was completed as the second Lancaster prototype with numerous modifications, including a tail with taller fins and rudders and no central fin, an improved mid-upper turret and refined air-

At first known as the Manchester Mk III, and retaining the original Manchester Mk I tail unit, the first prototype Lancaster (BT308) flew on 9 January 1941. The Lancaster would never have happened had not a Merlin 'power egg' capable of just being bolted on without further design work already been developed for the Beaufighter Mk II.

A row of small windows can be seen on the batch of 300 Lancaster Mk IIs built by Armstrong Whitworth with Hercules XVI engines. These aircraft had bulged bomb bays and originally the FN.64 ventral turret (the only turret to be really needed, and it was removed). The Mk II had good performance but high fuel consumption.

The serial ED912/G means a special aircraft which must be kept under armed guard when on the ground. It was one of the Mk III (Special) aircraft modified to drop the spinning-drum Upkeep device for destroying the German dams, and taken into action by No. 617 Sqn under Wing Commander Guy Gibson on the night of 17/18 May 1943.

HK793 was a B.I built by Vickers-Armstrong at Castle Bromwich, with the deep bomb bay of the Mk II. It is seen at the war's end as a Gee-H equipped lead aircraft (yellow fin stripes) with No. 149 (East India) Squadron. Gee, the RAF area-coverage navaid, was made more precise by the added H interrogation system.

frame with 'productionised' detail assemblies. Flight trials with the first Lancaster had gone with extraordinary smoothness; handling was superb, and performance was better even than predicted values – Chadwick was unable to account for the remarkably good figures turned in by the new four-engined machine. As early as 27 January, only 18 days from first flight, the first prototype was delivered to the Aeroplane and Armament Experimental Establishment at Boscombe Down, where it received the best assessment ever awarded a new aircraft, beginning: 'This aeroplane is eminently suitable for operational service.' Production of the Lancaster was ordered forthwith, starting with completion as Lancasters of the Manchesters already on the assembly line.

Further revamps

Chadwick was still not satisfied, and sent a team of draughtsmen from Chadderton to the flight sheds at Woodford where Avro bombers were actually assembled. Numerous further changes were made to improve systems, armour protection and many other details, Chadwick telling each worker: 'Imagine that six months hence you might have the job of repairing or overhauling this machine'. The changes made it more difficult to turn almost-finished Manchesters into Lancasters, but 243 Lancasters built by Avro and 57 by Metrovick started life as the twin-engined bombers. They were distinguished from true Lancasters by a row of small shallow windows along each side of the fuselage.

The first production Lancaster was L7527, flown on 31 October 1941 with 955-kW (1,280-hp) Merlin XX engines in place of the 854-kW (1,145-hp) Merlin Xs used previously, but somewhat slower because the gross weight had grown from 22680 to 27216 kg (50,000 to 60,000 lb). The mid-upper turret had a different appearance because of a surrounding aerodynamic fairing incorporating a 'taboo track' along which rode rollers which kept the twin guns at high angles when fore and aft to avoid firing at parts of the aircraft. Magazines in the mid-fuselage housed 2,000 rounds for this turret and 10,000 for the new Frazer-Nash FN.30 rear turret, less rounded than the FN.20 of the Manchester (almost the same as that of the Whitley V). Early Lancasters also retained the Manchester's FN.21A two-gun ventral turret, but this was rarely used and soon discarded. (Who was to know that in 1943-5, in the Lancaster's hour of need when dozens were being shot down each night by Junkers Ju 88s and Messerschmitt Bf 110Gs, that this would be the only turret that could have done any good?)

Production got into its stride in early 1942, with the formation of a

By the time production started the Lancaster had the tail of the Manchester Mk IA with wide-span tailplane carrying taller fins and rudders, and no central fin. The fuselage was at first that of the Manchester, with a row of small side windows, which are visible on this 1942 trio with No. 207 Sqn (ex-Manchesters).

Lancaster Production Group including A.V. Roe at Chadderton, Woodford, vast new shadow factories at Yeadon (today's Leeds/Bradford Airport) and Langar, Nottinghamshire; Metrovick at Trafford Park, Manchester; Austin Motors at Longbridge, Birmingham; Armstrong Whitworth at Baginton, Coventry (later at Bitteswell also); and Vickers-Armstrong at Castle Bromwich and Hawarden (Chester). This group grew to number over 131,000 including sub-contractors, and built up output until in August 1944 it delivered 293 new aircraft plus the equivalent of dozens more in spares and re-paired aircraft. The total was further swelled by Victory Aircraft of Toronto, a Crown company responsible to the Canadian Minister of Munitions and Supply. The Canadian aircraft was called Lancaster X (Mk 10 post-war) and took its Merlin engines off the newly set-up Packard Motors (USA) production line.

The RAF got a Lancaster in September 1941 when BT308 was lent to No. 44 (Rhodesia) Sqn at Waddington for trials. No. 44, a Handley Page Hampden unit, became the first squadron equipped with the new bomber in early 1942, having received the first machine on Christmas Eve. Next it was the turn of No. 97 Sqn, henceforth no longer the butt of jokes from other squadrons. The first operation, by No. 44 Squadron, was the laying of mines in the Heligoland Bight on the night of 3 March 1942. The first bombing raid came on 10 March, when two aircraft from No. 44 Squadron each took 2291 kg (5,050 lb) of incendiaries to Essen. The total was to grow to 618350 tonnes (608,612 long tons).

Electronic fit

News of the Lancaster burst on the world after a daring – and rather silly – daylight raid by 12 aircraft on 17 April 1942. The bombers were drawn from Nos 44 and 97 Sqns, and they flew right across Germany at low level to drop a few bombs on the MAN factory making diesel engines at Augsburg. The reason for this extra-ordinary mission, which cost seven aircraft and won Squadron Leader J.D. Nettleton a well-earned VC, was never explained, and it was never repeated. Thereafter the Lancaster settled down to patient slogging night after night in ever-larger forces whose techniques improved all the time. Soon Lancasters were carrying H2S mapping radar in a large blister where the ventral guns had been, as well as the vital Gee navaid and, by 1944, the even more accurate aid Gee-H (aircraft thus equipped had two horizontal yellow bands on their fins), used by Pathfinder and target-marking aircraft. A few Lancasters on special target-marking missions carried the Oboe

10 Fire extinguisher
11 Parachute emergency exit
12 F-24 camera
13 Glycol tank/step
14 Ventilator fairing
15 Bomb-bay doors forward actuating jacks
16 Bomb-bay doors forward actuating jacks
17 Control linkage
18 Rudder pedals
19 Instrument panel
20 Windscreen sprays
21 Windscreen
22 Dimmer switches
23 Flight-engineer's folding seat
24 Flight-engineer's control panel
25 Pilot's seat
26 Flight-deck floor level
27 Elevator and rudder control rods (underfloor)

Avro Lancaster Mk III cutaway drawing key

1 Two 0.303-in (7.7-mm) Browning machine-guns
2 Frazer-Nash power-operated nose turret
3 Nose blister
4 Bomb-aimer's panel (optically flat)
5 Bomb-aimer's control panel
6 Side windows
7 External air temperature thermometer
8 Pitot head
9 Bomb-aimer's chest support

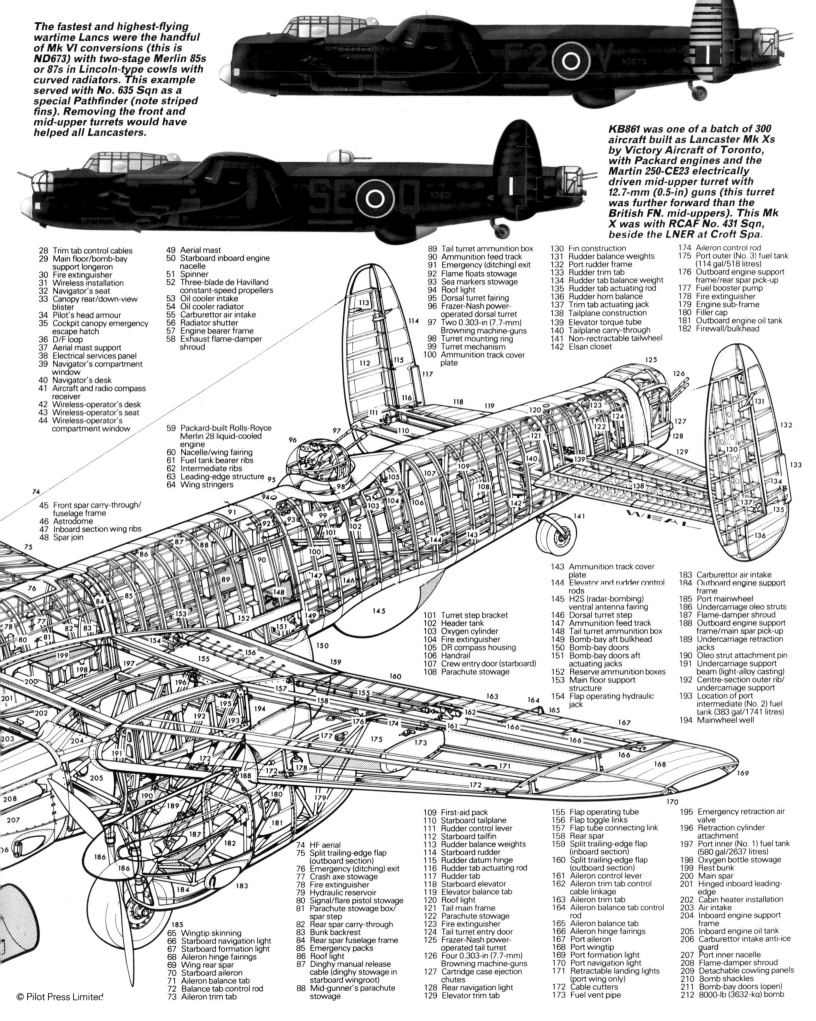

The fastest and highest-flying wartime Lancs were the handful of Mk VI conversions (this is ND673) with two-stage Merlin 85s or 87s in Lincoln-type cowls with curved radiators. This example served with No. 635 Sqn as a special Pathfinder (note striped fins). Removing the front and mid-upper turrets would have helped all Lancasters.

KB861 was one of a batch of 300 aircraft built as Lancaster Mk Xs by Victory Aircraft of Toronto, with Packard engines and the Martin 250-CE23 electrically driven mid-upper turret with 12.7-mm (0.5-in) guns (this turret was further forward than the British FN. mid-uppers). This Mk X was with RCAF No. 431 Sqn, beside the LNER at Croft Spa.

28 Trim tab control cables
29 Main floor/bomb-bay support longeron
30 Fire extinguisher
31 Wireless installation
32 Navigator's seat
33 Canopy rear/down-view blister
34 Pilot's head armour
35 Cockpit canopy emergency escape hatch
36 D/F loop
37 Aerial mast support
38 Electrical services panel
39 Navigator's compartment window
40 Navigator's desk
41 Aircraft and radio compass receiver
42 Wireless-operator's desk
43 Wireless-operator's seat
44 Wireless-operator's compartment window

45 Front spar carry-through/fuselage frame
46 Astrodome
47 Inboard section wing ribs
48 Spar join

49 Aerial mast
50 Starboard inboard engine nacelle
51 Spinner
52 Three-blade de Havilland constant-speed propellers
53 Oil cooler intake
54 Oil cooler radiator
55 Carburettor air intake
56 Radiator shutter
57 Engine bearer frame
58 Exhaust flame-damper shroud

59 Packard-built Rolls-Royce Merlin 28 liquid-cooled engine
60 Nacelle/wing fairing
61 Fuel tank bearer ribs
62 Intermediate ribs
63 Leading-edge structure
64 Wing stringers

65 Wingtip skinning
66 Starboard navigation light
67 Starboard formation light
68 Aileron hinge fairings
69 Wing rear spar
70 Starboard aileron
71 Aileron balance tab
72 Balance tab control rod
73 Aileron trim tab
74 HF aerial
75 Split trailing-edge flap (outboard section)
76 Emergency (ditching) exit
77 Crash axe stowage
78 Fire extinguisher
79 Hydraulic reservoir
80 Signal/flare pistol stowage
81 Parachute stowage box/spar step
82 Rear spar carry-through
83 Bunk backrest
84 Rear spar fuselage frame
85 Emergency packs
86 Roof light
87 Dinghy manual release cable (dinghy stowage in starboard wingroot)
88 Mid-gunner's parachute stowage

89 Tail turret ammunition box
90 Ammunition feed track
91 Emergency (ditching) exit
92 Flame floats stowage
93 Sea markers stowage
94 Roof light
95 Dorsal turret fairing
96 Frazer-Nash power-operated dorsal turret
97 Two 0.303-in (7.7-mm) Browning machine-guns
98 Turret mounting ring
99 Turret mechanism
100 Ammunition track cover plate
101 Turret step bracket
102 Header tank
103 Oxygen cylinder
104 Fire extinguisher
105 DR compass housing
106 Handrail
107 Crew entry door (starboard)
108 Parachute stowage

109 First-aid pack
110 Starboard tailplane
111 Rudder control lever
112 Starboard tailfin
113 Rudder balance weights
114 Starboard rudder
115 Rudder datum hinge
116 Rudder tab actuating rod
117 Rudder tab
118 Starboard elevator
119 Elevator balance tab
120 Roof light
121 Tail main frame
122 Parachute stowage
123 Fire extinguisher
124 Tail entry door
125 Frazer-Nash power-operated tail turret
126 Four 0.303-in (7.7-mm) Browning machine-guns
127 Cartridge case ejection chutes
128 Rear navigation light
129 Elevator trim tab

130 Fin construction
131 Rudder balance weights
132 Port rudder frame
133 Rudder trim tab
134 Rudder tab balance weight
135 Rudder tab actuating rod
136 Rudder horn balance
137 Trim tab actuating jack
138 Tailplane construction
139 Elevator torque tube
140 Tailplane carry-through
141 Non-rectractable tailwheel
142 Elsan closet

143 Ammunition track cover plate
144 Elevator and rudder control rods
145 H2S (radar-bombing) ventral antenna fairing
146 Dorsal turret step
147 Ammunition feed track
148 Tail turret ammunition box
149 Bomb-bay aft bulkhead
150 Bomb-bay doors
151 Bomb-bay doors aft actuating jacks
152 Reserve ammunition boxes
153 Main floor support structure
154 Flap operating hydraulic jack

155 Flap operating tube
156 Flap toggle links
157 Flap tube connecting link
158 Rear spar
159 Split trailing-edge flap (inboard section)
160 Split trailing-edge flap (outboard section)
161 Aileron control lever
162 Aileron trim tab control cable linkage
163 Aileron trim tab
164 Aileron balance tab control rod
165 Aileron balance tab
166 Aileron hinge fairings
167 Port aileron
168 Port wingtip
169 Port formation light
170 Port navigation light
171 Retractable landing lights (port wing only)
172 Cable cutters
173 Fuel vent pipe

174 Aileron control rod
175 Port outer (No. 3) fuel tank (114 gal/518 litres)
176 Outboard engine support frame/rear spar pick-up
177 Fuel booster pump
178 Fire extinguisher
179 Engine sub-frame
180 Filler cap
181 Outboard engine oil tank
182 Firewall/bulkhead

183 Carburettor air intake
184 Outboard engine support frame
185 Port mainwheel
186 Undercarriage oleo struts
187 Flame-damper shroud
188 Outboard engine support frame/main spar pick-up
189 Undercarriage retraction jacks
190 Oleo strut attachment pin
191 Undercarriage support beam (light-alloy casting)
192 Centre-section outer rib/undercarriage support
193 Location of port intermediate (No. 2) fuel tank (383 gal/1741 litres)
194 Mainwheel well

195 Emergency retraction air valve
196 Retraction cylinder attachment
197 Port inner (No. 1) fuel tank (580 gal/2637 litres)
198 Oxygen bottle stowage
199 Rest bunk
200 Main spar
201 Hinged inboard leading-edge
202 Cabin heater installation
203 Air intake
204 Inboard engine support frame
205 Inboard engine oil tank
206 Carburettor intake anti-ice guard
207 Port inner nacelle
208 Flame-damper shroud
209 Detachable cowling panels
210 Bomb shackles
211 Bomb-bay doors (open)
212 8000-lb (3632-kg) bomb

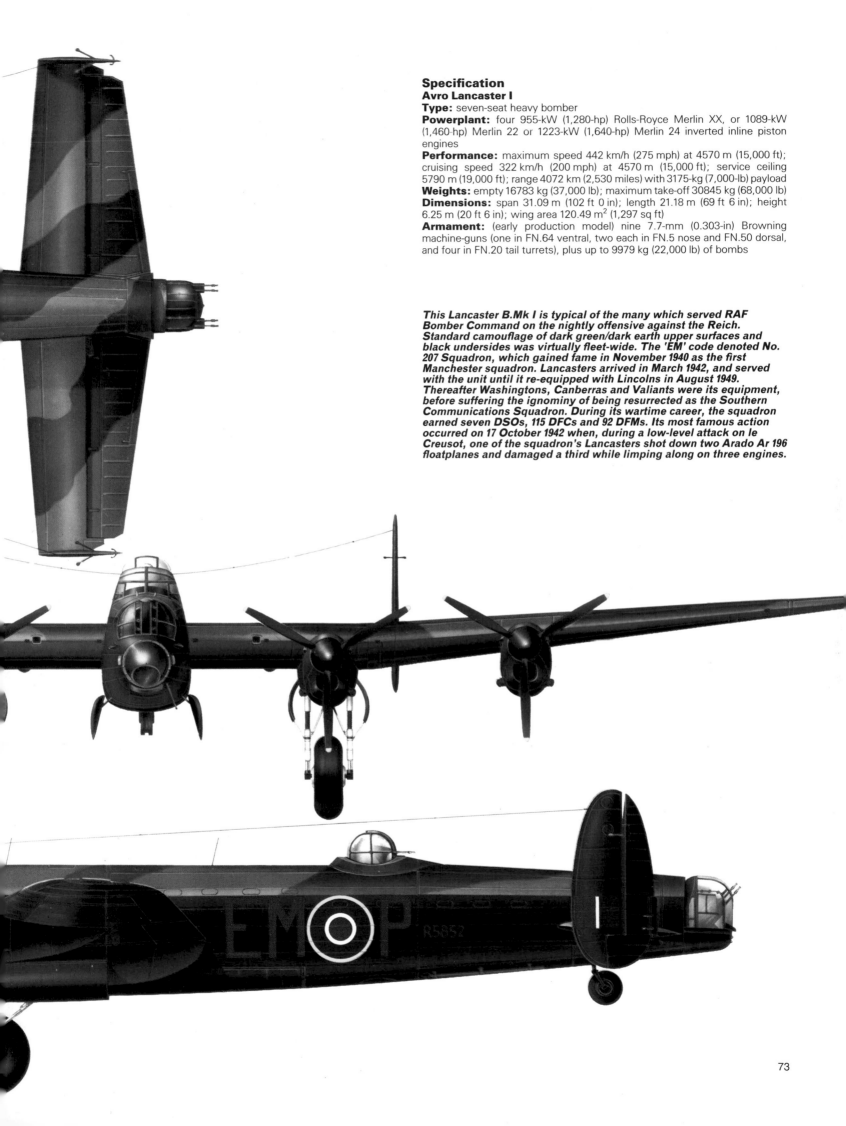

Specification
Avro Lancaster I
Type: seven-seat heavy bomber
Powerplant: four 955-kW (1,280-hp) Rolls-Royce Merlin XX, or 1089-kW (1,460-hp) Merlin 22 or 1223-kW (1,640-hp) Merlin 24 inverted inline piston engines
Performance: maximum speed 442 km/h (275 mph) at 4570 m (15,000 ft); cruising speed 322 km/h (200 mph) at 4570 m (15,000 ft); service ceiling 5790 m (19,000 ft); range 4072 km (2,530 miles) with 3175-kg (7,000-lb) payload
Weights: empty 16783 kg (37,000 lb); maximum take-off 30845 kg (68,000 lb)
Dimensions: span 31.09 m (102 ft 0 in); length 21.18 m (69 ft 6 in); height 6.25 m (20 ft 6 in); wing area 120.49 m^2 (1,297 sq ft)
Armament: (early production model) nine 7.7-mm (0.303-in) Browning machine-guns (one in FN.64 ventral, two each in FN.5 nose and FN.50 dorsal, and four in FN.20 tail turrets), plus up to 9979 kg (22,000 lb) of bombs

This Lancaster B.Mk I is typical of the many which served RAF Bomber Command on the nightly offensive against the Reich. Standard camouflage of dark green/dark earth upper surfaces and black undersides was virtually fleet-wide. The 'EM' code denoted No. 207 Squadron, which gained fame in November 1940 as the first Manchester squadron. Lancasters arrived in March 1942, and served with the unit until it re-equipped with Lincolns in August 1949. Thereafter Washingtons, Canberras and Valiants were its equipment, before suffering the ignominy of being resurrected as the Southern Communications Squadron. During its wartime career, the squadron earned seven DSOs, 115 DFCs and 92 DFMs. Its most famous action occurred on 17 October 1942 when, during a low-level attack on le Creusot, one of the squadron's Lancasters shot down two Arado Ar 196 floatplanes and damaged a third while limping along on three engines.

Heaviest bomb ever dropped in anger was the 9979-kg (22,000-lb) Grand Slam, which fell faster than sound and shook its targets apart by earthquake waves. To carry it the B.I (Special) had to be partly stripped. Most retained regular bomber (Night) colours, but this aircraft, with No. 617 Sqn's C Flight (code YZ) had this unusual scheme.

Shown in Tiger Force colours, the B.VII saw operational service during the war only in that force, this example being with No. 9 Sqn, which with No. 617 Sqn was then at Salbani, India. The B.VII(FE) (FE=Far East) had the Martin mid-upper turret, but this particular aircraft has the Bristol B.17 with twin 20-mm guns, à la Lincoln.

navaid, where errors were measured in feet, but Oboe was used mainly by de Havilland Mosquitoes. Dozens of Lancasters carried special communications gear in the first ECM (electronic counter-measures) and ECCM (electronic counter-countermeasures), such as the 'Airborne Cigar' radio jammer carried by No. 101 Sqn whose Lancasters had two large radio masts on top and another projecting down under the nose.

Like most of the best aircraft, most Lancasters looked almost identical to the first. Apart from special weapon and electronic fits, the only real difference in production machines was the Mk II, which had Bristol Hercules sleeve-valve radial engines. Avro built two (DR810 and 812) and then Armstrong Whitworth a batch of 300, used mainly by Canadian crews. It had a better take-off and climb, but though faster low down than the Merlin Lancaster it lost at altitude and also had a slightly lighter fuel consumption. Another feature of the Mk II was its bulged bomb bay, terminating at the rear in an improved FN.64A ventral turret.

Thanks to the original 1936 Specification calling for torpedoes, the Lancaster inherited from the Manchester a gigantic and unobstructed bomb bay. After some strengthening this was used to carry the heaviest and bulkiest bombs used in World War II, including the regular 1814-kg (4,000-lb) 'cookie' (the usual weapon, carried surrounded by a dozen or more cases of incendiaries), the double-length 3629-kg (8,000-lb) bomb and the rare 5443-kg (12,000-lb) size; the 5443-kg (12,000-lb) Tallboy deep-penetration streamlined bomb designed by B.N. (later Sir Barnes) Wallis at Vickers, and used to sink *Tirpitz*; the even bigger 9979-kg (22,000-lb) Grand Slam, which required substantial aircraft modifications resulting in the designation Mk I (Special); and the special weapon designed by Wallis to breach German dams.

Gibson's historic mission

The Dambusters' mission is perhaps the most famous exploit in the history of the RAF. Thanks again to the fertile brain of Wallis,

As a world-proved airframe, the Lancaster was well suited for civil test flying. The first such aircraft was G-AGJI, a converted Lancaster B.Mk I handed over to BOAC's Development Flight in January 1944. With faired-over nose and tail turret positions, it was extensively used for engine and equipment trials.

Project 'Upkeep' was launched in which large drum-like bombs were built, each weighing 4196 kg (9,250 lb) and fitting on trunnions built into Special Lancasters with a cut-away underside. The bomb was spun by an hydraulic motor at 500 rpm and released at exactly 402 km/h (250 mph) at 18.3 m (60 ft) between 366 and 411 m (400 and 450 yards) from the dam being attacked. Such tight limits, especially on a heavily defended target surrounded by mountains, meant special crews and Wing Commander Guy Gibson was detailed to form No. 617 Sqn for the task, accomplished on 21 March 1943.

The Dambusters' aircraft were called Mk III (Special). The Mk III was basically a Mk I with Packard engines and a modified nose. Had the war continued a few months longer, it would have out-numbered the Mk I: final totals were 3,440 Mk I and 3,020 Mk III. The Mk III had the V-1650-1 (Merlin 28) at first. This overheated, but the Packard Merlins 39 and 224 were as good as Rolls-Royce Merlins. From late 1943 the broad paddle-blade propeller became common, with better take-off and climb. Another addition was the Monica radar at the tail to warn of Luftwaffe night-fighters; not until a Ju 88 night-fighter was captured was it realised that this defence aid was in fact a deathtrap, the night-fighters homing in on its emissions! Most rear turrets eventually had plain apertures cut in the Perspex, despite

SW244, a Metrovick-built B.I, was one of two Lancasters converted with a saddle tank above the fuselage, raising fuel capacity from 2,158 to 3,360 Imp gal. The idea was to meet the range demands of Tiger Force in the Far East in 1945, but inflight-refuelling was eventually judged a better answer. VJ-Day came before such ranges were needed.

RF310 was one of the last B.IIIs delivered from Armstrong Whitworth at Coventry. After the war it was converted as an ASR.III (1948 designation, ASR.3) with an airborne lifeboat. Main contractor for this conversion, which involved a total gutting and re-equipping of the interior, was Cunliffe-Owen Aircraft at Southampton.

RF325 was the last Lancaster in service with the RAF, being withdrawn in October 1956 in the markings illustrated. The penultimate aircraft in a batch of B.IIIs built by Armstrong Whitworth, it was converted as an ASR.3 and then rebuilt in about 1949 as a GR.3 maritime reconnaissance aircraft for the MR School at St Mawgan.

One of the last Lancasters in use anywhere, this was built as PA342, one of 500 B.Is by Vickers-Armstrong at Chester. Rebuilt as a B.I(FE), it was handed to the Armée de l'Air and passed to the Aéronavale, with whom it served at Papeete and Noumea with Flottille 24F. Another 24F aircraft, a Mk VII, is preserved at East Kirkby.

bitter cold, to give the best view aft. By late 1944 the Lancaster VII came into production with the American Martin electrically driven mid-upper turret, further forward than the original turret and with two hard-hitting 12.7-mm (0.5-in) Brownings (also fitted to 50 late Mk III aircraft). Two of these guns were also fitted to the roomy new rear turret (made by Rose Bros of Gainsborough), which came into wide use from 1944 and greatly improved rear defence, by 1945 guided by AGLT (auto gun-laying turret) radar.

The Lancaster IV was later to enter service as the Lincoln, but a related machine, the Mk VI, received little publicity. Built as Mk Is or Mk IIIs, the small number of this high-performance mark were re-engined with the two-stage supercharged Merlin 85/87 in the circular cowling (with curved ventral radiator) that became familiar in the Lincoln and Shackleton. With four-bladed paddle propellers, the Mk VI had a tremendous performance, especially as armament was removed except for the tail turret, one being logged at 555 km/h (345 mph) in August 1943. These machines were used to carry special ECM and ECCM for the Pathfinder Force, operated by Nos 7 and 635 Sqns.

The last wartime marks were the Mks I(FE) and VII(FE), for Far East service with Tiger Force against Japan. These had special tropical and overseas equipment and were normally painted black below but white above. The FE Lancasters were the subject of various studies aimed at increasing range. Two aircraft (HK541 and SW244) were tested with grotesque 5455-litre (1,200-Imp gal) saddle tanks on top of the fuselage, but the final choice was inflight-refuelling. The war ended before the FE Lancasters got into action. The last Lancaster delivered was a Mk I (TW910), from Armstrong Whitworth, delivered on 2 February 1946. Total of all marks was 7,377.

Soldiering on

There were numerous oddball modifications during the war, as well as important post-war rebuilds. JB456 was fitted with the excellent Bristol B.17 dorsal turret with two 20-mm cannon that later became standard on the Lincoln. LL780 and RF268 had a sighting position in the tail controlling two 20-mm twin-cannon barbettes above and below. This work was aimed partly at perfecting the armament of the Windsor and Lincoln. The first post-war variant was the ASR.3 used by Coastal Command with an airborne lifeboat carried under the fuselage in a conversion by Cunliffe-Owen Aircraft. The GR.3 was a maritime reconnaissance version, later restyled MR.3. The PR.1 was a Bomber Command aircraft used for mapping and survey, with turrets removed; they completed detailed maps of most of West, Central and East Africa in 1946-52. The last Bomber Command Lancaster in service was a PR.1, PA427, struck off in December 1953. The last in the RAF was MR.3 (RF325), which after a ceremony at St Mawgan on 15 October 1956 was flown to Wroughton and scrapped.

The RAF Museum has R5868, with 137 missions and thought to be top-scorer in numbers of missions. But later it was discovered

that the true record holder (ED888, a veteran of more than 140 trips with Nos 103 and 576 Sqns from Elsham Wolds) had thoughtlessly been scrapped in 1947. The last Lancaster operators were the Canadian Armed Forces, which used the 10-MR until 1964, and the French Aéronavale, which kindly let the UK have its last Lancaster from its operational locale in the Pacific (Papeete and the New Hebrides). This aircraft has been maintained in airworthy condition, and so too has ex-RAF PA474, which is now painted in the markings of the aircraft used by Squadron Leader Nettleton in the Augsburg raid.

Avro Lancaster variants

Avro Type 683 Manchester III: Lancaster prototypes, in essence Manchesters with extended-span wings and four 854-kW (1,145-hp) Merlin Xs (total 2 – BT308 and DG595)
Avro Lancaster I: production version of the Type 683, with 955-kW (1,280-hp) Merlin XXs, 1089-kW (1,460-hp) Merlin 22s or 1223-kW (1,640-hp) Merlin 24s (total 3,440)
Avro Lancaster I (Special): Mk I modified to carry stores in excess of 5443 kg (12,000 lb), with radar and much other equipment removed (all conversions)
Avro Lancaster I(FE): variant for service in the Far East (all conversions)
Avro Lancaster PR.1: post-war aerial survey version (all conversions)
Avro Lancaster II: version re-engined with 1231-kW (1,650-hp) Bristol Hercules VI or 1294-kW (1,735-hp) Hercules XVI radial engines and incorporating many improvements (total 302 including two prototypes)
Avro Lancaster III: improved production version with 1089-kW (1,460-hp) or 1223-kW (1,640-hp) Packard Merlin 28, 38 or 224 inline engines (total 3,020)
Avro Lancaster III (Special): 'Dambuster' version (all conversions)
Avro Lancaster ASR.3: air-sea rescue version produced by Cunliffe-Owen with special equipment, including a Lifeboat Airborne Mk IIA, and Merlin 224 engines (all conversions)
Avro Lancaster GR.3: maritime-reconnaissance version of the ASR.3 (all conversions)
Avro Lancaster MR.3: redesignated version of the GR.3 (all conversions)
Avro Lancaster IV: prototype of the Avro Lincoln to Specification B.14/43
Avro Lancaster V: prototype of the Avro Lincoln II
Avro Lancaster VI: powered by 1313-kW (1,760-hp) Merlin 87s (total 9, all conversions: 2 from Mk Is and 7 from Mk IIIs)
Avro Lancaster VII: fitted with Martin dorsal turret, Rose tail turret, special equipment and Packard engines; all produced by Austin Motors (total 180)
Avro Lancaster VII(FE): tropicalised version for service in the Far East (all conversions)
Avro Lancaster X: production by Victory Aircraft in Canada with Packard engines (total 430)
Avro Lancaster 10-AR: aerial reconnaissance version of the Lancaster 10-P with special provision for operations over the Arctic (total 3, all conversions)
Avro Lancaster 10-BR: bomber-reconnaissance version (total 13, all conversions)
Avro Lancaster 10-DR: drone-carrying version (total 2), both conversions
Avro Lancaster 10-MP: Lancaster 10-MR re-designated
Avro Lancaster 10-MR: maritime-reconnaissance version of the Mk X (total more than 70, all conversions)
Avro Lancaster 10-P: photo-reconnaissance version (total 11, all conversions)
Avro Lancaster 10-SR: air-sea rescue version (total 8, all conversions)
Avro Civil Lancaster 10: mailplane conversion for Trans-Canada Airlines (total 5, all conversions)

The post-war RCAF retained RAF-integrated serial numbers, though this Lancaster B.10 has its serial (BK959) on the fins. Used for maritime patrol, this example has black rubber de-icer boots on all leading edges, and red-painted spinners and wingtips. AF was the post-war code of No. 404 Sqn, which converted to Neptunes in 1951.

Heinkel He 111

Although a 1934 design, the Heinkel He 111 not only provided the muscle of Germany's 'strategic' bombing force at the beginning of World War II but, with surprisingly little alteration to the basic aircraft, came to constitute its backbone until Hitler's eventual defeat in 1945.

Designed under the leadership of Siegfried and Walter Günter in response to demands at the time of the Luftwaffe's secret birth for a fast commercial transport capable of minimum adaptation for the bombing role, the He 111 was in effect a twin-engined, scaled-up version of the He 70 Blitz that had entered Lufthansa service in 1934, retaining its elliptical wing and tail surfaces. Powered by 448-kW (600-hp) B.M.W. VI 6,0Z engines, the first prototype was flown at Marienehe by Gerhard Nitschke on 25 February 1935, being followed by the second less than three weeks later. The third prototype, forerunner of the He 111A series bomber version, showed itself to possess a performance better than many then-current fighters.

As six commercial He 111C-0s entered service as 10-seat airliners with Lufthansa during 1936, the first of 10 military He 111A-0s were being evaluated at Rechlin but, owing to inadequate engine power when carrying a warload, were summarily rejected, all 10 aircraft being sold to China.

Anticipating the problem of power shortage, Heinkel produced the He 111B, of which the pre-production He 111B-0 series was powered by 746-kW (1,000-hp) Daimler-Benz DB 600A engines. Despite a considerable weight increase this version returned a top speed of 360 km/h (224 mph). By the end of 1936 the first production He 111B-1s with 656-kW (880-hp) DB 600C engines appeared and, following successful trials, joined 1./KG 154 (later renamed KG 157),

KG 152, KG 155, KG 253, KG 257 and KG 355. Thirty He 111B-1s were also shipped to Spain to provide the bomber force of K/88 of the Legion Cóndor fighting in the Civil War. The He 111B-2 was produced in 1937 with 709-kW (950-hp) DB 603CG engines.

Few examples of the He 111D-0 and D-1, with 709-kW (950-hp) DB 600Ga engines, were built as a result of a shortage of this engine, and in 1938 production switched to the He 111E with 746-kW (1,000-hp) Junkers Jumo 211A-1s. Some 200 of these aircraft were produced, and they proved capable of lifting a 2000-kW (4,409-lb) bombload – roughly similar to that of the RAF's much slower Armstrong Whitworth Whitley III heavy bomber.

Meanwhile efforts had been made to simplify the He 111's wing structure for ease of production, and a new planform with straight leading and trailing edges had appeared on the seventh prototype. This wing was introduced into production with the He 111F, which emerged from the shops of Heinkel's new showpiece factory at Oranienburg in 1938; powered by 821-kW (1,100-hp) Jumo 211A-3s, 24 He 111F-1s were sold to Turkey, while the Luftwaffe's version was the F-4. The He 111G series comprised nine examples, of which five (powered variously by B.M.W.132Dc and B.M.W.132H-1 radials

Armourers handling an SC 500 (500-kg/1,102-lb) bomb on an airfield at the Eastern Front during the summer of 1941, with a Heinkel He 111H-6 of Kampfgeschwader 55 in the background. The He 111 provided the Luftwaffe's main heavy bomber strength for much of World War II.

Above: Two examples of the Günter brothers' design art in flight during tests from the Heinkel works. Escorting this He 111P is an He 100 single-seat fighter, a type which was produced in only small numbers and which was never deployed to an operational squadron.

and DB 600G inlines) were delivered to Lufthansa and the remainder went to Turkey as He 111G-5s. Produced simultaneously with the He 111G series, the He 111J series was developed as a torpedo-carrying version, of which about 90 were produced, but in fact served as a normal bomber with the Kriegsmarine-allocated KGr 806 in 1939.

Hitherto all He 111s had featured a conventional 'stepped' windscreen profile but, following the appearance of the eighth prototype in January 1938, the He 111P adopted the smooth nose profile with extensive glazing that so characterised the aircraft thereafter. This design incorporated a nose gun mounted offset to port, and a small hinge-up windscreen to improve the pilot's view during landing. The He 111P series entered production before the end of 1938, the type joining KG 157 in the following April. Although this series was intended as an interim version pending arrival of the He 111H, it survived in Luftwaffe service long after the outbreak of war in 1939.

Devastation of Poland

By September that year the He 111H was well established with operational units, the Luftwaffe deploying 400 such aircraft compared with 349 He 111P series, 38 He 111E series and 21 He 111J series aircraft. Of this total of 808 aircraft, 705 were serviceable on the eve of Germany's attack on Poland. In that fateful campaign the Heinkels of KG 1, KG 4, KG 26, KG 27, KG 53, KG 152 and II/LG1 were in constant action, starting with raids far beyond the front line, but as the Poles fell back towards Warsaw, were launching devastating raids on the Polish capital.

First prototype of the He 111 was the He 111a (later styled the He 111V1) flown by Gerhard Nitschke at Marienehe on 24 February 1934 and powered by 492-kW (660-hp) BMW VI 6.0Z engines. Although built as a bomber, British intelligence authorities persisted in believing it to be a high-speed commercial aircraft.

Owing to the lack of suitable airfields, only three He 111-equipped units (KG 4, KG 26 and KGr 100) operated in the Norwegian campaign, the other Geschwäder deploying in readiness for the German attack in the West, which opened on 10 May 1940. Four days later 100 Heinkels of KG 54 attacked Rotterdam – now known to have occurred owing to the fact that a recall message was not received by many of the bombers, whose radio operators were already manning their front guns; as it was 57 aircraft dropped 97 tons of bombs in the centre of the city, killing 814 Dutch civilians.

By the beginning of the Battle of Britain the He 111H had almost entirely replaced the He 111P series (although most staff crews still flew the older aircraft, and it was in an He 111P that Oberst Alois Stoeckl, commanding KG 55, was shot down and killed near Middle Wallop on 14 August 1940). From the outset the He 111H, with its

Displaying three white bars on the rudder for fighter escort identification during the Battle of Britain, this He 111H-2 of the Geschwaderstab, KG 55 'Legion Cóndor' with additional nose and ventral MG 15 guns, was based at Lille-Nord, Belgium, in 1940.

He 111 variants

He 111a (He 111 V1): 1st prototype; two 448-kW (600-hp) B.M.W. VI6, OZ with two-bladed propellers
He 111 V2: 2nd prototype (D-ALIX); reduced trailing-edge curvature
He 111 V3: 3rd prototype (D-ALES); span reduced to 22.61 m (74 ft 1¾ in)
He 111 V4: 34th prototype (D-AHAO); 10-passenger airliner; three-bladed propellers
He 111C-0: six aircraft (D-ABYE, -AMES, -AQUY, -AQYF, -ATYL, -AXAV); two delivered to Kommando Rowehl for clandestine reconnaissance
He 111A-1: 10 aircraft based on V3; rejected by Luftwaffe and sold to China
He 111 V5: DB 600A; all-up weight 8600 kg (18,959 lb)
He 111B-0: pre-production version accepted by Luftwaffe; one aircraft with Jumo 210Ga
He 111B-1: production bombers; early aircraft with DB.600Aa, later DB.600C; all-up weight 9323 kg (20,536 lb); maximum bombload 1500 kg (3,307 lb)
He 111B-2: supercharged DB.600CG engines; all-up weight 10000 kg (22,046 lb)

He 111 V7: prototype with straight tapered wing
He 111G-01: also termed **He 111 V12** (D-AEQU); B.M.W. VI 6,0Zu; passed to DLH
He 111G-02: also termed **He 111 V13** (D-AYKI); passed to DLH
He 111G-3: two aircraft, **V14** (D-ACBS) with B.M.W.132Dc and **V15** (D-ADCF) with B.M.W.132H-1; both passed to DLH and re-styled **He 111L**
He 111G-4: also termed **He 111 V16** (D-ASAR); DB 600G; used by Milch as personal transport
He 111G-5: four aircraft with DB.600Ga engines; sold to Turkey
He 111 V9: modified from B-2 airframe with DB.600Ga; became He 111D prototype with wing radiators
He 111D-0: pre-production batch with DB.600Ga and radiators moved to engine nacelles
He 111D-1: small number of production aircraft; abandoned due to shortage of DB engines
He 111 V6: prototype (D-AXOH) from modified B-0 with Jumo 610Ga

He 111 V10: prototype He 111E (D-ALEQ) from modified D-0 with Jumo 211A-1
He 111E-0: pre-production aircraft, 1700-kg (3,748-lb) bombload; all-up weight 10315 kg (22,740 lb)
He 111E-1: production bombers, 2000-kg (4,409-lb) bombload; all-up weight 10775 kg (23,754 lb)
He 111E-3: minor internal alterations; internal bombload only
He 111E-4: half bombload carried externally
He 111E-5: as E-4 but introduced extra internal fuel tanks
He 111 V11: prototype He 111F with straight-tapered wing; Jumo 211A-3
He 111F-0: pre-production aircraft; all-up weight 11000 kg (24,250 lb)
He 111F-1: 24 aircraft sold to Turkey in 1938
He 111F-4: 40 aircraft for Luftwaffe with E-4 bombload arrangement
He 111J-0: pre-production aircraft; DB 600CG; external bombload only
He 111J-1: 90 producion aircraft intended as torpedo-bombers but several served as bombers only
He 111 V8: modified B-0 (D-AQUO) with stepped cockpit profile
He 111P-0: pre-production batch similar to V8, following J-1 in factory
He 111P-1: production; DB.601A-1; maximum speed 398 km/h (247 mph)
He 111P-2: as P-1 but with FuG 10 radio
He 111P-3: P-1s and P-2s modified as dual-control trainers
He 111P-4: provision for additional defensive armament; extra internal fuel; external bombload
He 111P-6: introduced DB.601N engines; reverted to internal bombload; P-6/R2 was later conversion to glider tug; others transferred to Hungary
He 111 V19: prototype (D-AUKY); Jumo 211 engines
He 111H-0: pre-production batch similar to P-2 (FuG10) but with Jumo 211
He 111H-1: production version of H-0
He 111H-2: as H-1 but with Jumo 211A-3 engines
He 111H-3: introduced anti-shipping role with forward-firing 20-mm gun in gondola; Jumo 211D-1 engines
He 111H-4: early aircraft had Jumo 211D-1, but later 211F-1 engines

He 111H-5: provision for 2500-kg (5,511-lb) bombloads; all-up weight increased to 14055 kg (30,982 lb)
He 111H-6: included all previous modifications and provision for two 765-kg (1,686-lb) LT5b torpedoes and increased defensive armament; Jumo 211F-1; He 111H-7 and H-9 were similar but with minor equipment changes
He 111H-8: H-3 and H-5 airframes with balloon cable-fender and cutters; H-8/R2 had fenders removed and was modified as glider tug
He 111H-10: H-6 development with 20-mm gun removed from gondola to nose; Kuto-Nase balloon cable-cutters; Jumo 211F-2
He 111H-11: fully enclosed dorsal gun position with increased armament and armour; H-11/R1 had twin MG 81 guns in beam positions; H-11/R2 was glider tug
He 111H-12: ventral gondola omitted to allow carriage of Hs 293A missiles; FuG 230b and FuG 203b radio equipment
He 111H-14: pathfinder development of H-10; 20 H-14/R2s were glider tugs
He 111H-16: 'standard' bomber; H-16/R1 had electric dorsal turret; H-16/R2 was glider tug with rigid boom; H-16/R3 was pathfinder with reduced bombload
He 111H-18: pathfinder similar to He 111H-16/R3 with special flame-damped exhausts
He 111H-20: built as glider tug/transport; H-20/R1 was paratrooper with jump hatch; H-20/R2 was freighter/tug with 30-mm gun in electric dorsal turret; H-20/R3 modified as bomber; H-20/R4 modified as bomber with external load of 20 50-kg (110-lb) bombs
He 111H-21: introduced Jumo 213; maximum speed 480 km/h (298 mph); bombload 3000 kg (6,614 lb); all-up weight increased to 16000 kg (35,275 lb); *Rüstsatzas* for He 111H-20
He 111H-23: similar to H-20/R1 with Jumo 213 engines
He 111 V32: single H-6 modified with turbocharged DB.601U engines as prototype for proposed He 111R high-altitude bomber; **He 111R-1** and **R-2** were proposed but not built
He 111Z-1: two He 111 composited with fifth engine added; glider tug; all-up weight 28500 kg (62,831 lb)
He 111Z-2: long-range bomber project similar to Z-1 intended to carry four Hs283A missiles
He 111Z-3: proposed version of Z-1 for long-range reconnaissance

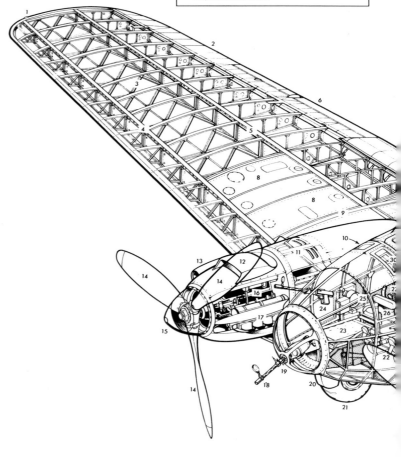

Large bombs were carried externally, this being a 1000-kg (2,204-lb) weapon. The aircraft is operating on the Eastern Front in January 1943, and has a soluble white distemper applied over the standard camouflage for winter operations.

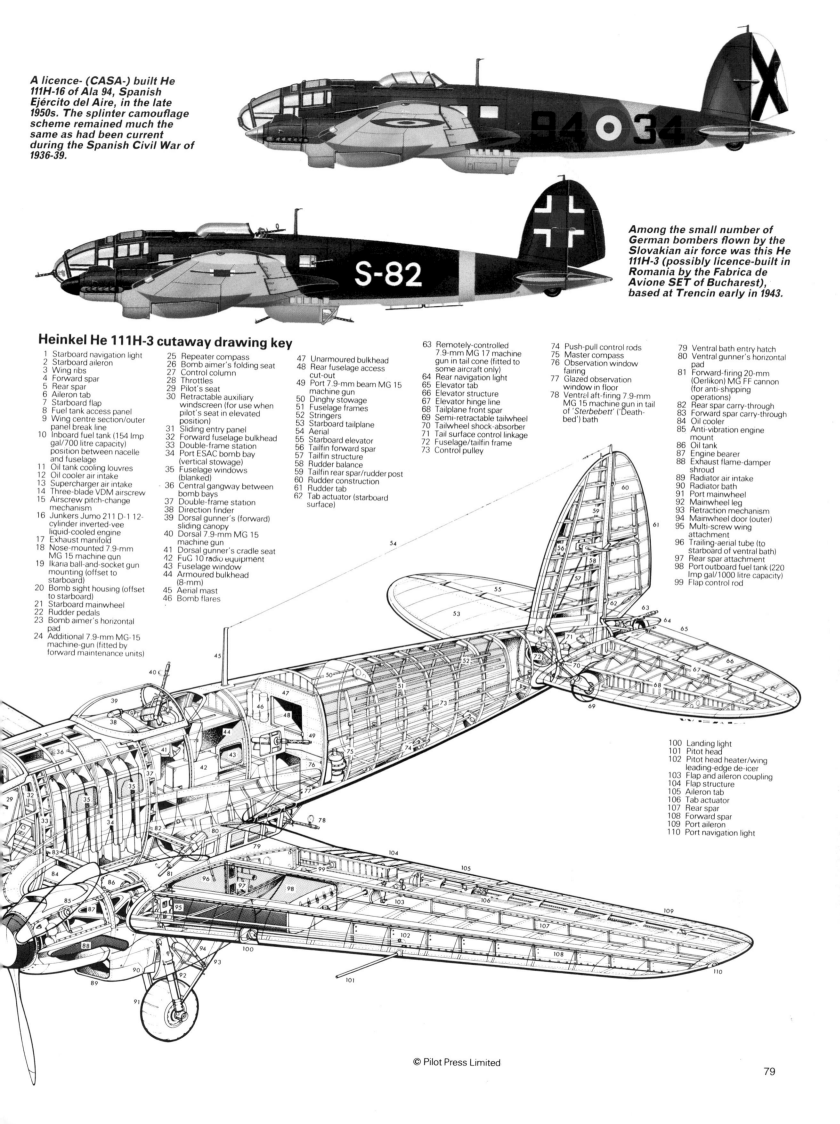

A licence- (CASA-) built He 111H-16 of Ala 94, Spanish Ejército del Aire, in the late 1950s. The splinter camouflage scheme remained much the same as had been current during the Spanish Civil War of 1936-39.

Among the small number of German bombers flown by the Slovakian air force was this He 111H-3 (possibly licence-built in Romania by the Fabrica de Avione SET of Bucharest), based at Trencin early in 1943.

Heinkel He 111H-3 cutaway drawing key

1 Starboard navigation light
2 Starboard aileron
3 Wing ribs
4 Forward spar
5 Rear spar
6 Aileron tab
7 Starboard flap
8 Fuel tank access panel
9 Wing centre section/outer panel break line
10 Inboard fuel tank (154 Imp gal/700 litre capacity) position between nacelle and fuselage
11 Oil tank cooling louvres
12 Oil cooler air intake
13 Supercharger air intake
14 Three-blade VDM airscrew
15 Airscrew pitch-change mechanism
16 Junkers Jumo 211 D-1 12-cylinder inverted-vee liquid-cooled engine
17 Exhaust manifold
18 Nose-mounted 7.9-mm MG 15 machine gun
19 Ikaria ball-and-socket gun mounting (offset to starboard)
20 Bomb sight housing (offset to starboard)
21 Starboard mainwheel
22 Rudder pedals
23 Bomb aimer's horizontal pad
24 Additional 7.9-mm MG-15 machine-gun (fitted by forward maintenance units)

25 Repeater compass
26 Bomb aimer's folding seat
27 Control column
28 Throttles
29 Pilot's seat
30 Retractable auxiliary windscreen (for use when pilot's seat in elevated position)
31 Sliding entry panel
32 Forward fuselage bulkhead
33 Double-frame station
34 Port ESAC bomb bay (vertical stowage)
35 Fuselage windows (blanked)
36 Central gangway between bomb bays
37 Double-frame station
38 Direction finder
39 Dorsal gunner's (forward) sliding canopy
40 Dorsal 7.9-mm MG 15 machine gun
41 Dorsal gunner's cradle seat
42 FuG 10 radio equipment
43 Fuselage window
44 Armoured bulkhead (8-mm)
45 Aerial mast
46 Bomb flares

47 Unarmoured bulkhead
48 Rear fuselage access cut-out
49 Port 7.9-mm beam MG 15 machine gun
50 Dinghy stowage
51 Fuselage frames
52 Stringers
53 Starboard tailplane
54 Aerial
55 Starboard elevator
56 Tailfin forward spar
57 Tailfin structure
58 Rudder balance
59 Tailfin rear spar/rudder post
60 Rudder construction
61 Rudder tab
62 Tab actuator (starboard surface)

63 Remotely-controlled 7.9-mm MG 17 machine gun in tail cone (fitted to some aircraft only)
64 Rear navigation light
65 Elevator tab
66 Elevator structure
67 Elevator hinge line
68 Tailplane front spar
69 Semi-retractable tailwheel
70 Tailwheel shock-absorber
71 Tail surface control linkage
72 Fuselage/tailfin frame
73 Control pulley

74 Push-pull control rods
75 Master compass
76 Observation window fairing
77 Glazed observation window in floor
78 Ventral aft-firing 7.9-mm MG 15 machine gun in tail of 'Sterbebett' ('Death-bed') bath

79 Ventral bath entry hatch
80 Ventral gunner's horizontal pad
81 Forward-firing 20-mm (Oerlikon) MG FF cannon (for anti-shipping operations)
82 Rear spar carry-through
83 Forward spar carry-through
84 Oil cooler
85 Anti-vibration engine mount
86 Oil tank
87 Engine bearer
88 Exhaust flame-damper shroud
89 Radiator air intake
90 Radiator bath
91 Port mainwheel
92 Mainwheel leg
93 Retraction mechanism
94 Mainwheel door (outer)
95 Multi-screw wing attachment
96 Trailing-aerial tube (to starboard of ventral bath)
97 Rear spar attachment
98 Port outboard fuel tank (220 Imp gal/1000 litre capacity)
99 Flap control rod

100 Landing light
101 Pitot head
102 Pitot head heater/wing leading-edge de-icer
103 Flap and aileron coupling
104 Flap structure
105 Aileron tab
106 Tab actuator
107 Rear spar
108 Forward spar
109 Port aileron
110 Port navigation light

Heinkel He 111

Though to some extent superseded by the H-series, the Heinkel He 111P continued in widespread service well into the war. This P-2 of Kampfgeschwader 55 flew from Villacoublay, France during the autumn of 1940 on night raids over Britain and displays the Geschwaderstab marking on the nose; crudely applied mottled camouflage has obscured Geschwaderzeichen and fin swastika.

435-km/h (270-mph) top speed, proved a difficult aircraft to shoot down (compared with the Dornier Do 17), and showed itself capable of weathering heavy battle damage. The 17 Gruppen flying the He 111H during the battle operated an average strength of about 500 aircraft (compared with He 111P series aircraft, of which some 40 served in the reconnaissance role with the Auffklärungsgruppen), losing some 246 of their number in air combat in the course of the four-month battle. Among the outstanding attacks by He 111s were those by KG 55 on the Bristol aircraft factory on 25 September, and the same unit's devastating raid on Supermarine's factory at Southampton the following day.

The majority of the He 111Hs employed during the Battle of Britain were He 111H-1s, -2s, -3s, and -4s, the latter two initially powered by 821-kW (1,100-hp) Jumo 211D engines. Perhaps the main significance of their losses lay in their five-man crews, whereas the other bombers, the Junkers Ju 88 and Do 17, were crewed by only four.

Heavy He 111H-5

The next variant to join the Kampfgechwäder was the He 111H-5, which incorporated additional fuel tanks in place of the wing bomb cells, and featured two external racks each capable of lifting a 1000-kg (2,205-lb) bomb; its maximum all-up weight was increased to 14055 kg (30,985 lb). He 111H-5s were widely used during the winter Blitz of 1940-1, these aircraft carrying the majority of the heavy bombs and parachute mines to fall on British cities in that campaign. The He 111H-5 could also carry a single 1800-kg (3,968-lb) bomb externally.

The He 111H-6 came to be the most widely-used of all He 111s, entering production at the end of 1940. With provision to carry a pair of 765-kg (1,687-lb) LT F5b torpedoes, this version was armed with six 7.92-mm (0.31-in) MG 15 machine-guns and a forward-firing 20-mm cannon, and some aircraft featured a remotely-operated grenade launcher in the extreme tail. Despite its torpedo-carrying ability, most He 111H-6s were used as ordinary bombers, the first unit to fly torpedo-equipped He 111H-6s being I/KG 26, flying these

aircraft from Bardufoss and Banak in northern Norway against the North Cape convoys from June 1942 onwards and participating in the virtual annihilation of the convoy PQ 17.

The He 111H-7 and He 111H-9 designations covered minor equipment alterations in the He 111H-6, while the He 111H-8 featured an outsize balloon fender designed to deflect barrage balloon cables to cutters in the wing tips; these were found to be of little use so surviving He 111H-8s were later converted to glider tugs, as He 111H-8/R2s.

The He 111H-10 was similar to the He 111H-6 but included a 20-mm MG FF cannon in the ventral gondola and Kuto-Nase cable cutters in the wings.

Varied roles

Following the successful use of He 111Hs as pathfinders by KGr 100, this role featured prominently in subsequent development of the aircraft, the He 111H-14, He 111H-16/R3 and He 111H-18 being specially fitted with FuG Samos, Peil-GV, APZ5 and FuG Korfu radio equipment for the task; He 111H-14s were flown on operations by Sonderkommando Rastedter of KG 40 in 1944.

As the He 111 was joined by such later bombers as the Heinkel He 177 Greif, Dornier Do 217 and others, it underwent parallel development as a transport; the He 111H-20/R1 was fitted out to accommodate 16 paratroops and the He 111H-20/R2 was equipped as a freight-carrying glider tug. Nevertheless, bomber versions continued to serve, particularly on the Eastern Front where the He 111H-20/R3 with a 2000-kg (4,410-lb) bombload and the He 111H-20/R4, carrying 20 50-kg (110-lb) fragmentation bombs, operated by night.

Perhaps the most outstanding, albeit forlorn, of all operations by the He 111H bombers and transports was that in support of the Wehrmacht's attempt to relive the Germany 6th Army at Stalingrad between November 1942 and February 1943. As the entire available force of Junkers Ju 52/3m transports was inadequate for the supply task, He 111 bombers of KG 27, KG 55 and I/KG 100 joined KGrzb V 5 and KGrzb V 20 (flying an assortment of He 111D, F, P and H trans-

Serving with the Legion Cóndor's bomber element, Kampfgruppe 88, during the Spanish Civil War in 1937, this He 111B-1 carried a variety of individual markings, including the name Holzauge (literally 'Wooden Eye') and a black scottie-dog on the fin.

A Jumo-powered He 111E-1 whose maximum bombload (carried internally) had been increased to 2000 kg (4,410 lb); this version eventually equipped all four bomber Staffeln of Kampfgruppe 88 of the Legion Cóndor in Spain during 1938.

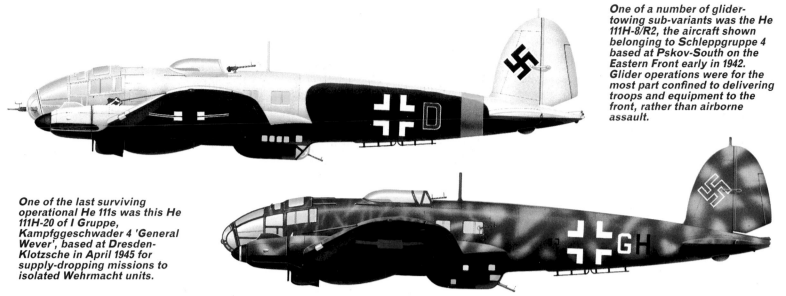

One of the last surviving operational He 111s was this He 111H-20 of I Gruppe, Kampfgeschwader 4 'General Wever', based at Dresden-Klotzsche in April 1945 for supply-dropping missions to isolated Wehrmacht units.

ports) and embarked on the job of flying in food and ammunition to the beleaguered army. Although the bombers were occasionally able to attack the Russian armour as it tightened its grip on the city, bad weather severely hampered the supply operations, and by the end of the Stalingrad campaign the Luftwaffe had lost 165 He 111s, a sacrifice from which the Kampfgeschwader never fully recovered.

Last ditch measures

The Heinkel He 111 also underwent two of what were unquestionably the most bizarre of all the Luftwaffe's wartime operational experiments. The first involved the carriage of a Fieseler Fe 103 flying-bomb (the V-1) under one wing. Following trials at Peenemünde in 1943, about 20 He 111H-6s, He 111H-16s and He 111H-21s (all re-designated He 111H-22s) were modified and delivered to III/KG 3 in July 1944. Within six weeks this unit, based in the Netherlands, had launched 300 flying-bombs against London, 90 against Southampton and 20 against Gloucester, the tactics being to approach the British shoreline at low level to escape radar detection before the aircraft climbed to about 450 m (1,475 ft) to release the weapon and then dived to make good their escape.

Believing this campaign to have achieved worthwhile results, the Luftwaffe equipped all three Gruppen of KG 53 with about 100 He 111H-22s and, based in western Germany, these joined the assault on the UK in December, one raid being launched against far-distant Manchester on Christmas Eve. In the seven months of operations the four Gruppen launched 1,200 flying-bombs but lost 77 aircraft; moreover, not more than 20 per cent of the bombs reached their intended target cities.

The other experiment involving the He 111 resulted in the extraordinary five-engined He 111Z (Z denoting Zwilling, or twin), achieved by joining together two He 111s by means of a new wing centre-section carrying a fifth engine. The resulting aircraft, with a span of 35.20 m (115 ft 6 in), was intended to tow the huge Messerschmitt Me 321 Gigant glider or three Gotha Go 242 gliders at 225 km/h (140 mph) at 4000 m (13,125 ft). Trials proved fairly successful, and the He 111Z-1 served with Grossraumlastenseglerkommando 2 based at Obertraubling in 1943 for supply missions on the Eastern Front. The He 111Z-2, which is not thought to have been flown operationally, was equipped to carry four Henschel Hs 293A rocket bombs over long distances, and the projected He 111Z-3 was to have been a long-range reconnaissance version. The He 111Z had a crew of seven, of which four members (including the pilot) were located in the port fuselage, the others in the starboard fuselage.

Outstanding among the final operations by He 111 bombers was the attack on Poltava airfield in the Soviet Union on the night of 21-22 June 1944. The previous day 114 USAAF Boeing B-17s and their escorting North American P-51s had flown to the USSR after bombing Berlin. Heinkel He 111s of KG 4, KG 27, KG 53 and KG 55 caught the Americans unawares and, by the light of flares, the bombers destroyed 43 B-17s and 15 P-51s on the ground.

He 111 transports equipped Transportgruppe 30 at the end of 1944, these aircraft dropping paratroops behind the American lines at the beginning of the Ardennes campaign. By the end of the war the aircraft was being used solely in the transport role, flown by KG 4, TGr 30 and Schleppgruppe 1 in the last days of the Third Reich.

Total He 111 production exceeded 7,300 aircraft.

The Heinkel He 111H-6 was the most widely-used version of the aircraft and is pictured here carrying a pair of practice torpedoes on fuselage PVC racks. Among the operational units to employ torpedo-carrying He 111s was KG 26, based in Norway for attacks on the Allied Murmansk-bound convoys.

The Heinkel He 111H-11 with 13-mm (0.51-in) MG 131 heavy machine-gun in the extreme nose and five 250-kg (550-lb) bombs on a special rack-plate under the fuselage; this version also featured considerably increased armour protection, some of which could be jettisoned in the interests of speed in an emergency.

Heinkel He 111

Specification
Heinkel He 111H-16

Type: five-seat medium night bomber/pathfinder and glider tug

Powerplant: two 1006-kW (1,350-hp) Junkers Jumo 211F-2 inline piston engines

Performance: maximum speed 435 km/h (270 mph) at 600 m (19,685 ft); service ceiling 8500 m (27,890 ft); normal range 1950 km (1,212 miles)

Weights: empty 8680 kg (19,136 lb); maximum take-off 14000 kg (30,864 lb)

Dimensions: span 22.60 m (74 ft 1¾ in); length 16.40 m (53 ft 9½ in); height 4.00 m (13 ft 1¼ in); wing area 86.50 m² (931.1 sq ft)

Armament: one 20-mm MG FF cannon, one 13-mm (0.51-in) MG 131 and up to seven 7.92-mm (0.31-in) MG 15 and MG 81 machine-guns, plus one 2000-kg (4,409-lb) bomb carried externally and one 500-kg (1,102-lb) bomb internally, or eight 250-kg (551-kg) bombs all internally

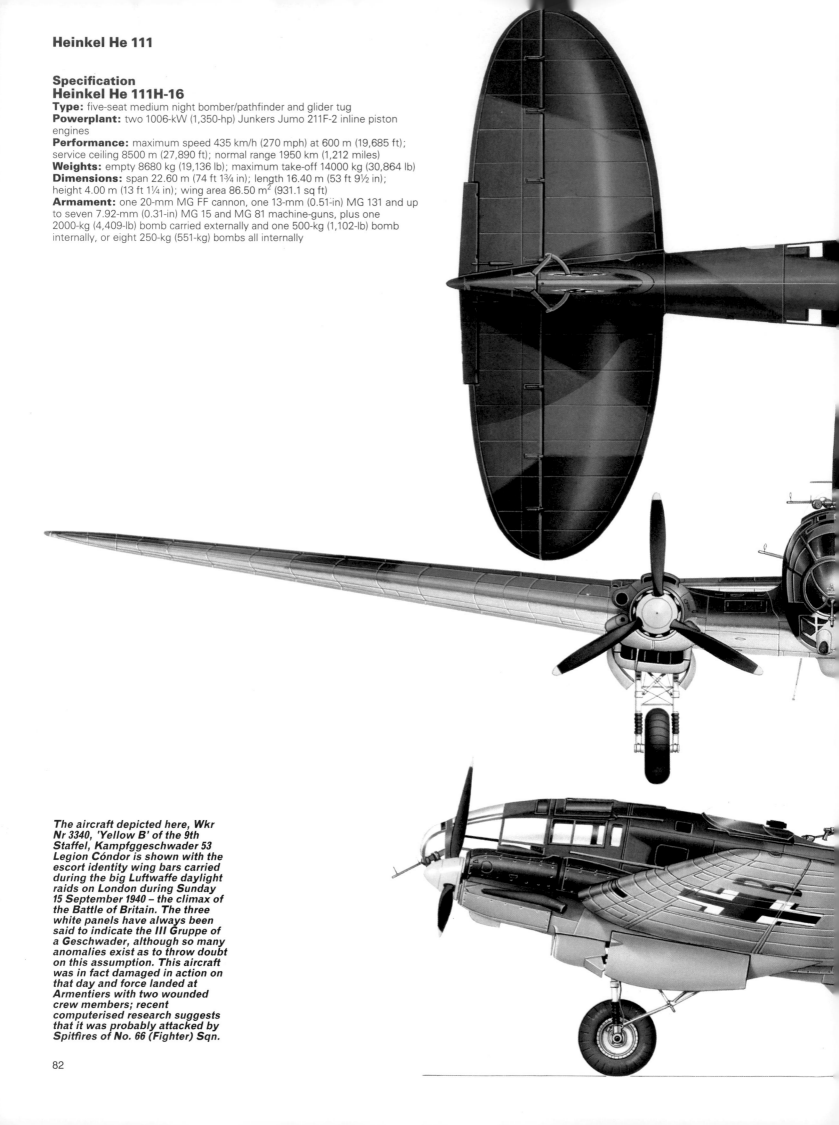

The aircraft depicted here, Wkr Nr 3340, 'Yellow B' of the 9th Staffel, Kampfggeschwader 53 Legion Cóndor is shown with the escort identity wing bars carried during the big Luftwaffe daylight raids on London during Sunday 15 September 1940 – the climax of the Battle of Britain. The three white panels have always been said to indicate the III Gruppe of a Geschwader, although so many anomalies exist as to throw doubt on this assumption. This aircraft was in fact damaged in action on that day and force landed at Armentiers with two wounded crew members; recent computerised research suggests that it was probably attacked by Spitfires of No. 66 (Fighter) Sqn.

Savoia-Marchetti S.M.79

The fast and rugged S.M.79, while never fully escaping from its airliner looks, was one of the Italian air force's most potent wartime aircraft, taking a high toll on Allied shipping in the Mediterranean.

As the seeds of the Axis partnership were being sown in Europe, and Germany's Lufthansa was being presented with dual-role bomber-transports for commercial operation, a similar philosophy was being pursued, albeit with less malice aforethought, in the other dictatorship. When Alessandro Marchetti proposed a cleaned-up, high-speed, eight-passenger development of his S.M.81 early in 1934, ostensibly to participate in the forthcoming prestigious 'MacRobertson' race from England to Australia, it was immediately clear that in such an aircraft lay the basis of an efficient heavy bomber.

In the event the commercial S.M.79P (I-MAGO) was not completed in time for the great race, being flown at Cameri airport in October 1934, powered by three 455-kW (610-hp) Piaggio P.IX Stella RC.2 nine-cylinder radials. Deprived of the possible laurels of the 1934 race, I-MAGO went on to demonstrate its potential in a record-breaking flight from Milan to Rome in June 1935 and, soon afterwards, with three 560-kW (750-hp) Alfa Romeo 125 RC.35 engines, established world records over 1000-km (621-mile) and 2000-km (1,243-mile) closed circuits with various loads; the following year, with 582-kW (780-hp) Alfa Romeo 126 RC.34 engines, I-MAGO raised its own record for carrying 2000 kg (4,409 lb) over 1000 km (621 miles) to 420 km/h (261 mph).

Development of the commercial S.M.79 was now simultaneously pursued along several paths: the S.M.79C (C for *Corsa*, or race), the S.M.79T (T for *Transatlantica*) and the twin-engine S.M.79B. Eleven S.M.79Ts with additional fuel for prestigious transatlantic flights and five racing S.M.79Cs were built, all with 746-kW (1,000-hp) Piaggio P.XI RC.40 radials. Among the outstanding achievements of these fine aircraft was their gaining of the first three places

in the 1937 Istres-Damascus-Paris race, in which they beat the 'MacRobertson' race winner, the D.H.88 Comet G-ACSS, into fourth place. Early in 1938 three S.M.79s were flown from Rome to Rio de Janeiro, covering the 9842 km (6,116 miles) at an average speed of 404 km/h (251 mph). Further world speed-distance-payload records fell to S.M.79s in 1938.

Development of the S.M.79B as a commercial aircraft was short-lived, principally on account of the supposed public prejudice against twin engines on the grounds of safety. However, after the prototype S.M.79B flew in 1936 with two 768-kW (1,030-hp) Fiat A.80 radials, it became clear that the twin-engine layout was still being looked on with favour by some foreign air forces, and Savoia-Marchetti eventually sold four military examples to Iraq in 1938 (all of which were destroyed during the anti-British rebellion of 1941), and three to Brazil. Romania, on the other hand, adopted the S.M.79B on a much larger scale, purchasing 24 in 1938 with 746-kW (1,000-hp) Gnome-Rhône Mistral Major radials, followed later by 24 more powered by 910-kW (1,220-hp) Junkers Jumo 211Da inline engines. Romania also negotiated to build the aircraft under licence (as the S.M.79-JR) at the Bucharest plant of Industria Aeronautica Romana, these aircraft later serving as medium bombers with the Romanian forces on the Russian front in large numbers in 1942, while the earlier S.M.79Bs were relegated to transport duties. The IAR-built S.M.79-JR had a top speed of 445 km/h (277 mph) at 5000 m (16,405 ft), time to 3000 m (9,845 ft) was 8 minutes 40 seconds, and the service ceiling was 7400 m (24,280 ft).

Seen in October 1940, these aircraft of the 229ᵃ Squadriglia are regular bombers. The S.M.79 took part in the assault on France, that against Greece and against the British in the Western Desert.

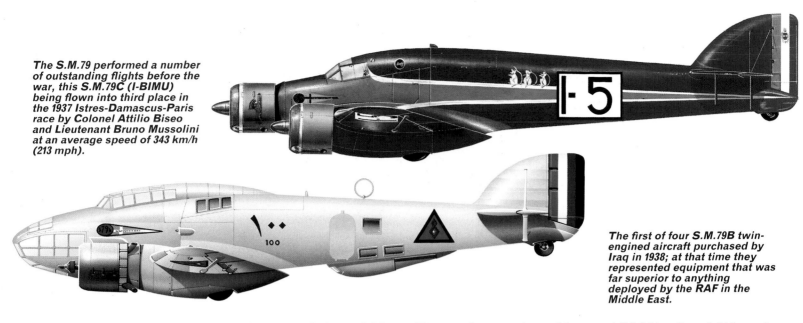

The S.M.79 performed a number of outstanding flights before the war, this *S.M.79C (I-BIMU)* being flown into third place in the 1937 Istres-Damascus-Paris race by Colonel Attilio Biseo and Lieutenant Bruno Mussolini at an average speed of 343 km/h (213 mph).

The first of four *S.M.79B* twin-engined aircraft purchased by Iraq in 1938; at that time they represented equipment that was far superior to anything deployed by the RAF in the Middle East.

Such was the early recognition of military potential in the S.M.79 that the second prototype was completed in 1935 as a bomber. Construction was largely of wood, the three-spar low wing being built as a single unit with only 1½° of dihedral. The big fuselage was a welded steel-tube structure, the forward part being duralumin- and plywood-covered, and the rear section covered with ply and fabric. Two pilots were normally accommodated, and a single fixed forward-firing machine-gun (initially 7.7 mm/0.303 in, but later 12.7-mm/0.5-in) was located over the cockpit. The bomb-bay, offset slightly to starboard, occupied the mid-fuselage, and aft of it was a ventral fairing containing the bomb aimer's station and a rear-firing gunner with 7.7-mm (0.303-in), later 12.7-mm (0.5-in) Breda-SAFAT machine-gun. Another machine-gun position was located at the rear of the prominent dorsal hump (which gave the S.M.79 its service nickname 'il Gobbo', or the hunchback), and a single 7.7-mm (0.303-in) machine-gun in the rear fuselage could be swung from side to side to fire through beam hatches.

From the outset the Regia Aeronautica test pilots expressed enthusiasm for the S.M.79, and production orders were placed before the end of 1935. Early aircraft, S.M.79-Is, with three 582-kW (780-hp) Alfa Romeo 126 RC.34 radials, entered service with the 8° and 111° Stormi Bombardamento Veloce (fast bomber groups) in 1936. In 1937 these units were sent to Spain to serve with the Aviacion del Tercio, flying during the Spanish Civil War as the 27° and 28° Gruppi ('Falchi delle Baleari', 'Hawks of Balearics', based in the Balearic Islands), and the 29° and 30° Gruppi ('Sparvieri', or 'Sparrows').

These units, together with two of S.M.81s, flew 5,318 sorties, dropped 12040 tonnes (11,850 tons) of bombs and scored 224 direct hits on government vessels. At the end of the Civil War the new Spanish government took over 80 S.M.79s and these came to provide a major portion of the Spanish air force's bombing arm for many years to come.

Racing into service

Meanwhile the introduction of the S.M.79 (now officially named the Sparviero) into service with the Regia Aeronautica had gone ahead at full speed. By the beginning of World War II some 11 *stormi*, each of four *squadriglie* (squadrons), were deployed with a total of 389 aircraft in Italy, Albania and in the Aegean. However, it was in a new role that the S.M.79 was being examined. Given the geographical location in the Mediterranean, Italy had for some years worked to gain a justified reputation in torpedo warfare and technology, and in 1937 had conducted trials at Gorizia with an S.M.79 carrying a single torpedo. Although these trials showed great promise, it was decided to pursue a dual torpedo installation, at the same time fitting more powerful engines, initially the 642-kW (860-hp) Alfa Romeo 128 RC.18 (this producing the prototype S.M.84) and later the 746-kW (1,000-hp) Piaggio P.XI RC.40 radial. In the latter configuration the aircraft entered production as the S.M.79-II, starting delivery to the Regia Aeronautica in 1940; later sub-variants were powered by 1007-kW (1,350-hp) Alfa Romeo 135 RC.32 18-cylinder radials, and also 746-kW (1,000-hp) Fiat A.80 RC.41 engines.

An S.M.79 waits for a mission while armourers prepare bombs, which are yet to have fins attached. The Sparviero had an unusual bomb-bay arrangement as it was offset to starboard within the fuselage.

A crew disembark their aircraft, displaying Italian flying gear of the early war period. Also displayed is the sliding hatch for the upper gun, and the hump that gave the S.M.79 its 'Il Gobbo' (the hunchback) nickname.

Savoia-Marchetti S.M.79

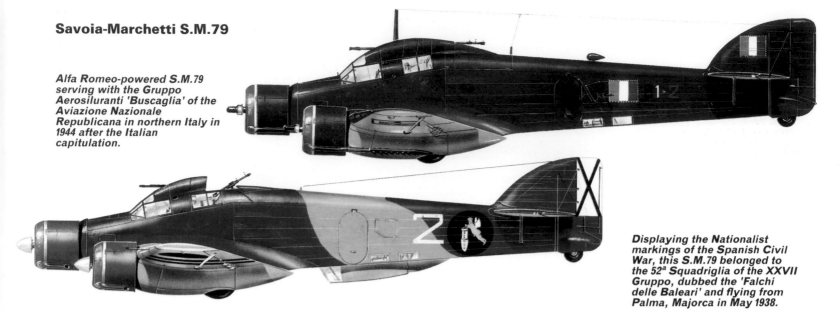

Alfa Romeo-powered S.M.79 serving with the Gruppo Aerosiluranti 'Buscaglia' of the Aviazione Nazionale Republicana in northern Italy in 1944 after the Italian capitulation.

Displaying the Nationalist markings of the Spanish Civil War, this S.M.79 belonged to the 52ª Squadriglia of the XXVII Gruppo, dubbed the 'Falchi delle Baleari' and flying from Palma, Majorca in May 1938.

When Italy entered World War II on 10 June 1940, the Regia Aeronautica possessed 14 S.M.79 *stormi* with 575 aircraft: three *stormi* (the 9°, 12° and 46°) were deployed in Italy, four (the 10°, 14°, 15° and 33°) in Libya, five (the 11°, 30°, 34°, 36° and 41°) in Sicily, and two (the 8° and 32°) in Sardinia. The 9° and 46° Stormi took part in the brief campaign against metropolitan France, while the S.M.79s of the 10°, 13° and 33° Stormi (of the Aeronautica della Libia) operated against French forces in Tunisia.

When the Greek campaign broke out four *squadriglie* of S.M.79s based in Albania were joined by aircraft of the Aerosiluranti (torpedo-bombing arm) deployed in the Aegean. In the 11-day campaign against Yugoslavia in April 1941, 30 S.M.79-Is of the Regia Aeronautica's 92° Gruppo and 281ª Squadriglia were opposed by 42 similar aircraft of the Yugoslav 7th Bombing Wing and 81st Independent Bombing Group, survivors of an order for 45 aircraft placed with Italy in 1939. During the operations against Crete, S.M.79s of the Aerosiluranti were in constant action against British and Greek shipping in the eastern Mediterranean.

Fighting in Africa

In the Western Desert Marshal Graziani's land forces were in the main ill-served by the Regia Aeronautica, the Italian pilots bestowing unwarranted respect on the hotch-potch of RAF forces available in Egypt. A total of four *stormi* with 125 S.M.79s was available, based at Castel Benito, Bir el Bhera, Benina and El Adem; yet few effective raids were flown, very small numbers of Sparvieri attacking targets at Halfaya, Mersa Matruh, Sidi Barrani and Sollum with heavy escorts of Fiat CR.42s. A number of combats were fought with RAF Gloster Gladiators, but few S.H.79s were lost in the air. The main attrition resulted from unservicability, and this was difficult to rectify at the end of a long supply route for spares, with the result that many Italian aircraft were destroyed or captured on the ground when General Wavell's forces advanced.

During the campaigns in East Africa, 12 S.M.79-Is of the 44° Gruppo were reinforced by 16 more aircraft flown from Libya, but in the final loss of Italian territories about six were lost on the ground in

A torpedo-bomber S.M.79-II of the 278ª Squadriglia, 132° Gruppo Autonomo Aerosiluranti, based at Sicily during the spring of 1942, wears one of the most widely adopted camouflage schemes.

British air raids at Addis Ababa, three were shot down and the remainder captured more or less intact; one of these later carried RAF markings (HK848) to join four others flown to the Middle East (AX702-705) by escaping Yugoslav pilots.

The Sparviero's outstanding role in the Mediterranean was in maritime operations, both as a bomber and in the torpedo attack role. During the early months of the war, attacks were carried out against Malta and shipping in the Sicilian narrows by aircraft of the 30° Stormo and the 279ª Squadriglia, later joined by the 10° Stormo. When the Allies sailed the famous Malta convoy of August 1942 (Operation Pedestal), the Regia Aeronautica and Aerosiluranti deployed 74 torpedo and bomber S.M.79-IIs, of which 50 belonged to the 32° Stormo at Villacidro, Sardinia, 10 for the 105ª Squadriglia at Decimomannu, Sardinia, and 14 to the 132ª Squadriglia on Pantelleria. From the moment the convoy of 14 merchantmen with heavy naval escort came within range, these S.M.79s (with a number of

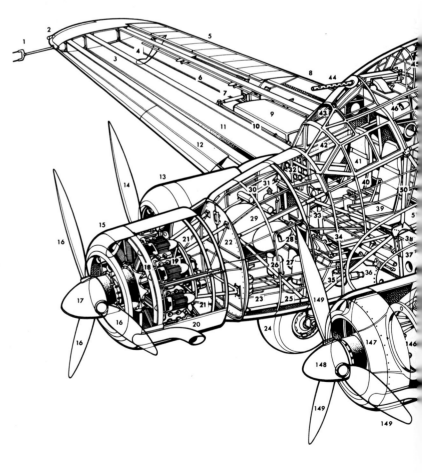

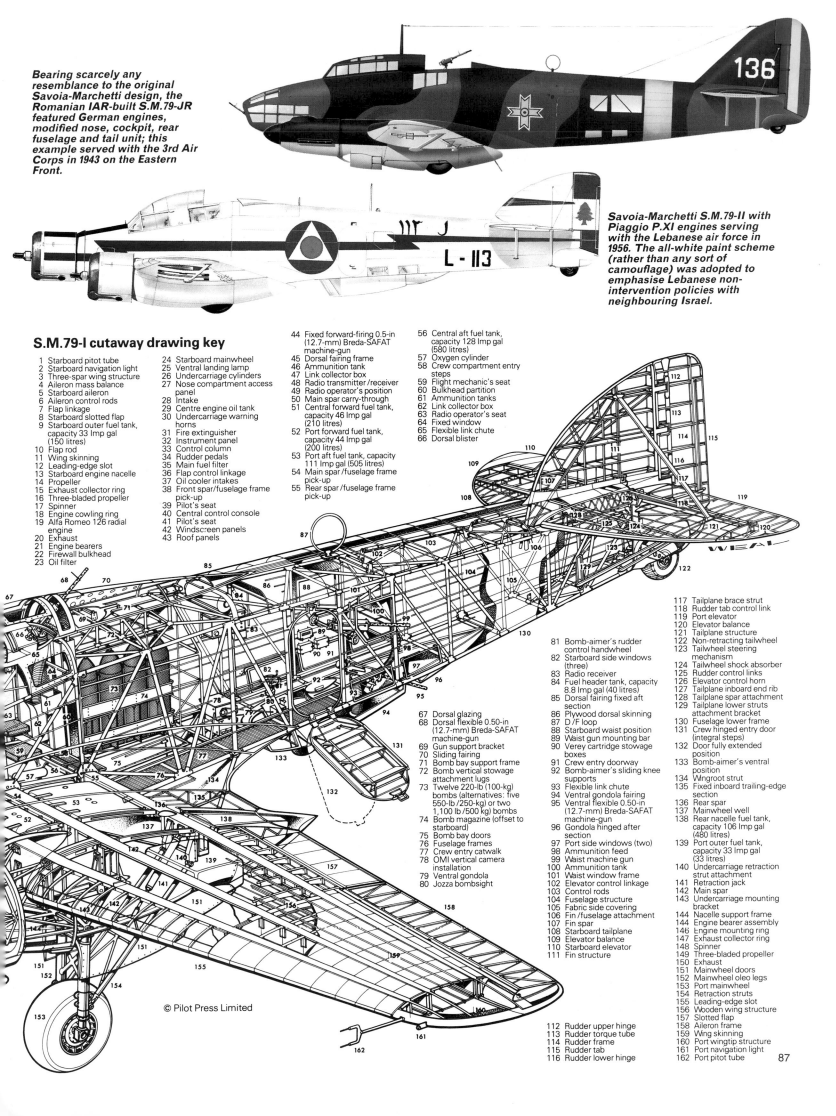

Bearing scarcely any resemblance to the original Savoia-Marchetti design, the Romanian IAR-built S.M.79-JR featured German engines, modified nose, cockpit, rear fuselage and tail unit; this example served with the 3rd Air Corps in 1943 on the Eastern Front.

Savoia-Marchetti S.M.79-II with Piaggio P.XI engines serving with the Lebanese air force in 1956. The all-white paint scheme (rather than any sort of camouflage) was adopted to emphasise Lebanese non-intervention policies with neighbouring Israel.

S.M.79-I cutaway drawing key

1 Starboard pitot tube
2 Starboard navigation light
3 Three-spar wing structure
4 Aileron mass balance
5 Starboard aileron
6 Aileron control rods
7 Flap linkage
8 Starboard slotted flap
9 Starboard outer fuel tank, capacity 33 Imp gal (150 litres)
10 Flap rod
11 Wing skinning
12 Leading-edge slot
13 Starboard engine nacelle
14 Propeller
15 Exhaust collector ring
16 Three-bladed propeller
17 Spinner
18 Engine cowling ring
19 Alfa Romeo 126 radial engine
20 Exhaust
21 Engine bearers
22 Firewall bulkhead
23 Oil filter
24 Starboard mainwheel
25 Ventral landing lamp
26 Undercarriage cylinders
27 Nose compartment access panel
28 Intake
29 Centre engine oil tank
30 Undercarriage warning horns
31 Fire extinguisher
32 Instrument panel
33 Control column
34 Rudder pedals
35 Main fuel filter
36 Flap control linkage
37 Oil cooler intakes
38 Front spar/fuselage frame pick-up
39 Pilot's seat
40 Central control console
41 Pilot's seat
42 Windscreen panels
43 Roof panels

44 Fixed forward-firing 0.5-in (12.7-mm) Breda-SAFAT machine-gun
45 Dorsal fairing frame
46 Ammunition tank
47 Link collector box
48 Radio transmitter/receiver
49 Radio operator's position
50 Main spar carry-through
51 Central forward fuel tank, capacity 46 Imp gal (210 litres)
52 Port forward fuel tank, capacity 44 Imp gal (200 litres)
53 Port aft fuel tank, capacity 111 Imp gal (505 litres)
54 Main spar/fuselage frame pick-up
55 Rear spar/fuselage frame pick-up

56 Central aft fuel tank, capacity 128 Imp gal (580 litres)
57 Oxygen cylinder
58 Crew compartment entry steps
59 Flight mechanic's seat
60 Bulkhead partition
61 Ammunition tanks
62 Link collector box
63 Radio operator's seat
64 Fixed window
65 Flexible link chute
66 Dorsal blister

67 Dorsal glazing
68 Dorsal flexible 0.50-in (12.7-mm) Breda-SAFAT machine-gun
69 Gun support bracket
70 Sliding fairing
71 Bomb bay support frame
72 Bomb vertical stowage attachment lugs
73 Twelve 220-lb (100-kg) bombs (alternatives: five 550-lb/250-kg or two 1,100 lb/500 kg) bombs
74 Bomb magazine (offset to starboard)
75 Bomb bay doors
76 Fuselage frames
77 Crew entry catwalk
78 OMI vertical camera installation
79 Ventral gondola
80 Jozza bombsight
81 Bomb-aimer's rudder control handwheel
82 Starboard side windows (three)
83 Radio receiver
84 Fuel header tank, capacity 8.8 Imp gal (40 litres)
85 Dorsal fairing fixed aft section
86 Plywood dorsal skinning
87 D/F loop
88 Starboard waist position
89 Waist gun mounting bar
90 Verey cartridge stowage boxes
91 Crew entry doorway
92 Bomb-aimer's sliding knee supports
93 Flexible link chute
94 Ventral gondola fairing
95 Ventral flexible 0.50-in (12.7-mm) Breda-SAFAT machine-gun
96 Gondola hinged after section
97 Port side windows (two)
98 Ammunition feed
99 Waist machine gun
100 Ammunition tank
101 Waist window frame
102 Elevator control linkage
103 Control rods
104 Fuselage structure
105 Fabric side covering
106 Fin/fuselage attachment
107 Fin spar
108 Starboard tailplane
109 Elevator balance
110 Starboard elevator
111 Fin structure

112 Rudder upper hinge
113 Rudder torque tube
114 Rudder frame
115 Rudder tab
116 Rudder lower hinge

117 Tailplane brace strut
118 Rudder tab control link
119 Port elevator
120 Elevator balance
121 Tailplane structure
122 Non-retracting tailwheel
123 Tailwheel steering mechanism
124 Tailwheel shock absorber
125 Rudder control links
126 Elevator control horn
127 Tailplane inboard end rib
128 Tailplane spar attachment
129 Tailplane lower struts attachment bracket
130 Fuselage lower frame
131 Crew hinged entry door (integral steps)
132 Door fully extended position
133 Bomb-aimer's ventral position
134 Wingroot strut
135 Fixed inboard trailing-edge section
136 Rear spar
137 Mainwheel well
138 Rear nacelle fuel tank, capacity 106 Imp gal (480 litres)
139 Port outer fuel tank, capacity 33 Imp gal (33 litres)
140 Undercarriage retraction strut attachment
141 Retraction jack
142 Main spar
143 Undercarriage mounting bracket
144 Nacelle support frame
145 Engine bearer assembly
146 Engine mounting ring
147 Exhaust collector ring
148 Spinner
149 Three-bladed propeller
150 Exhaust
151 Mainwheel doors
152 Mainwheel oleo legs
153 Port mainwheel
154 Retraction struts
155 Leading-edge slot
156 Wooden wing structure
157 Slotted flap
158 Aileron frame
159 Wing skinning
160 Port wingtip structure
161 Port navigation light
162 Port pitot tube

© Pilot Press Limited

87

It was as a torpedo-bomber that the Sparviero achieved the greatest success. These attacks continued even after 1943, with aircraft flying with the German-controlled Aviazione Nazionale Republicana.

The S.M.79 was a good bomber when it first appeared in military service, but by the time of World War II was largely outclassed; nevertheless, it fared well in the early days of the Mediterranean fighting.

An unusual view of 'il Gobbo' in flight, photographed from the upper gun position of another S.M.79. Nestling under the centre-section is a torpedo, ready to be dropped from ultra low-level.

Luftwaffe units) flew constant attacks and, despite desperate opposition from carrierborne fighters, hit with torpedoes and bombs nine merchantmen, two cruisers, a carrier and a destroyer. In the course of the Mediterranean air-sea war Sparvieri were credited with sinking the destroyers HMS *Husky, Jaguar, Legion* and *Southwall,* as well as severely damaging the battleship HMS *Malaya* and the

carriers HMS *Indomitable, Victorious* and *Argus.* HMS *Malaya* and *Argus* were attacked and hit in attacks by the 130° and 132° gruppi flying S.M.79s from Gerbini and Castelvetrano in Sicily; the former *Gruppo* included pilots such as Cimicchi, Di Bella and Melley whose names, together with Capitano Buscaglia, commanding the 132° Gruppo, became famous throughout Italy.

Improved torpedo-bomber

Towards the end of 1943 a new version of the Sparviero, the S.M.79-III, began appearing in small numbers with torpedo *gruppi* of the Aerosiluranti. This version dispensed with the ventral gondola (the bomb-aimer's position being superfluous) and the forward-firing 12.7-mm (0.5-in) machine-gun was replaced by a fixed 20-mm cannon, the latter being fired as a 'Flak deterrent' during torpedo attacks. One of the greatest torpedo exponents of this era was Capitano Faggioni, who commanded a *gruppo* of S.M.79-IIIs.

At the time of the Allied landings in Algeria of November 1942 the Sparviero force was declining, partly through combat losses but also as a result of Allied air attacks on the Italian aircraft industry, which severely restricted the supply of spare engines and other replacements. At that date 10 S.M.79 *gruppi* remained operational with 153 aircraft, of which only 112 were combat-ready. Eight of these flew Sparviero torpedo aircraft, and in an effort to retain some semblance of respectable performance in the face of Allied air superiority in the central Mediterranean, it became customary for the S.M.79s to carry only one torpedo. Nevertheless, by the eve of the invasion of

The first prototype Savoia-Marchetti S.M.79P I-MAGO after the original Piaggio P.IX engines had been replaced by 559-kW (750-hp) Alfa Romeo 125 radials. This photo was probably taken late in 1935.

One of the five racing S.M.79C aircraft which achieved such success in the Istres-Damascus-Paris race of 1937; the significance of the I-11 marking denoted the aircraft as being the 11th Italian entry.

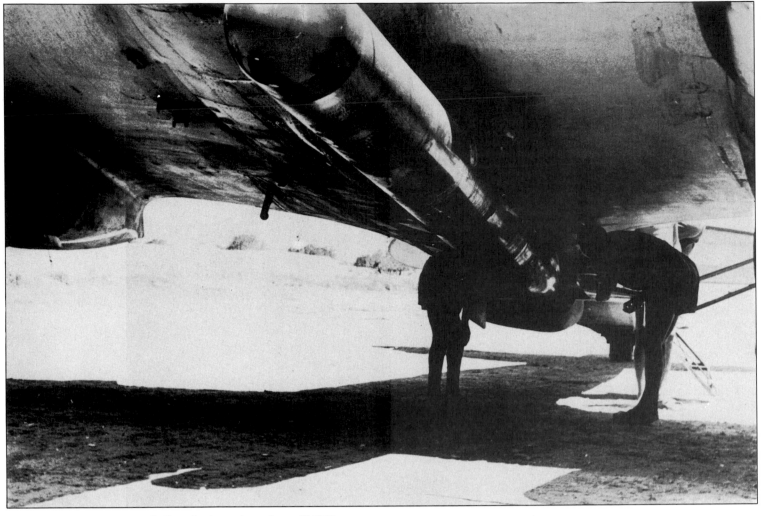

A close-up details the installation of a torpedo under an S.M.79. Although fittings were available for two weapons, performance was so impaired that one was the normal operational load.

Sicily the Sparviero force had further dwindled to the equivalent of four fragmented *gruppi* and two *squadriglie* with a total of no more than 27 serviceable aircraft. One of the reasons that so many aircraft were lying unserviceable on Italian airfields (estimated at around 50) was that for some months, in an effort to gain short bursts of extra speed, S.M.79s had been using a system of ethyl injection into the Alfa Romeo 128 engines (which admittedly increased the speed to well over 480 km/h; 298 mph), and this had taken its toll in worn-out engines.

At the time of the Italian capitulation 36 serviceable S.M.79s stood on the airfields at Capodichino, Littoria, Pisa and Siena; 21 of those eventually managed to fly south to the Allied lines to form part

of the Italian Co-Belligerent Air Force, while some of the others flew in Luftwaffe markings in which they were relegated to transport duties. Faggioni continued to command his *gruppo aerosiluranti* of S.M.79-IIIs in operations against the Allies, however, one of his outstanding operations being at the head of an attack on shipping at Gibraltar on the night of 4/5 June 1944. He was killed later, leading a strike against shipping at Nettuno.

After the war surviving Sparvieri were converted to transports and flew services with the interim Corrieri Aerei Militari before the resumption of formal commercial services. After that a few were employed as target tugs in Italy and three were sold as military transports to the Lebanese air force in 1950.

Total production of the S.M.79 in Italy between 1934 and 1944 was 1,330.

The twin-engined S.M.79B was produced as a cheap version of the basic aircraft to sell for export to Brazil, Iraq and Romania. The British encountered the aircraft during the Iraqi insurrection of 1941 and the Romanians used theirs on the Eastern Front in the same year.

S.M.79-I bombers of XXVII Gruppo Bombardamento Terrestre, Aviacion del Tercio ('Falchi delle Baleari'), during the Spanish Civil War, 1938. The green blotching on sand camouflage of the nearest aircraft contrasts with the brown and sand schemes of the other aircraft.

Savoia-Marchetti S.M.79

Specification
Savoia-Marchetti S.M.79-I
Type: four/five-crew medium bomber/torpedo-bomber
Powerplant: three 582-kW (780-hp) Alfa Romeo 126 RC.34 9-cylinder air-cooled radial piston engines
Performance: maximum speed 430 km/h (267 mph) at 4000 m (13,125 ft); climb to 4000 m (13,125 ft) in 13 minutes 15 seconds; service ceiling 6500 m (21,325 ft); maximum range at 340 km/h (211 mph) 3300 km (2,050 miles)
Weights: empty 6950 kg (15,322 lb); maximum take-off 10730 kg (23,655 lb)
Dimensions: span 21.20 m (69 ft 6¾ in); length 15.60 m (51 ft 2 in); height 4.60 m (15 ft 1 in); wing area 61.70 m² (664.2 sq ft)
Armament: one fixed 12.7-mm (0.5-in) machine-gun firing forward over cabin roof, guns of the same calibre in dorsal position and in rear of ventral position, one 7.7-mm (0.303-in) machine-gun for beam defence, plus a maximum bomb-load of five 250-kg (551-lb) bombs or one 45-cm (17.7-in) naval torpedo

Savoia-Marchetti S.M.79 variants

S.M.79P: commercial prototype (I-MAGO); originally with Piaggio P.IX Stella RC.2, later with Alfa Romeo 125 RC.35, and Alfa Romeo 126 RC.34 engines
S.M.79C: five racing aircraft; 746-kW (1,000-hp) Piaggio P.XI RC.40 engines
S.M.79T: 11 transatlantic aircraft, plus three S.M.79-1 (BISE, I-BRUN and I-MONI) modified to S.M.79T standard; Piaggio P.XI RC.40 engines
S.M.79B: twin-engine variant; prototype with 768-kW (1,030-hp) Fiat A.80 RC.41 radials; four similar aircraft to Iraq in 1938, and three to Brazil with 694-kW (930-hp) Alfa Romeo 128 RC.18 radials
S.M.79B: (Romanian): 24 Italian-built aircraft with 746-kW (1,000-hp) Gnome-Rhône K-14 Mistral Major radials, and 24 Italian-built aircraft with 910-kW (1,220-hp) Junkers 211 Da inline engines
S.M.79-JR: (Romanian): licence-built (by IAR

in Bucharest) aircraft with Junkers Jumo 211Da inverted V-12 engines
S.M.79-I: military protoype for Regia Aeronautica; Piaggio P.IX Stella RC.2 radials
S.M.79-I: production version with Alfa Romeo 126 RC.34 radials for Regia Aeronautica and Aerosiluranti; also 45 aircraft to Yugoslavia; some late-series aircraft with 642-kW (860-hp) Alfa Romeo 128 RC.18 radials; in production 1936-40
S.M.79-II: production version (bombers and torpedo-bombers) with 746-kW (1,000-hp) Piaggio P.XI RC.40 radials; in production 1940-43
S.M.79-III: (sometimes designated **S.579**): production version (bombers and torpedo-bombers) with increased armament; most aircraft without ventral gondola; alternative engines were 746-kW (1,000-hp) Fiat A.80 RC.41 or 1007-kW (1,350-hp) Alfa Romeo 135 RC.32 radials

Savoia-Marchetti S.M.79-II of the 205ª Squadriglia, displaying the Sorci Verdi (Green Mice) emblem adopted from the pre-war S.M.79 record-breaking Sparviero flight led by Colonel Attilio Biseo. Although early in the war Italian bombers tended to be deployed and operated in gruppo strength, battle losses during the final stages of the North African campaign resulted in many such units being disbanded. The 205ª Squadriglia was, however, re-formed as an autonomous unit at Milis, Sardinia, on the eve of the invasion of Sicily in July 1943, albeit with only four serviceable Sparvieri.

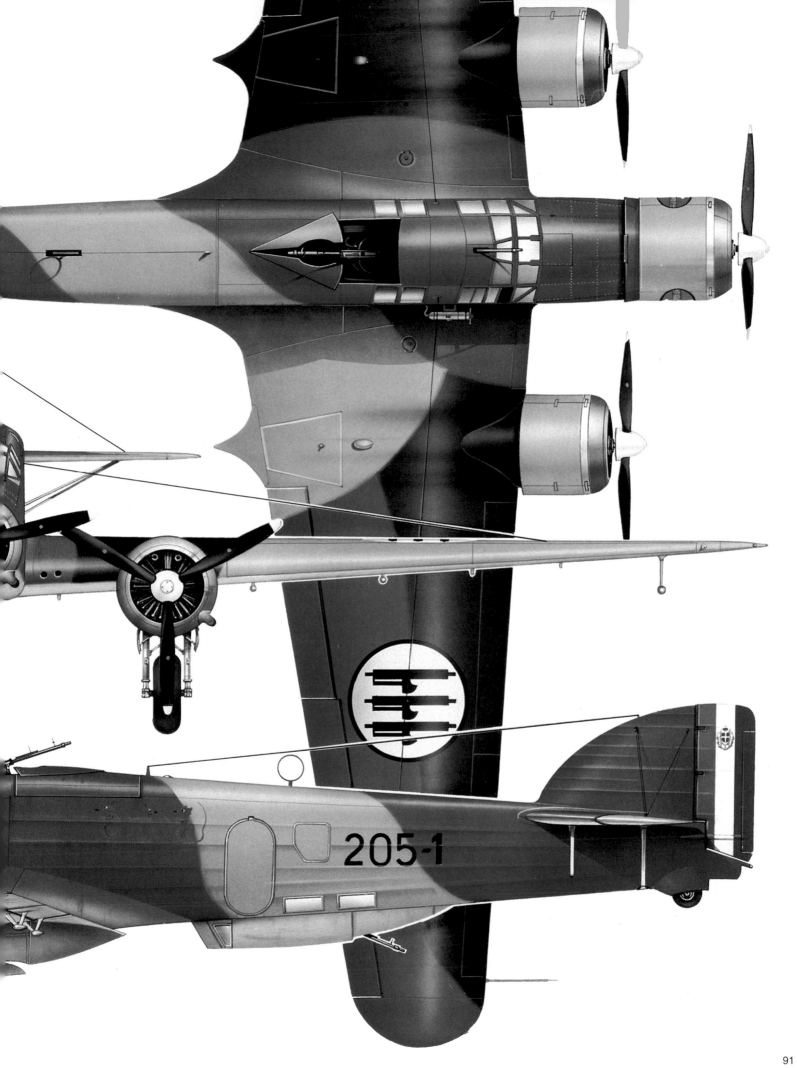

205-1

Short Sunderland

Developed from the great 'Empire' flying-boats, the Sunderland became a wartime legend as the chief patrol aircraft of the Commonwealth forces. It was tough, reliable and could turn its hand to almost any maritime task, from air-sea rescue to sinking U-boats. The Germans found it a very prickly customer and dubbed it 'The Flying Porcupine'.

Just as the Short S.23 C-class 'Empire' flying-boat marked a startling advance on all previous civil transport aircraft in Imperial Airways, so did its military derivative, the Sunderland, mark an equally great advance on marine aircraft in the RAF. Sometimes called 'The Pig' (not unkindly) by its crews, it was dubbed 'The Flying Porcupine' by Luftwaffe pilots who tried to attack it. When the last of these well-loved 'boats was retired from the RAF on 20 May 1959 it had set a record of 21 years' continuous service in the same oceanic duty. On the side, it had performed many other remarkable feats.

The Sunderland had its origins in a 1933 Air Ministry specification, R.2/33, calling for a new maritime reconnaissance flying-boat to replace the Short Singapore III biplane then just coming off the production line at the Rochester works of Short Brothers. The same company's chief designer Arthur (later Sir Arthur) Gouge immediately began to prepare a tender to the new requirement. He was already well advanced with planning a new civil transport flying-boat. Almost alone among British designers, Gouge realised that the all-metal stressed-skin monoplanes being built in the USA and Germany were a better species of flying machine, and he designed the S.23 as a

stressed-skin cantilever monoplane with a smooth skin and the greatest attention to the reduction of drag. It was an ideal basis for the new RAF machine, the S.25.

Military changes

Gouge made his submission in 1934, the specified armament being a 37-mm Coventry Ordnance Works gun in a bow cockpit or turret and a single Lewis machine-gun in the extreme tail. Compared with the civil S.23, the military 'boat had a completely new hull of much deeper cross-section, and with a long nose projecting ahead of a flight deck quite near the wing. When construction was well advanced it was decided to alter the armament to a nose turret with one machine-gun and a tail turret with four, a complete reversal of original thoughts on firepower. The shift in centre of gravity could only be countered by moving back the wing or altering the planform so that taper

This photograph - enough to quicken the pulse of anyone who remembers the sound of a Sunderland riding on the step at full power - was probably taken at Lough Erne, Northern Ireland, in the final year of the war. The aircraft is Z-Zebra, a Mk V of No. 201 Sqn, which had previously used code letters ZM.

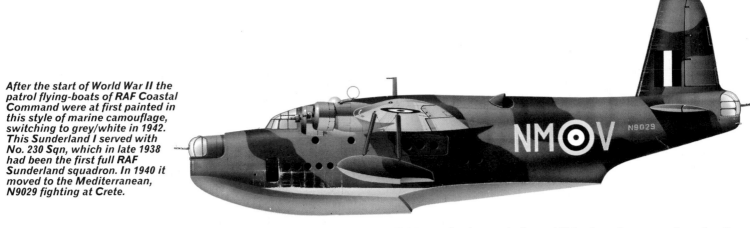

was mainly on the leading edge. The first prototype, K4774, now named Sunderland, was completed with the original wing, basically similar to that of the C-class transport, and flown without armament by J. Lankester Parker from the River Medway on 16 October 1937. After preliminary trials it went back into the factory to have the 'swept-back' wing fitted, flying again on 7 March 1938.

Powered by 753-kW (1,010-hp) Bristol Pegasus XXII engines, more powerful than those of the civil machine, the Sunderland was far more capable than any previous RAF aircraft. Fuel was housed in six vertical drum tanks between the spars with a capacity of 9206 litres (2,025 Imp gal), later increased to 11602 litres (2,552 Imp gal) by four further cells aft of the rear spar. In the original Sunderland I the normal crew was seven, accommodated basically on two decks and with comprehensive provision for prolonged habitation, with six bunks, galley with cooking stove, workshops and stowage for a considerable quantity of equipment including four rifles and three spare propeller blades. At the upper level it was possible to walk aft from the two-pilot flight deck past the cubicles of the radio operator (left) and navigator (right) and through the deep front spar into the domain of the flight engineer with extensive instrument panels inside the wing centre section. One could crawl through the rear spar to an aft upper deck filled with reconnaissance flares, smoke and flame floats, marine markers and other pyrotechnics.

The main offensive load, comprising up to 907 kg (2,000 lb) of bombs, depth charges, mines or other stores, was hung beneath the centre-section on carriers running on lateral tracks. In combat, large side hatches were opened beneath the wing and the weapons run out under the wings by a drive motor which cut out when the bomb carriages had reached full travel on each side. Defensive armament was concentrated in a Nash and Thompson FN.13 hydraulic tail turret, with four of the new Browning 0.303-in (7.7-mm) guns. In the bows was an FN.11 turret with a single VGO (Vickers gas-operated) machine-gun with a winching system for retracting the turret aft so that the big anchor could be passed out through a bow hatch.

Despite its great bulk the hull was well shaped, and drag at the nominal 30.5 m (100 ft) per second was actually lower than for the much smaller biplane Singapore III. Wing loading was, of course, in the order of twice that common on RAF aircraft of the mid-1930s, but Gouge's patented flaps (which had broad chord and rotated aft about a part-cylindrical upper surface) provided increased area and added 30 per cent to lift co-efficient for landing. Hydrodynamically, a new feature was the bringing of the planing bottom to a vertical knife-edge at the rear (second) step, thereafter sweeping the bottom line smoothly up and back to the tail. Flight-control surfaces were fabric-covered and driven manually, with no servotab assistance, but the Sunderland responded admirably to powerful control demands. A twin-wheel beaching chassis could be attached under the main spar and at the rear of the planing bottom.

RAF service began in June 1938 when the second production Mk I (L2159) was ferried out to No. 230 Sqn at Seletar, Singapore. About 40 were in service at the outbreak of war, and by late 1941 the total output of the Mk I had risen to 90, of which 15 were built by a second-source supplier, a works set up at the Denny shipyard at Dumbarton and run by Blackburn. From late 1939 until 1942 Sunderlands were camouflaged, though in their harsh environments paint flaked off rapidly. Early home-based units, such as Nos 204, 210 and 228 Sqns, plus No. 10 Sqn of the RAAF which arrived to collect its aircraft and stayed in the UK for the next 62 years, were intensively in action from the first day of the war. Successes against U-boats were at first non-existent, but rescues of torpedoed crews made the headlines, starting on 18 September 1939 when two of No. 228 Sqn's aircraft had the whole crew of 34 from the Kensington Court in hospital an hour after their ship sank off the Scillies.

Strengthening the defenses

By 1940 Sunderlands were being improved in various ways, notably by the addition of two VGO guns aimed from hatches at the rear of the upper deck on each side, with the front part of each hatch opening into the slipstream to give the gunner a calmer area for aiming. Other changes included the progressive addition of a second gun to the nose turret, replacement of the bracket-type (Hamilton-licence) de Havilland propellers by 3.81-m (12 ft 6 in) constant-speed propellers with spinners, addition of pulsating rubber-boot de-icers to the wings and tail and, from October 1941, ASV Mk II radar which covered the upper rear of the hull with matched dipole Yagi aerials in groups of four and added long dipole-equipped horizontal poles under the outer wings to give azimuth (homing) guidance. At the 241 km/h (150 mph) speeds which were hardly ever exceeded on patrol, these

Four Pegasus XXII engines of 783 kW (1,050 hp) each were deemed of ample power for early Sunderlands, but later the portly 'boats were burdened by tons of extra gear and festooned with radar dipole arrays. This example was the third production Sunderland, L.2160, photographed about June 1938.

Short Sunderland

Another early-war Sunderland was this Mk II of No. 201 Squadron, one of the first to have both ASV radar and the dorsal turret (which was offset to starboard). By this time the mid-upper and tail guns were belt-fed Brownings, though the nose guns were usually Vickers. Propellers were fitted with spinners, and the engines had flame-damped exhausts.

prominent arrays had little effect on performance.

In any case, though the defensive armament was actually quite light, and contained no gun greater than rifle calibre, the Sunderland soon gained the great respect of the enemy. On 3 April 1940 a Sunderland off Norway was attacked by six Ju 88s, shot one down, forced another to land immediately, and drove the rest off. Later another was attacked by eight Ju 88s over the Bay of Biscay and shot down three (confirmed by the convoy it was escorting).

Further development

In late 1941 production switched to the Mk II, with Pegasus XVIIIs with two-speed superchargers and, in the last few examples of this mark, improved armament in a twin-Browning nose turret, two more Brownings in an FN.7 dorsal turret on the right side of the hull at the trailing edge, and four Brownings in an FN.4A tail turret with ammunition doubled to 1,000 rounds per gun. Only 43 of this mark were produced, 15 of them at a third source, the Short & Harland company at Queen's Island, Belfast (later the home of the parent company). This limited production resulted from the fact that in June 1941 a Mk I had begun testing an improved planing bottom, with the Vee-type main step smoothly faired to reduce drag in the air. This hull resulted in the designation Mk III, and it succeeded the Mk II from December 1941. No fewer than 461 were delivered, 35 coming from a fourth assembly shop on Lake Windermere. The Mk III was effectively the standard wartime boat, and its exploits were legion in all theatres.

In the Mediterranean, Sunderlands were called upon to undertake many dangerous missions, none worse than the prolonged evacuation from Crete when many trips were made

A fine study of a Blackburn-built MK III, ML868 (also shown in a colour profile), with full ASV Mk II radar. It is seen serving with RAF No. 230 Sqn after the unit's return to the Far East in 1944. No. 280 ranged over vast areas of Japanese-occupied South East Asia.

Short Sunderland III cutaway drawing key

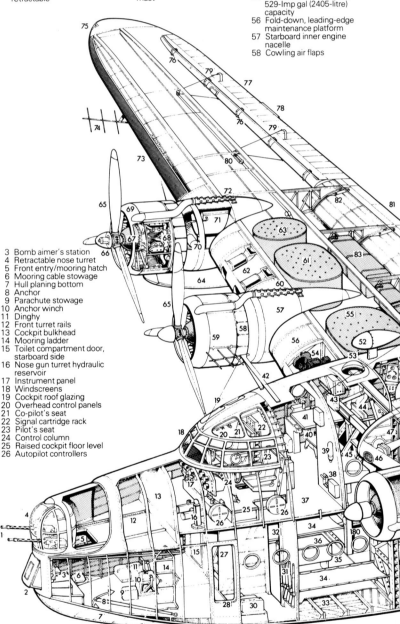

1 Twin Vickers 0.303-in (7.7-mm) machine guns
2 Bomb aiming window, retractable
3 Bomb aimer's station
4 Retractable nose turret
5 Front entry/mooring hatch
6 Mooring cable stowage
7 Hull planing bottom
8 Anchor
9 Parachute stowage
10 Anchor winch
11 Dinghy
12 Front turret rails
13 Cockpit bulkhead
14 Mooring ladder
15 Toilet compartment door, starboard side
16 Nose gun turret hydraulic reservoir
17 Instrument panel
18 Windscreens
19 Cockpit roof glazing
20 Overhead control panels
21 Co-pilot's seat
22 Signal cartridge rack
23 Pilot's seat
24 Control column
25 Raised cockpit floor level
26 Autopilot controllers
27 Stairway between upper and lower decks
28 Front entry door
29 Fuselage chine member
30 Crew luggage locker
31 Rifle rack
32 Wardroom door
33 Planing bottom hull construction
34 Wardroom bunks
35 Window panels
36 Folding table
37 Upper deck floor level
38 Parachute stowage
39 Fire extinguisher
40 Navigator's seat
41 Chart table
42 Forward ASV radar aerial mast
43 Navigator's instrument panel
44 Flight engineer's aft facing seat
45 Radio operator's station
46 Air intake duct
47 Wing/fuselage attachment main frames
48 Wing root rib cut-outs
49 Air conditioning plant
50 Engineer's control panels
51 Carburettor de-icing fluid tank
52 D/F loop aerial
53 Astrodome observation hatch
54 Auxiliary Power Unit
55 Forward inner fuel tank, 529-Imp gal (2405-litre) capacity
56 Fold-down, leading-edge maintenance platform
57 Starboard inner engine nacelle
58 Cowling air flaps
59 Detachable engine cowlings
60 Flame suppressor exhaust pipe
61 Forward inner fuel tank, 325-Imp gal (1477-litre) capacity
62 Oil coolers
63 Forward outer fuel tank, 132-Imp gal (600-litre) capacity
64 Starboard wing tip float
65 De Havilland three-bladed, constant speed propeller, 12ft 9in (3.89 m) diameter

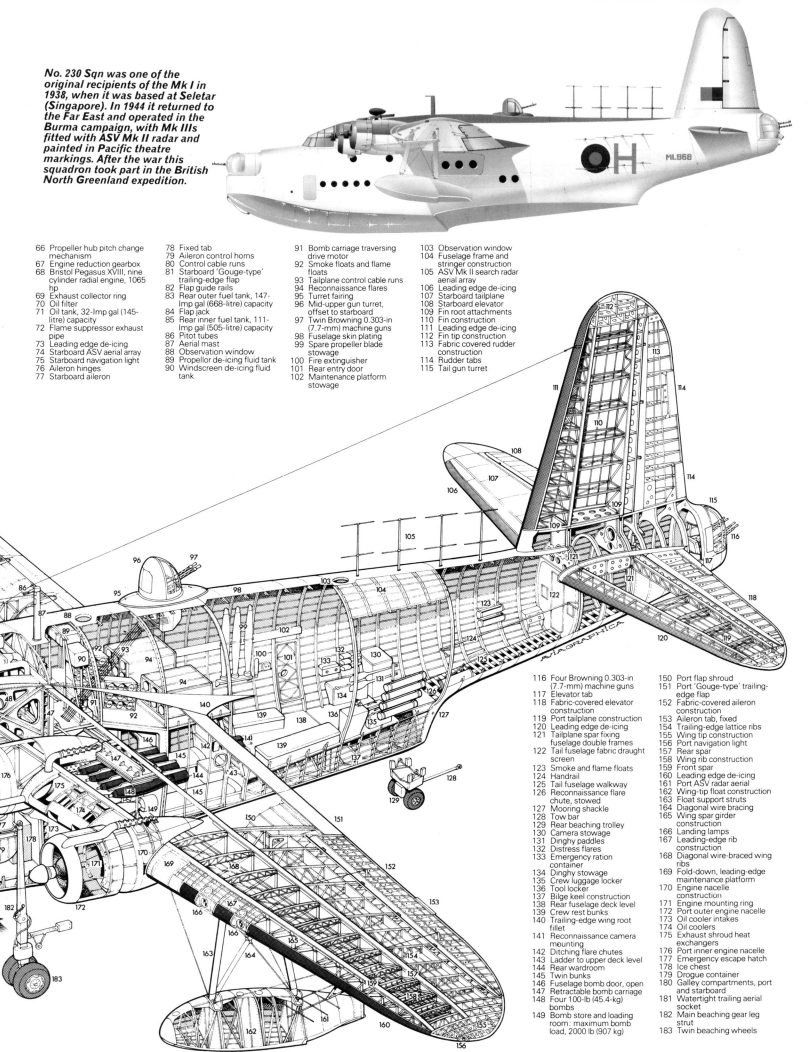

No. 230 Sqn was one of the original recipients of the Mk I in 1938, when it was based at Seletar (Singapore). In 1944 it returned to the Far East and operated in the Burma campaign, with Mk IIIs fitted with ASV Mk II radar and painted in Pacific theatre markings. After the war this squadron took part in the British North Greenland expedition.

66 Propeller hub pitch change mechanism
67 Engine reduction gearbox
68 Bristol Pegasus XVIII, nine cylinder radial engine, 1065 hp
69 Exhaust collector ring
70 Oil filter
71 Oil tank, 32-Imp gal (145-litre) capacity
72 Flame suppressor exhaust pipe
73 Leading edge de-icing
74 Starboard ASV aerial array
75 Starboard navigation light
76 Aileron hinges
77 Starboard aileron

78 Fixed tab
79 Aileron control horns
80 Control cable runs
81 Starboard 'Gouge-type' trailing-edge flap
82 Flap guide rails
83 Rear outer fuel tank, 147-Imp gal (668-litre) capacity
84 Flap jack
85 Rear inner fuel tank, 111-Imp gal (505-litre) capacity
86 Pitot tubes
87 Aerial mast
88 Observation window
89 Propellor de-icing fluid tank
90 Windscreen de-icing fluid tank

91 Bomb carriage traversing drive motor
92 Smoke floats and flame floats
93 Tailplane control cable runs
94 Reconnaissance flares
95 Turret fairing
96 Mid-upper gun turret, offset to starboard
97 Twin Browning 0.303-in (7.7-mm) machine guns
98 Fuselage skin plating
99 Spare propeller blade stowage
100 Fire extinguisher
101 Rear entry door
102 Maintenance platform stowage

103 Observation window
104 Fuselage frame and stringer construction
105 ASV Mk II search radar aerial array
106 Leading edge de-icing
107 Starboard tailplane
108 Starboard elevator
109 Fin root attachments
110 Fin construction
111 Leading edge de-icing
112 Fin tip construction
113 Fabric covered rudder construction
114 Rudder tabs
115 Tail gun turret

116 Four Browning 0.303-in (7.7-mm) machine guns
117 Elevator tab
118 Fabric-covered elevator construction
119 Port tailplane construction
120 Leading edge de-icing
121 Tailplane spar fixing fuselage double frames
122 Tail fuselage fabric draught screen
123 Smoke and flame floats
124 Handrail
125 Tail fuselage walkway
126 Reconnaissance flare chute, stowed
127 Mooring shackle
128 Tow bar
129 Rear beaching trolley
130 Camera stowage
131 Dinghy paddles
132 Distress flares
133 Emergency ration container
134 Dinghy stowage
135 Crew luggage locker
136 Tool locker
137 Bilge keel construction
138 Rear fuselage deck level
139 Crew rest bunks
140 Trailing-edge wing root fillet
141 Reconnaissance camera mounting
142 Ditching flare chutes
143 Ladder to upper deck level
144 Rear wardroom
145 Twin bunks
146 Fuselage bomb door, open
147 Retractable bomb carriage
148 Four 100-lb (45.4-kg) bombs
149 Bomb store and loading room: maximum bomb load, 2000 lb (907 kg)

150 Port flap shroud
151 Port 'Gouge-type' trailing-edge flap
152 Fabric-covered aileron construction
153 Aileron tab, fixed
154 Trailing-edge lattice ribs
155 Wing tip construction
156 Port navigation light
157 Rear spar
158 Wing rib construction
159 Front spar
160 Leading edge de-icing
161 Port ASV radar aerial
162 Wing-tip float construction
163 Float support struts
164 Diagonal wire bracing
165 Wing spar girder construction
166 Landing lamps
167 Leading-edge rib construction
168 Diagonal wire-braced wing ribs
169 Fold-down, leading-edge maintenance platform
170 Engine nacelle construction
171 Engine mounting ring
172 Port outer engine nacelle
173 Oil cooler intakes
174 Oil coolers
175 Exhaust shroud heat exchangers
176 Port inner engine nacelle
177 Emergency escape hatch
178 Ice chest
179 Drogue container
180 Galley compartments, port and starboard
181 Watertight trailing aerial socket
182 Main beaching gear leg strut
183 Twin beaching wheels

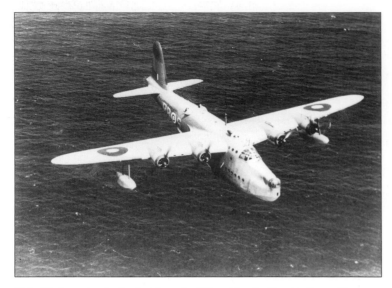

This Mk I serving in the hard-worked Royal Australian Air Force No. 10 Sqn, based at Mount Batten (plymouth), was photographed in 1941 with ASV radar fitted. The wartime censor retouched out this highly secret apparatus before releasing the photograph for publication. Note the two hooded open dorsal gun positions.

Sunderlands were flown by the French Aéronavale until 1960. Flotille 7E inherited a number of aircraft at the end of World War II, but added 19 reconditioned Mk 5s from the RAF in 1951.

with as many as 82 armed passengers in addition to the crew, which by this time had grown to 10. A Sunderland made the necessary visual reconnaissance of Taranto before the Fleet Air Arm attack of 11 November 1940. Over the Atlantic the Sunderland shared with the Consolidated Catalina the main effort against U-Boats, but when the latter received Metox passive receivers tuned to ASV Mk II they received ample warning of the presence of British aircraft and kills dropped sharply. The RAF response was the new ASV Mk III, operating in the band well below 50 cm and with the aerials neatly faired into blisters under the outer wings. When thus fitted the Sunderland became a Mk IIIA.

The U-boat sensors could not pick up this radar, and once again, in early 1943, kills became frequent. The response of the U-Boats was to fit batteries of deadly flak, typically one or two

The final production Sunderland was the Mk V, with American Twin Wasp engines giving more power than the old nine-cylinder Pegasus. This example was serving at the end of the war with No. 4 OTU (Operational Training Unit); its serial number was SZ568. The Mk V was fitted as standard with ASV Mk VIc radar with scanners faired into underwing blisters.

37-mm and two quadruple 20-mm, and fight it out on the surface. The odds were then heavily against the flying-boat, which needed forward-firing firepower. Curiously, although the bow was ideally arranged for it, really heavy forward-firing armament was never fitted to the Sunderland, nor was the Leigh light, although many aircraft received four fixed 0.303-in (7.7-mm) Brownings, firing straight ahead, together with a pilot gunsight. The one thing these guns did sometimes succeed in doing was to knock out the U-Boat gunners as they ran from the conning-tower hatch the few metres to their guns.

Keeping the wolf from the door

In addition, heavier lateral armament became common, to combat the more numerous and more heavily armed Luftwaffe long-range fighters. Although the latter's cannon always gave a considerable edge in stand-off range, Sunderlands did at least fit locally contrived installations of single VGOs or Brownings from the escape hatches in the galley compartments (last but one in the main row of portholes). This became a standard fit in late 1943, at which time Short also added an installation of one or two of the much more effective 0.5-in (12.7-mm) Brownings from upper rear hatches behind the trailing edge. Thus, the number of guns rose in a year from five to 18, believed the greatest number of guns carried by any regular British service aircraft.

In late 1942 severe shortage of equipment by BOAC, the national civil airline, resulted in six Sunderland IIIs being stripped of all armament (turrets were replaced by bulbous fairings) and put into joint BOAC/RAF service between Poole and Lagos (West Africa) and Calcutta (India). BOAC investigated the engine installation and cruising angle of attack to such effect that mean cruising speed, which had seldom bothered the RAF, was improved by more than 40 per cent. Spartan bench seats for seven passengers, the main payload being mail, gradually gave way in the BOAC Hythe class to an excellent airline interior for 24 passengers (16 with sleeping accommodation), plus 2950 kg (6,500 lb) of mail, and the engines were modified to Pegasus 38 (later 48) standard. By 1944 the number of civil Sunderland IIIs had grown to 24, and after the war the Hythes, eventually totalling 29, were supplemented by a complete civil rebuild - the S.26 Sandringham - which went into production as a basic war transport for BOAC (as the Plymouth class) and its airlines.

It was not until the appearance of the Wellington GR.Mk VIII (the Wellington Mk VII was a cancelled Merlin-powered bomber) that the Wellington came to play a regular part in Coastal Command's contribution to the Battle of the Atlantic. A total of 394 of this version was produced and, being powered by Pegasus XVIII radials, it was generally similar to the Wellington Mk IC, roughly half the total in fact being contributed from Wellington Mk IC production lines. The main feature was the installation of ASV Mk II radar with its associated array of dorsal aerials, a radar developed to detect surfaced submarines whose forays in the Atlantic were costing the UK so dearly. The first Wellington GR.Mk VIIIs joined No. 172 Squadron at Chivenor in April 1942, the unit being formed from the Leigh Light Flight. Some of the Wellington GR.Mk VIIIs were also equipped with a retractable Leigh Light fitted in the old 'dustbin' aperture, and on the night of 3/4 June 1942 a No. 172 Squadron Wellington made the first Leigh Light attack on a surfaced U-boat; the first enemy submarine to be despatched in such an attack was sunk on 6 July of that year. Wellington GR.Mk VIIIs equipped eight squadrons.

Proliferation of versions

This mark was followed in Coastal Command by the Wellington GR.Mk XI (180 produced at Blackpool), which used a Mk X airframe powered by Hercules VI radials and equipped with ASV Mk II; the Wellington GR.Mk XI equipped six squadrons. The Wellington GR.Mk XII (58 built at Chester and Weybridge) was similar but also included a Leigh Light; it served with Nos 36 and 172 Squadrons. Wellington GR.Mk XIII (843 built at Blackpool) featured Hercules XVIIs, ASV Mk III and provision for two 45.7-mm (18-in) torpedoes for daylight maritime duties; it equipped 13 squadrons. The Wellington GR.Mk XIV (841 produced at Blackpool and Chester) was similar to the Wellington GR.Mk XIII but carried the Leigh Light in place of the torpedoes for night patrols; it was flown by 10 squadrons.

In the autumn of 1944 some of the Wellington GR.Mk XIs and GR.Mk XIIIs that had been replaced by later versions were modified as night-fighter nav-radar operator trainers, the former redesignated the Wellington T.Mk XVII with Mosquito-style radar and two-seat training provision, and the latter the Wellington T.Mk XVIII redesigned to accommodate four pupils training on the Mosquito radar. After the war numerous Wellington Mk X bombers underwent con-

version (without redesignation) for use as radar and navigation trainers, remaining in service with operational conversion units and advanced flying schools until 1953.

As the Wellington began its phasing out of Bomber Command's front line and the old Wellington Mk IAs and Mk ICs were replaced by Wellington Mk IIIs and Mk Xs at the OCUs, the Wellington Mk Is were converted for use as transports by the RAF. From *ad hoc* use of the Wellington to move troops (particularly in the Middle East) as early as 1941 stemmed a major requirement to modify large numbers of Wellington Mk Is as 18-seat troop transports. The majority of conversions was carried out 'in the field', the modifications including the removal of all turrets, oxygen system and bomb gear, and the installation of rudimentary seating. The resulting aircraft (after discarding the designations Wellington C.Mk IA and C.Mk IC) became the Wellington C.Mk XV and C.Mk XVI, and these served with Nos 24, 99, 162, 196, 232 and 242 Squadrons. At the same time the Wellington underwent clearance trials for towing General Aircraft Hotspur, Airspeed Horsa and Waco Hadrian gliders though, as far as is known, the aircraft was not employed in this role on operations. Another series of trials involved Wellingtons towing Spitfire and Hurricane fighters for possible reinforcement of Malta from Gibraltar, but no detailed account of these trials has ever been made available.

Among the large number of experimental tasks undertaken by Wellingtons were the flight testing of armament and engine in-

Vickers Wellington

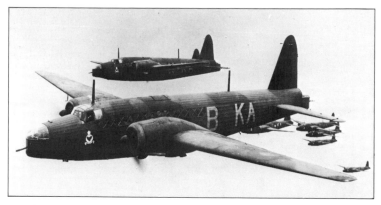

Wellington Mk Is of No. 9 (Bomber) Sqn. The first RAF squadron to be equipped with the Wellington, this unit was one of those to suffer heavy losses to enemy fighters in the disastrous daylight raids of the first four months of the war. This picture was taken shortly before the outbreak of hostilities.

stallations. In the former category were the trials with models of Dr Barnes Wallis' 'Highball' and 'Upkeep' spinning bombs that were used to such good effect by Bomber Command. In another series of trials a dorsal turret mounting a 40-mm Vickers gun was tested in a Wellington Mk II; in conjunction with Vickers' F.22/39 fighter project a 40-mm gun was tested in another Wellington Mk II.

Testing of experimental engines in the Wellington continued throughout and after the war, and of these the early flights by jet engines were the most noteworthy. In 1942 Vickers were asked to undertake the installation of early Whittle turbojets in Wellingtons for flight trials, and between 1942 and 1945 some 15 types of engine were flown in the rear fuselages of a pair of Wellington Mk IIs; powered by Merlin 62s and fitted with Wellington Mk VI wings, these Wellingtons made a total of 366 flights at heights up to 10970 m (36,000 ft) and mounted every one of the pioneer British turbojets. Engine testbed work continued after the war, perhaps the most important being that for the Rolls-Royce Dart turboprop, which flew in a Wellington Mk X (LN715) in 1948 in preparation for the Vickers 630 Viscount airliner whose prototype flew on 16 July that year.

The 'Wimpey' continued to give sterling service as a trainer in the RAF, and the Wellington T.Mk 10 served with air navigation schools until replaced by the Vickers Valetta T.Mk 3, and with No. 201 AFS where it eventually gave place to the Vickers Varsity. The last Wellington delivered to the RAF was a Hercules XVI-powered Wellington Mk X, which left Blackpool on 25 October 1945. In nine years the three Vickers factories had built a grand total of 11,461 Wellingtons – the largest number of any bomber ever produced in the UK.

T2501 was a Wellington Mk IC (IN-F) of a bomber OTU that landed in enemy-occupied territory during bombing operations; it was given German markings and underwent evaluation at the experimental station at Rechlin.

Vickers Wellington B.Mk III cutaway drawing key

1 Forward navigation light
2 Two 0.303-in (7.7-mm) Browning machine-guns
3 Frazer Nash FN 5 power-operated nose turret
4 Turret fairing
5 Parachute stowage
6 Bomb-aimer's control panel
7 Nose turret external rotation valve
8 Bomb-aimer's window
9 Bomb-aimer's cushion (hinged entry hatch)
10 Parachute stowage
11 Rudder control lever
12 Fuselage forward frame
13 Camera
14 Elevator and aileron control levers
15 Bomb-bay forward bulkhead (canted)
16 Cockpit bulkhead frame
17 Pilot's seat
18 Control column
19 Nose compartment/cabin step
20 Instrument panel
21 Co-pilot's folding seat
22 Windscreen
23 Hinged cockpit canopy section (ditching)
24 Electrical distributor panel
25 Aerial mast
26 R.3003 controls mounting
27 Tail unit de-icing control unit
28 Armour-plate bulkhead
29 Wireless-operator's seat
30 Wireless-operator's desk
31 Motor generator (wireless installation) and HT battery stowage
32 Bomb-bay doors
33 T.R.9F wireless unit crate
34 Aldis signal lamp stowage
35 Navigator's desk
36 Navigational instrument and map stowage
37 Navigator's seat
38 Folding doors (sound-proof bulkhead)
39 Fire extinguisher (on leading-edge fuselage frame)
40 Flying-controls locking bar ('nuisance bar') stowage
41 Wing inboard geodetic structure
42 Cooling duct exit louvre
43 Flame-damper exhaust tailpipe extension
44 Engine cooling controllable gills
45 Bristol Hercules XI radial engine
46 Exhaust collector ring
47 Three-blade Rotol electric propeller
48 Three-piece engine wrapper cowl
49 Carburettor air intake scoop
50 Engine mounting bearers
51 Starboard oil tank
52 Starboard nacelle fuel tank, capacity 58 Imp gal (284 litres)
53 Wing forward fuel tank train, capacity 52 Imp gal (236 litres) inboard, 55 Imp gal (250 litres) centre, 43 Imp gal (195 litres) outboard
54 Twin-boom inboard wing spar
55 Wing aft fuel tank train, capacity 60 Imp gal (273 litres) inboard, 57 Imp gal (259 litres) centre, 50 Imp gal (227 litres) outboard
56 Fuel filler caps
57 Spar twin/single boom transition
58 Pitot head piping
59 Cable cutters
60 Pitot head
61 Spar construction
62 Starboard navigation light
63 Starboard formation light
64 Aileron control rod stop bracket
65 Ball-bearing brackets
66 Starboard aileron
67 Aileron control rod
68 Aileron control articulated lever

69 Aileron trim tab control cable linkage
70 Aileron trim tab
71 Trim cables
72 Aileron control rod joint
73 Fuel jettison pipe
74 Flap operating shaft
75 Flap links
76 Flap trailing-edge
77 Aileron control rod adjustable joint
78 Dinghy stowage
79 Flotation gear CO_2 bottles
80 Fuel lines
81 D/F loop fairing
82 Dorsal identification light
83 Hand grips
84 Oxygen cylinders
85 'Floating'-spar centre-section carry-through
86 Reconnaissance flares
87 Wing forward pivot fixing
88 Spar/rib pick-up
89 Spar aperture
90 Rest bunk (stowed against port wall)
91 Sextant steadying frame
92 Astrodome
93 Flap actuating cylinder
94 Flame float/sea marker stowage
95 Flap synchronizing mechanism
96 Parachute stowage
97 Reconnaissance flare launching tube
98 Trailing-edge fuselage frame
99 Geodetic construction
100 Whip aerial
101 HF aerial
102 Beam gunner's heated-clothing/oxygen supply/intercom sockets
103 Starboard beam gun, 0.303-in (7.7-mm) Browning
104 Ammunition box
105 Gun mounting
106 Fuselage upper longeron
107 Tail turret ammunition boxes
108 Parachute stowage
109 Rudder tab control cables
110 Ammunition feed tracks
111 Roof light
112 Tail turret external rotation valve
113 Starboard tailplane lower geodetic panel
114 Tailplane spar
115 Elevator balance

116 Starboard elevator
117 Elevator trim tab
118 Trim tab control cables
119 Fin geodetic structure (lower section)
120 Fin de-icing overshoe
121 Fin upper section
122 Non-kink de-icing connector hose
123 Rudder mass balance weights
124 Rear navigation/formation lights
125 Rudder combined trim/balance tab
126 Rudder post
127 Tab actuating rod
128 Tab control cables
129 Rudder actuating lever
130 Tail turret entry door
131 Frazer Nash FN.20A tail turret
132 Four 0.303-in (7.7-mm) Browning machine-guns
133 Cartridge case ejection chute
134 Elevator tab
135 Port elevator
136 Elevator balance
137 Tailplane structure

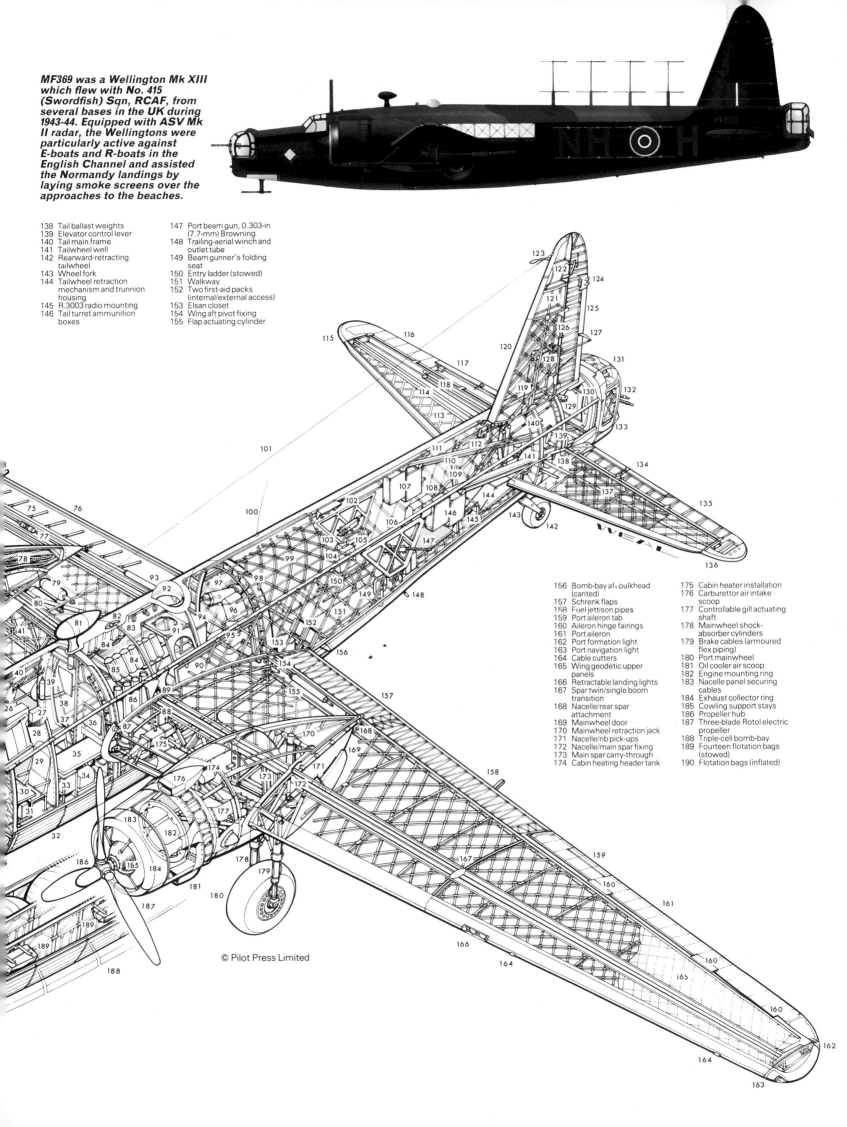

MF369 was a Wellington Mk XIII which flew with No. 415 (Swordfish) Sqn, RCAF, from several bases in the UK during 1943-44. Equipped with ASV Mk II radar, the Wellingtons were particularly active against E-boats and R-boats in the English Channel and assisted the Normandy landings by laying smoke screens over the approaches to the beaches.

138 Tail ballast weights
139 Elevator control lever
140 Tail main frame
141 Tailwheel well
142 Rearward-retracting tailwheel
143 Wheel fork
144 Tailwheel retraction mechanism and trunnion housing
145 R.3003 radio mounting
146 Tail turret ammunition boxes

147 Port beam gun, 0.303-in (7.7-mm) Browning
148 Trailing-aerial winch and outlet tube
149 Beam gunner's folding seat
150 Entry ladder (stowed)
151 Walkway
152 Two first-aid packs (internal/external access)
153 Elsan closet
154 Wing aft pivot fixing
155 Flap actuating cylinder

156 Bomb-bay aft bulkhead (canted)
157 Schrenk flaps
158 Fuel jettison pipes
159 Port aileron tab
160 Aileron hinge fairings
161 Port aileron
162 Port formation light
163 Port navigation light
164 Cable cutters
165 Wing geodetic upper panels
166 Retractable landing lights
167 Spar twin/single boom transition
168 Nacelle/rear spar attachment
169 Mainwheel door
170 Mainwheel retraction jack
171 Nacelle/rib pick-ups
172 Nacelle/main spar fixing
173 Main spar carry-through
174 Cabin heating header tank

175 Cabin heater installation
176 Carburettor air intake scoop
177 Controllable gill actuating shaft
178 Mainwheel shock-absorber cylinders
179 Brake cables (armoured flex piping)
180 Port mainwheel
181 Oil cooler air scoop
182 Engine mounting ring
183 Nacelle panel securing cables
184 Exhaust collector ring
185 Cowling support stays
186 Propeller hub
187 Three-blade Rotol electric propeller
188 Triple-cell bomb-bay
189 Fourteen flotation bags (stowed)
190 Flotation bags (inflated)

Mitsubishi G4M 'Betty'

So lightly protected that it was known to US fighter pilots as the 'Honourable One-Shot Lighter', the G4M (called 'Betty' by the Allies) tried to get too much range from too small an aircraft. Despite this, it was by far the most important bomber of the Imperial Japanese navy, seeing action throughout the vast Pacific theatre.

Probably the rock-bottom moment of World War II for the British was 10 December 1941, when the Japanese, whose aircraft were, as we all knew, copied from Western designs but made of bamboo and rice-paper, sank two of the Royal Navy's greatest warships by air attack. What could have done such a thing? The only answer seemed to be the ancient Yokosuka B4Y biplane torpedo bomber. Only much later was it realised the great battleship and battle-cruiser had been sent to the bottom by Mitsubishi G3M and G4M long-range bombers. The latter was totally unknown to the Allies, because nobody had read the reports on it sent back from China; they had not read the reports on the Mitsubishi A6M fighter, either, and this was an even bigger shock.

In the context of the war in the Pacific a Japanese twin-engined bomber was unlikely ever again to be more than a thorn in the side of the Allies, and in fact the G4M did little to influence the course of events and suffered heavy casualties. At the same time, a front-line force of more than 2,000 aircraft flown with immense courage and determination could hardly be ignored, and on occasion 'Betty' did inflict damaging blows. It must be remembered that this modest aircraft, in most respects in the class of Douglas A-20 or North American B-25 but with a much lower gross weight than a B-25, was used for missions which really demanded a four-engine 'heavy'. Perhaps shortsightedly, it was not until 1943 that the Imperial Japanese

Navy gave up its insistence on twin-engined bombers and instructed Nakajima to build the formidable G7N. Starting so late, only four of these were completed before the Japanese collapse.

Development of the G4M began with the issue, in September 1937, of a specification (known as a 12-*shi* specification, because it was in the 12th year of Emperor Hirohito's reign) for a new long-range bomber to succeed the very successful G3M. The latter had gone into action over China only two months previously, and had delighted navy officials by having a combat range in excess of 3700 km (2,300 miles); from the start of the war these bombers had demonstrated their ability to carry heavy bombloads to targets deep inside China, operating from some 2415 km (1,500 miles) away in Japan. Not unnaturally the Koku Hombu (navy air HQ) considered it would be possible to do even better, though it suggested Mitsubishi should use just two engines of 746 kW (1,000 hp) each. Other numerical demands were a speed of 398 km/h (247 mph), a range with an 800-kg (1,746-lb) torpedo or similar bombload of 3700 km (2,299 miles) and all-round defensive guns needing a crew of seven to nine.

*Aircrews relax before a mission, with an **Ohka**-carrying **G4M2e Model 24J** in the background. Bomb-bay doors were removed and shackles attached to carry the piloted missile, but the combination was slow and an easy target for enemy aircraft.*

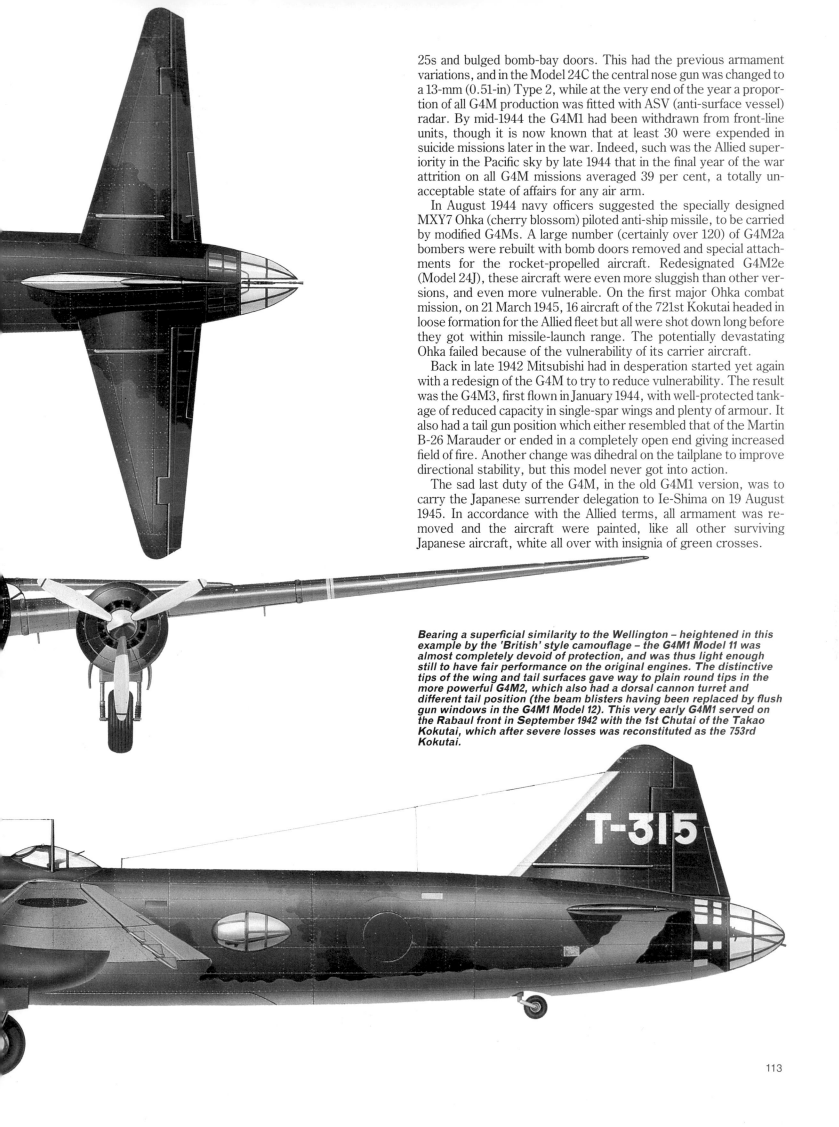

25s and bulged bomb-bay doors. This had the previous armament variations, and in the Model 24C the central nose gun was changed to a 13-mm (0.51-in) Type 2, while at the very end of the year a proportion of all G4M production was fitted with ASV (anti-surface vessel) radar. By mid-1944 the G4M1 had been withdrawn from front-line units, though it is now known that at least 30 were expended in suicide missions later in the war. Indeed, such was the Allied superiority in the Pacific sky by late 1944 that in the final year of the war attrition on all G4M missions averaged 39 per cent, a totally unacceptable state of affairs for any air arm.

In August 1944 navy officers suggested the specially designed MXY7 Ohka (cherry blossom) piloted anti-ship missile, to be carried by modified G4Ms. A large number (certainly over 120) of G4M2a bombers were rebuilt with bomb doors removed and special attachments for the rocket-propelled aircraft. Redesignated G4M2e (Model 24J), these aircraft were even more sluggish than other versions, and even more vulnerable. On the first major Ohka combat mission, on 21 March 1945, 16 aircraft of the 721st Kokutai headed in loose formation for the Allied fleet but all were shot down long before they got within missile-launch range. The potentially devastating Ohka failed because of the vulnerability of its carrier aircraft.

Back in late 1942 Mitsubishi had in desperation started yet again with a redesign of the G4M to try to reduce vulnerability. The result was the G4M3, first flown in January 1944, with well-protected tankage of reduced capacity in single-spar wings and plenty of armour. It also had a tail gun position which either resembled that of the Martin B-26 Marauder or ended in a completely open end giving increased field of fire. Another change was dihedral on the tailplane to improve directional stability, but this model never got into action.

The sad last duty of the G4M, in the old G4M1 version, was to carry the Japanese surrender delegation to Ie-Shima on 19 August 1945. In accordance with the Allied terms, all armament was removed and the aircraft were painted, like all other surviving Japanese aircraft, white all over with insignia of green crosses.

Bearing a superficial similarity to the Wellington – heightened in this example by the 'British' style camouflage – the G4M1 Model 11 was almost completely devoid of protection, and was thus light enough still to have fair performance on the original engines. The distinctive tips of the wing and tail surfaces gave way to plain round tips in the more powerful G4M2, which also had a dorsal cannon turret and different tail position (the beam blisters having been replaced by flush gun windows in the G4M1 Model 12). This very early G4M1 served on the Rabaul front in September 1942 with the 1st Chutai of the Takao Kokutai, which after severe losses was reconstituted as the 753rd Kokutai.

113

de Havilland Mosquito

The Mosquito was born in an uncertain fashion during wartime, with few real supporters. Within five years it became one of the RAF's most versatile and valued assets. More versions of the Mosquito were built than of any other aircraft in history, and to the pilots it was the 'Wooden Wonder'.

The all-wooden de Havilland Mosquito was possibly the most useful single type of aircraft produced by the Allies in World War II. Like so many other great aircraft it owed nothing to any official specification and was created in the teeth of often fierce opposition by the officials. Even after a prototype had been ordered, the limited nature of the programme (a mere 50 aircraft) caused it to be removed entirely from future plans three times after the Dunkirk evacuation. Each time it was daringly put back by a single believer, Patrick (later Sir Patrick) Hennessy, brought in from Ford Motors by Lord Beaverbrook to help run British aircraft production. So in November 1940 a single prototype at last took the air. Once that had happened the fantastic performance of the Mosquito carried all before it.

The de Havilland Aircraft Company was famed chiefly for light-planes and rather primitive mixed-construction light transports, but in 1936 it designed the aerodynamically superb (but technically disastrous) D.H.91 Albatross airliner with structure entirely of wood. A few months later work was started on a military derivative with two Merlin engines to meet the requirements of specification P.13/36, but this was not accepted, largely because of the wooden structure which was hardly taken seriously. Undeterred, the project staff

under R. E. Bishop, R. M. Clarkson and C. T. Wilkins continued to study a new species of high-speed bomber able to evade hostile fighters and thus dispense with gun turrets. The concept appeared to make sense. Doing away with turrets reduced the crew from six to two, comprising a pilot on the left in the nose cockpit with the navigator/bombardier on his right. Either could work the radio. Thanks to the scale effect, in that saving weight enabled the aircraft to be smaller and burn less fuel, it was calculated the twin-Merlin unarmed bomber could carry 454 kg (1,000 lb) of bombs 2400 km (1,500 miles) for a weight of just over 6800 kg (15,000 lb), so that with good streamlining the speed could reach almost 655 km/h (400 mph), getting on for twice the speed of other British bombers.

The aircraft could have flown in early 1939 but officials, including the Air Staff, showed either disinterest or hostility. Literally dozens of objections were raised to show that an unarmed bomber would be useless, that a crew of only two could not fly the mission, and that the company's proposals were pointless. At a major meeting at the Air

Second operator of the Mosquito B.IV was RAF No. 139 Sqn, based at Horsham St Faith until late September 1942, and subsequently at Marham. These aircraft may have been photographed on their way to disrupt a major speech by Dr Goebbels in January 1943.

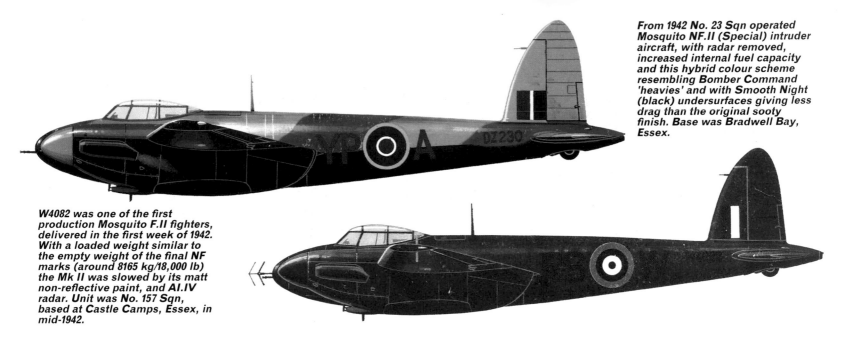

From 1942 No. 23 Sqn operated Mosquito NF.II (Special) intruder aircraft, with radar removed, increased internal fuel capacity and this hybrid colour scheme resembling Bomber Command 'heavies' and with Smooth Night (black) undersurfaces giving less drag than the original sooty finish. Base was Bradwell Bay, Essex.

W4082 was one of the first production Mosquito F.II fighters, delivered in the first week of 1942. With a loaded weight similar to the empty weight of the final NF marks (around 8165 kg/18,000 lb) the Mk II was slowed by its matt non-reflective paint, and AI.IV radar. Unit was No. 157 Sqn, based at Castle Camps, Essex, in mid-1942.

Ministry just after the Munich crisis, in October 1938, the officials declined to study the proposals but asked if de Havilland would build wings for one of the existing bomber programmes. Even after the outbreak of war, no member of the Air Staff saw in the proposals anything but a pointless diversion. It was not until long after the outbreak of war that, partly because of support by Air Marshal Sir Wilfred Freeman, the Air Staff began to concede that a twin-Merlin aircraft, provided it was built solely for reconnaissance, might possibly be unarmed and might even be made of wood. With great efforts the point was reached on 1 March 1940 at which a contract could be signed for a prototype plus 49 production machines.

The basic Mosquito

The first D.H.98 Mosquito (W4050) was secretly built at Salisbury Hall, about 8 km (5 miles) from the Hatfield works, to which it was taken by road on 3 November 1940. Geoffrey de Havilland Jr made the first flight on 25 November. It had been estimated that, with twice the power of a Spitfire, twice the wetted (skin) area and more than twice the weight, the Mosquito would be 32 km/h (20 mph) faster. Nobody in the Air Ministry believed this; they were amazed when the prototype was officially tested at Boscombe Down in February 1941 and found to reach 631 km/h (392 mph), somewhat over 32 km/h (20 mph) more than the fastest British fighter.

The basic design was a beautifully streamlined monoplane, with the sharply tapered wing mounted in the mid position above a bomb bay for four 113-kg (250-lb) bombs. The pilot sat just ahead of the leading edge, where he had a fine view except where blocked by the engine cowlings which extended aft to the trailing edge. Almost the entire structure was wood, the wing having two spars and ply skins (double on the upper surface) with spruce stringers, while the fuselage was made in left and right halves moulded on concrete formers from sandwich structure comprising light balsa between inner and outer skins of plywood. Flying-control surfaces were light alloy, with metal skin on the ailerons and fabric on the tail, but the hydraulic plain flaps were wood. Unusual features included coolant radiators occupying the wing leading edge between engines and fuselage, which with development could give positive thrust in cruising flight, and simple landing gears with twin shock struts filled with rubber blocks. This eliminated much need for precision metalwork, and the total weight of castings (113 kg/250 lb) and forgings (13.6 kg/30 lb) was less than for any other twin-engined combat aircraft of its day.

Flight development showed the need for an increase in span from 16.00 m (52 ft 6 in) to 16.51 m (54 ft 2 in), a larger tailplane, improved cowlings and exhaust systems, and lengthened nacelles which divided the flaps into four small sections joined by torque tubes. The leading-edge slats were judged unnecessary and

The yellow prototype actually carried Class B serial number E0234 until the end of 1940. This photograph may have been taken with a tail number added for the new types display at Hatfield on 20 April 1941. Six months later W4050 was flying in full camouflage, with long nacelles, a larger tailplane and Merlin 61 engines.

ML963 was one of the main run B.XVI high-flying bombers delivered from Hatfield in 1944. This example, in day bomber camouflage with medium sea grey underside, served with No. 571 Sqn, and with a 1814-kg (4,000-lb) 'cookie' and underwing tanks could take off at over 11340 kg (25,000 lb).

de Havilland Mosquito

LR508 was one of the small initial batch of Hatfield-built B.IX high-altitude bombers which set up a fantastic record on night missions with No. 105 Sqn. This particular machine made 96 combat missions, but 10 of 105's Mk IXs exceeded 100 missions, LR504 reaching 200 and LR503 possibly setting a record with 213.

ML963 was a B.XVI built at Hatfield in 1944 and seen serving with No. 571 Sqn based at Oakington, Cambridgeshire. The Mk XVI was a development of the Mk IX but with a pressurised cockpit and increased internal fuel. Most could carry a 1814-kg (4,000-lb) bomb.

The Mosquito was one of the most heavily armed aircraft operated by the Allies during World War II, and its capacity to accommodate each new innovation of the armourers never ceased. The standard fighter aircraft, like this FB Mk VI, carried four .303-in machine-guns in addition to a further four 20-mm cannon. At the same time, they were also intended to carry four 500-lb bombs. Operating at night, the FB.VIs made places like the Falaise gap a far worse place to be after the sun had set for the retreating Wermacht armies. For a month after D-Day, Mosquitoes flew over France every night attacking German lines of communication. Even when the weather was too bad for them to attack their targets, the knowledge that they were waiting above the clouds was enough to prevent the Germans from moving.

A particularly versatile mark, the Royal Navy's TR.33 could carry a wide range of offensive stores, including (as shown) a 457-mm (18-in) torpedo. It also had radar, four cannon and full carrier equipment. Prior to delivery of this fully-developed, Leavesden-built series, the Fleet Air Arm used 'hooked' Mk VIs.

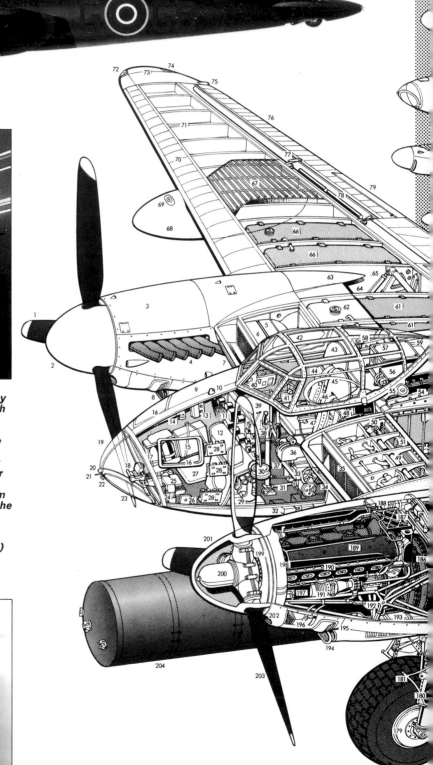

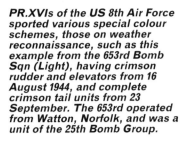

PR.XVIs of the US 8th Air Force sported various special colour schemes, those on weather reconnaissance, such as this example from the 653rd Bomb Sqn (Light), having crimson rudder and elevators from 16 August 1944, and complete crimson tail units from 23 September. The 653rd operated from Watton, Norfolk, and was a unit of the 25th Bomb Group.

de Havilland Mosquito B.XVI cutaway drawing key

1 Three-bladed de Havilland type 5000 hydromatic propeller
2 Spinner
3 Starboard engine cowling panels, Merlin 73 engine
4 Exhaust stubs
5 Starboard oil radiator
6 Coolant radiator
7 Radiator air intake
8 Carburettor air intake and guard
9 Fuselage nose skinning
10 Windscreen de-icing fluid nozzle
11 Instrument panel
12 Parachute stowage
13 Junction box
14 Fire axe
15 SYKO apparatus stowage
16 Nose compartment side windows
17 Portable oxygen bottles
18 Mk XIV bombsight
19 Nose glazing
20 Forward navigation/ identification light
21 Temperature probe
22 Windscreen de-icing fluid nozzle
23 Optically flat bomb aiming window
24 Bomb sight mounting
25 Bomb selector switches
26 Camera remote control box
27 Bomb aimer's kneeling cushion
28 Signal pistol cartridge racks
29 Rudder pedals
30 Compass
31 Control linkages

32 Oxygen system economizer units
33 Elevator trim handwheel
34 Port radiator ram air intake
35 Oil and coolant radiators
36 Engine throttle levers
37 Ventral entry hatch
38 Control column handwheel
39 Folding chart table
40 Windscreen panels
41 Trailing aerial winch
42 Cockpit roof escape hatch
43 Seat back armour plate
44 Navigator/bombadier's seat
45 Rearward vision blister fairing
46 Pilot's seat
47 Intercom socket

48 Portable fire extinguisher
49 Cabin pressurization and heating air ducts
50 Non-return air valve
51 Engine control runs
52 Wing root rib
53 Centre section fuel tanks (two), capacity 68-Imp gal (309 litres) each (restricted to 46-Imp gal (209 litres) port and 47½-Imp gal (216 litres) starboard with 4000-lb (1815-kg) bomb load)
54 Wing upper surface attachment joint
55 Centre fuel tank filler cap
56 ARI-5083 receiver
57 IFF transmitter/receiver
58 Signal pistol aperture
59 Cockpit aft glazing
60 Rear pressure bulkhead

61 Starboard inboard fuel tanks, capacity 78 Imp gal (355 litres) inner and 65.5 Imp gal (298 litres) outer
62 Fuel filler cap
63 Nacelle fairing
64 Starboard main undercarriage bay
65 Hydraulic retraction jack
66 Outboard fuel tanks, 34-Imp gal (155 litres) inner and 24-Imp gal (109 litres) outer
67 Wing stringers
68 Starboard auxiliary fuel tank, capacity 50-Imp gal (227 litres)
69 Fuel filler cap
70 Plywood leading edge skinning
71 Wing top skin panelling, double plywood sandwich construction
72 Starboard navigation light
73 Wing tip fairing
74 Formation light
75 Resin light
76 Starboard aileron
77 Aileron hinge control
78 Mass balance weights
79 Aileron tab
80 Underside view showing bulged (increased volume) bomb bay doors
81 Ventral entry hatch with drift sight aperture
82 Trailing aerial fairing
83 Starboard outer plain flap segment
84 Flap hydraulic jack
85 Nacelle tail fairing
86 Flap inboard segment
87 Oil filler cap
88 Dinghy access panel
89 Two-man dinghy stowage compartment
90 Wing fixing bearer
91 Rear fuselage equipment heater air ducting
92 Long range oil tank, capacity 10 Imp gal (45 litres)
93 Hydraulic reservoir
94 TR1143 transmitter/ receiver
95 Mk XIV bomb sight computer

96 Batteries
97 Hydraulic and pneumatic systems servicing panel
98 Pneumatic system air bottle
99 De-icing fluid reservoir
100 Picketing equipment stowage
101 Camera motor
102 TR1143 aerial
103 Fuselage stringers, between inner and outer skin laminations
104 Heat conserving canvas bulkhead cover
105 Fuselage half shell sandwich skin construction (plywood/balsa/plywood)
106 Diagonal graining pattern
107 Centreline fuselage half shell joint strip
108 Rudder control linkage
109 Fin attachment bulkhead
110 Rudder mass balance weight
111 Ferrite aerial rod
112 Tailfin construction
113 Starboard tailplane
114 Elevator horn balance
115 Pitot tube
116 Rudder horn balance
117 Fabric covered rudder construction
118 Rudder tab
119 Tab operating rod
120 Elevator tabs
121 Tailcone
122 Tail navigation lights
123 Fabric covered elevator construction
124 Tailplane construction
125 Ferrite aerial rod
126 Elevator operating linkage
127 Tailwheel housing
128 Tailplane spar attachment joint
129 Tailwheel leg strut
130 Retracting tailwheel
131 Levered suspension tailwheel forks
132 Fuselage skin fabric covering
133 Identification code lights, white, amber and green
134 Beam approach aerial
135 Camera mounting
136 F.24 Camera
137 Tailplane control cables
138 Rear fuselage entry hatch
139 Crew equipment stowage bag
140 Bulged bomb bay tail fairing
141 Bomb door hydraulic jacks
142 Beam approach receiver
143 Oxygen bottles

144 Flap shroud ribs
145 Inboard fuel tank bay ventral access panel
146 Bomb carriers
147 500-lb (227-kg) short-finned HE bombs (4)
148 Port engine nacelle top fairing
149 Main undercarriage hydraulic retraction jack
150 Undercarriage leg rear strut mounting
151 Flap hydraulic jack
152 Nacelle tail fairing
153 Port plain flap segments
154 All-wooden flap construction
155 Port outer fuel tanks
156 Fuel filler cap
157 Retractable landing lamp
158 Aileron tab control linkage
159 Rear spar
160 Aileron hinge control
161 Aileron tab
162 Aluminium aileron construction
163 Resin lamp
164 Port formation lamp
165 Detachable wing tip fairing
166 Port navigation light
167 Leading edge nose ribs
168 Front spar, box beam construction
169 Wing lower surface single skin/stringer panel
170 Wing rib construction
171 Plywood leading edge skinning, fabric covered
172 Port auxiliary fuel tank, capacity 50 Imp gal (227 litres)
173 Fuel filler cap
174 Main undercarriage rear strut
175 Mudguard
176 Mainwheel doors
177 Port mainwheel
178 Mainwheel leg strut
179 Pneumatic brake disc
180 Rubber compression block shock absorber
181 Spring loaded door guides
182 Main undercarriage pivot fixing
183 Engine oil tank, capacity 16 Imp gal (73 litres)
184 Cabin heater
185 Fireproof bulkhead
186 Two-stage supercharger
187 Intercooler
188 Heywood compressor
189 Rolls-Royce Merlin 72, 12-cylinder Vee engine
190 Exhaust ports
191 Alternator
192 Engine bearers
193 Carburettor air intake duct
194 Intake guard
195 Intercooler radiator exhaust
196 Intercooler radiator
197 Engine mounting block
198 Coolant header tank
199 Spinner armoured backplate
200 Propeller hub pitch change mechanism
201 Spinner
202 Intercooler radiator intake
203 Port 3-bladed de Havilland hydromatic propeller
204 4000-lb (1815-kg) HC bomb

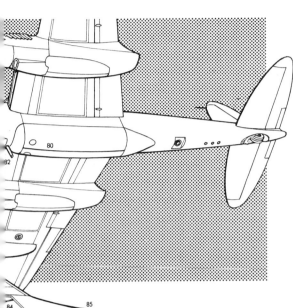

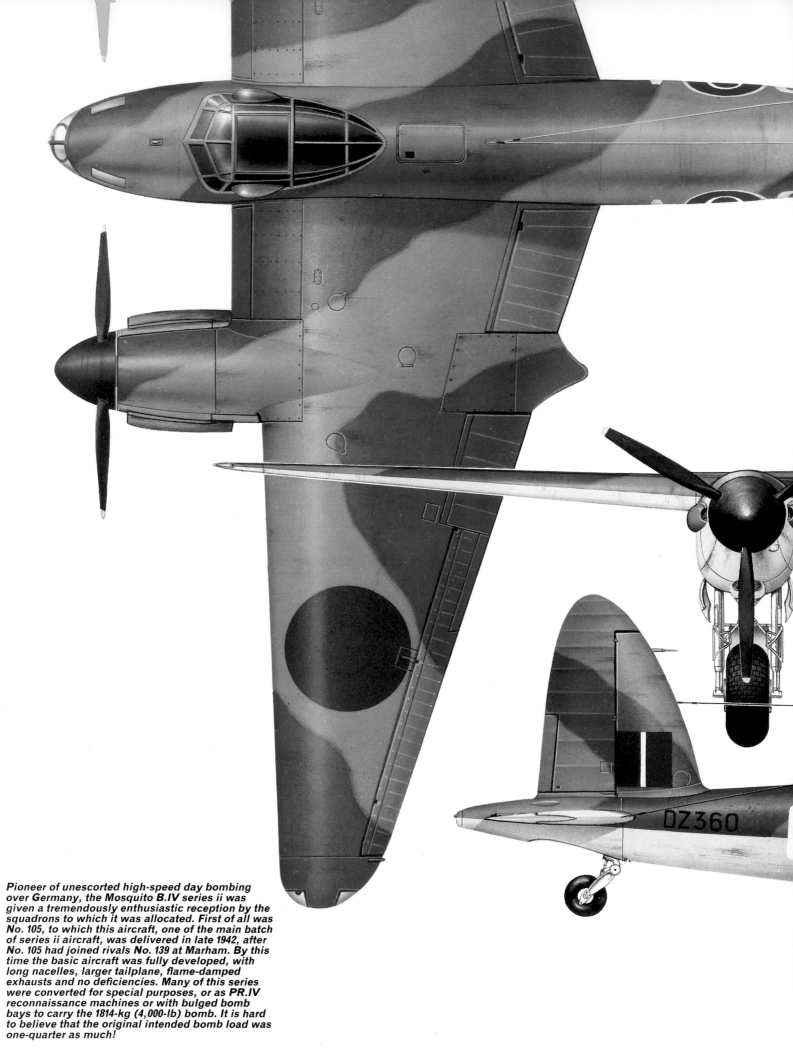

Pioneer of unescorted high-speed day bombing over Germany, the Mosquito B.IV series ii was given a tremendously enthusiastic reception by the squadrons to which it was allocated. First of all was No. 105, to which this aircraft, one of the main batch of series ii aircraft, was delivered in late 1942, after No. 105 had joined rivals No. 139 at Marham. By this time the basic aircraft was fully developed, with long nacelles, larger tailplane, flame-damped exhausts and no deficiencies. Many of this series were converted for special purposes, or as PR.IV reconnaissance machines or with bulged bomb bays to carry the 1814-kg (4,000-lb) bomb. It is hard to believe that the original intended bomb load was one-quarter as much!

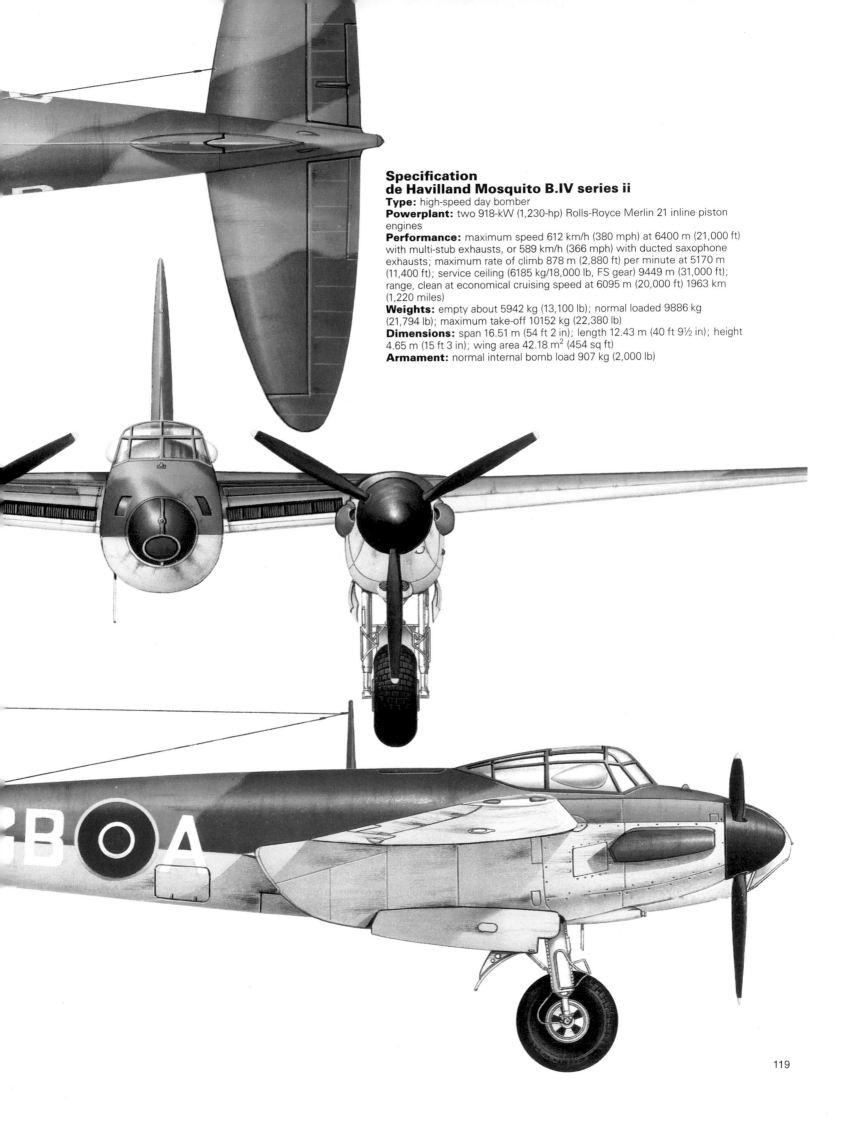

**Specification
de Havilland Mosquito B.IV series ii**

Type: high-speed day bomber

Powerplant: two 918-kW (1,230-hp) Rolls-Royce Merlin 21 inline piston engines

Performance: maximum speed 612 km/h (380 mph) at 6400 m (21,000 ft) with multi-stub exhausts, or 589 km/h (366 mph) with ducted saxophone exhausts; maximum rate of climb 878 m (2,880 ft) per minute at 5170 m (11,400 ft); service ceiling (6185 kg/18,000 lb, FS gear) 9449 m (31,000 ft); range, clean at economical cruising speed at 6095 m (20,000 ft) 1963 km (1,220 miles)

Weights: empty about 5942 kg (13,100 lb); normal loaded 9886 kg (21,794 lb); maximum take-off 10152 kg (22,380 lb)

Dimensions: span 16.51 m (54 ft 2 in); length 12.43 m (40 ft 9½ in); height 4.65 m (15 ft 3 in); wing area 42.18 m² (454 sq ft)

Armament: normal internal bomb load 907 kg (2,000 lb)

de Havilland Mosquito

Though the RAAF took virtually all the 212 Mosquitoes produced (with increasing local content) by DH Australia at Sydney Bankstown, this machine was one of 38 FB.VI imported from Britain and assigned to RAAF No. 1 Sqn. The RAAF serial number system reflects the aircraft type, A52 as a prefix indicating a Mosquito.

Mosquitoes were also active at sea. Usually operating in pairs and armed with rockets, they hunted Kriegsmarine U-boats and made short work of any that were unlucky enough to be found on the surface.

By far the most important mark, the FB.VI (here belonging to No. 143 Sqn, Banff, 1945) combined the full forward-firing armament of four 20-mm cannon and four machine-guns with the ability to carry two 113-kg (250-lb) bombs in the rear bomb bay plus two of 227 kg (500 lb) or, as seen here, eight rockets, under the outer wings.

eliminated. Though the aircraft had only managed to survive by being a reconnaissance machine, its brilliant performance now opened the way to bomber and fighter roles. By summer 1941 many ideas were being drawn or tested, including the fitting of Merlin 60-series two-stage engines; four-bladed propellers; span increased to pointed tips at 19.81 m (65 ft 0 in), though in fact only half this extension was the limit, flown on the high-altitude MP469 in 1942 and leading to the F.XV; and, most importantly, fitting guns and bombs. Bishop had always ensured there was room under the floor for four 20-mm Hispano cannon, and in 1942 the F.II night-fighter went into production with these guns plus four 7.7-mm (0.303-in) Brownings in the nose, plus the new AI Mk IV radar. The fighter had a side door instead of a hatch in the underside of the nose, and a flat armoured windscreen.

B.IV – bombing and reconnaissance

As for the bomber, in October 1941 Wilkins suggested that the 227-kg (500-lb) bomb should have short or retractable tailfins; then four could be carried. This was at first rejected, but after prolonged tests it was found to be perfectly feasible and the standard bomb was made with shorter fins. Thus the bombload was doubled at a stroke, and the B.IV went into production alongside the fighter in 1942. The T.III dual trainer flew in January 1942 but was mainly built post-war, such was the demand for operational Mosquitoes. Meanwhile, the

NS777 was a Hatfield-built PR.XVI, very similar to the B.XVI but with cameras instead of bombs in the main internal bay. It is seen in PRU Blue, with D-Day 'invasion stripes' as carried by all aircraft of the Allied Expeditionary Air Forces.

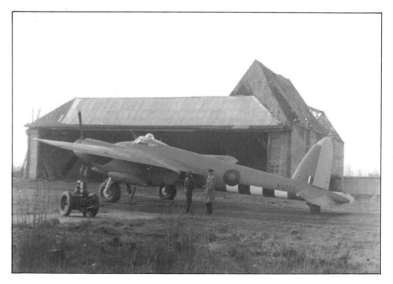

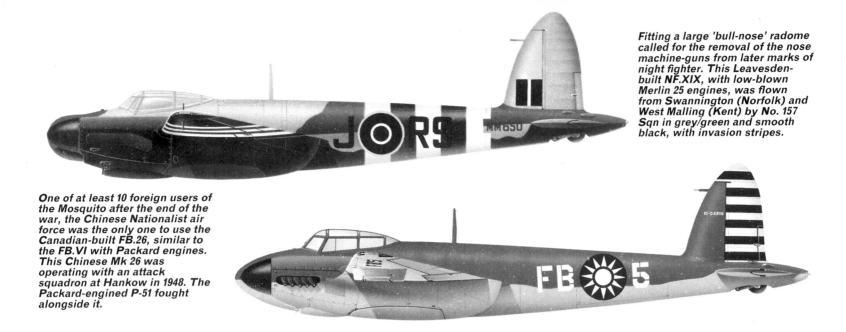

Fitting a large 'bull-nose' radome called for the removal of the nose machine-guns from later marks of night fighter. This Leavesden-built NF.XIX, with low-blown Merlin 25 engines, was flown from Swannington (Norfolk) and West Malling (Kent) by No. 157 Sqn in grey/green and smooth black, with invasion stripes.

One of at least 10 foreign users of the Mosquito after the end of the war, the Chinese Nationalist air force was the only one to use the Canadian-built FB.26, similar to the FB.VI with Packard engines. This Chinese Mk 26 was operating with an attack squadron at Hankow in 1948. The Packard-engined P-51 fought alongside it.

original 49 short-nacelle aircraft entered service in summer 1941 as photo-reconnaissance machines or as conversions to B.IV series i bombers, all with the 907-kg (2,000-lb) bomb load. The first mission was a camera trip to Bordeaux and La Pallice on 17 September 1941 by W4055 of No. 1 PRU (Photographic Reconnaissance Unit).

Full-scale RAF service began with the B.IV series ii, the first definitive bomber version, which entered service with No. 105 Sqn of No. 2 Group at Swanton Morley in November 1941. Next came No. 139 Sqn at Marham. The first bomber mission was flown by just one aircraft, W4072 (a series i) of No. 105 Sqn at the end of the '1,000-bomber' raid on Cologne on 30-31 May 1942. After various ineffective sorties a daring attack was made on Gestapo HQ in Oslo, thwarted by the performance of the bombs; one failed to explode, though inside the building, while three others went out through the far wall before detonating. For the rest of the war the old B.IV, usually with 227-litre (50-Imp gal) underwing drop tanks, made daring precision attacks throughout Europe from tree-top height. More important even than this, 'Mossies' (pronounced Mozzies) were fitted with the precision navaid known as 'Oboe' and used as Pathfinder target markers, or on occasion to drop bombs with great accuracy on point targets. No. 109 Sqn was the first Oboe-Mosquito unit in No. 8 Group (PFF, or Pathfinder Force), later joined by nine other squadrons. They marked the targets for Bomber Command's 'Main Force'

on all subsequent heavy night raids, and formed the Light Night Striking Force for quite damaging nuisance raids on German cities.

By 1943 bomber production switched to the high-flying B.IX with two-stage Merlins, paddle-blade propellers and much increased high-altitude performance. In 1944 the B.IX and B.IV Special were fitted with modified bomb beams and bulged bomb bays to carry a 1814-kg (4,000-lb) bomb, four times the design bomb load. The B.XVI, first flown in November 1943, was a high-altitude bomber designed to carry this bomb from the start, and also fitted with a pressure cabin for routine operations at up to 10670 m (35,000 ft).

Special missions

The PR.IV was a camera variant of the B.IV series ii (32 delivered), but the B.V bomber was not built. Next came the FB.VI fighter-bomber, built in larger numbers (2,584) than any other of the 43 marks. First flown in June 1942, it had single-stage engines, the guns of the F.II, a short bomb bay for two 113-kg (250-lb) bombs and wing racks for two more 113-kg (250-lb) bombs or two 227-litre (50-Imp gal) drop tanks. With the FB.VI series ii the bomb size in the bomb bay and underwing was doubled, and other wing loads could be 455-litre (100-Imp gal) tanks or eight rockets. The versatile FB.VI ranged throughout Europe, hitting such point targets as the walls of Amiens prison, the Gestapo HQ at The Hague, Gestapo HQ at

A Mosquito Mk VI (formerly FB.VI) of British Overseas Airways takes off on a night transport mission to Sweden from RAF Leuchars. These aircraft flew VIPs and escaped POWs into and out of this neutral country (hence the 'civil' insignia), plus other vital cargoes including Swedish ball bearings.

After the war the Royal Norwegian air force was one of numerous foreign air forces that operated Mosquitoes. This FB.VI served with RNorAF No. 334 Squadron from Stavanger/Sola. This unit was originally B Flight of No. 333 Sqn operating the same aircraft with the RAF strike wing from Banff, Scotland, in 1943.

de Havilland Mosquito

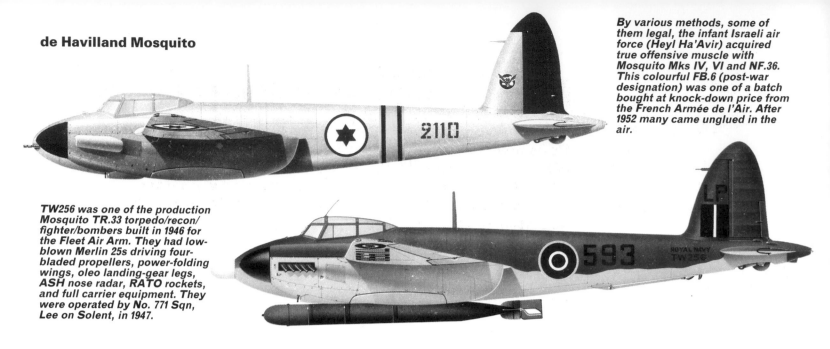

By various methods, some of them legal, the infant Israeli air force (Heyl Ha'Avir) acquired true offensive muscle with Mosquito Mks IV, VI and NF.36. This colourful FB.6 (post-war designation) was one of a batch bought at knock-down price from the French Armée de l'Air. After 1952 many came unglued in the air.

TW256 was one of the production Mosquito TR.33 torpedo/recon/fighter/bombers built in 1946 for the Fleet Air Arm. They had low-blown Merlin 25s driving four-bladed propellers, power-folding wings, oleo landing-gear legs, ASH nose radar, RATO rockets, and full carrier equipment. They were operated by No. 771 Sqn, Lee on Solent, in 1947.

Copenhagen, and numerous V-weapon sites; they were among various Mosquitoes that destroyed 428 V-1 flying bombs in the air, and this mark, backed up by the Mk XVIII with a 57-mm gun, was the chief attack weapon of Coastal Command against surface ships from mid-1943, using guns, bombs and rockets.

After the F.II the chief night-fighters were the NF.XII and NF.XIII, in which the harpoon-like aerials of AI Mk II gave way to bluff radomes on the nose which required removal of the machine-guns. In the NF.XII the radar was the British AI Mk VIII, while the NF.XIII had a blunter 'bull nose' which alternatively could accommodate American AI Mk X (SCR-720). A handful were built of the long-span F.XV already mentioned, and the designation NF.XVII was allotted to 100 NF.XIIIs with SCR-720. The NF.XIX was an improved but heavier NF.XIII (230 built in late 1944). A big jump in performance came when a fighter Mosquito was fitted with two-stage engines, the resulting NF.XXX (or NF.30) becoming extremely important and effective in the final year of the European war. Though weighing up to 10730 kg (23,650 lb), it reached 682 km/h (424 mph) and carried many EW (electronic warfare) devices such as 'Perfectos' and 'Airborne Cigar' spoofing/jamming gear; six squadrons of NF.XXXs operated with No. 100 Group on bomber support missions, as well as with night-fighter units.

Many marks flew with all Allied air forces, including the Red air force and the USAAF, the latter using Canadian-built aircraft as the F-8 reconnaissance version as well as the British-built T.III and PR.XVI. De Havilland Aircraft of Canada at Downsview built a series of variants from Mks 21 to 29, with Packard engines (see variants list) while DH Australia at Bankstown built the Mks 40 to 43. All these were based on the FB.VI. At home, production was supported by a vast array of subcontractors, furniture and piano makers and even tiny groups in cottage back rooms, with assembly lines at DH Hatfield, DH Plant 2 at Leavesden (Watford), Percival Aircraft at Luton, Standard Motors at Canley (Coventry) and Airspeed at Portsmouth.

Post-war variants

In addition to 10 civil Mosquitoes (a B.IV 'ii' and nine FB.VIs) used by BOAC on urgent services with cargo and passengers between the UK and Sweden (and occasionally other places), there were various later marks that did not see war service. The heaviest and highest-performing of all versions were the closely related PR.34, B.35 and NF.36. All had the high-altitude Merlin 113A/114A and broad paddle-bladed propellers. The PR.34 was the longest-ranged of all marks, with a swollen belly housing some of the remarkable load of 5769 litres (1,269 Imp gal) of fuel. Though it weighed up to 11567 kg (25,500 lb), it could reach 684 km/h (425 mph) and cruise for 5633 km (3,500 miles). A PR.34A made the RAF's last Mosquito mission with No. 81 Sqn in Malaya on 15 December 1955. The B.35

was the ultimate bomber mark, with a pressurised cockpit and weighing up to 11431 kg (25,200 lb) with a 1814-kg (4,000-lb) bomb and 2714 litres (597 Imp gal) internal fuel for a range of about 3220 km (2,000 miles) at over 483 km/h (300 mph), maximum speed being 679 km/h (422 mph). It just missed the war and served until replaced by Canberras from 1951, many being converted into PR.35s or TT.35s. The corresponding night-fighter was the NF.36, with American AI Mk 10 radar; the NF.38 export variant for Yugoslavia had British AI Mk IX. There were also numerous Sea Mosquito variants, of which the most important was the TR.33. The last of 7,781 Mosquitoes was VX916, an NF.38 delivered from Chester on 28 November 1950. It was the 6,439th built in England; Canadian production totalled 1,034 and Australian 212. Post-war air forces using Mosquitoes, included those of Belgium, China, Czechoslovakia, Denmark, Dominica, France, Israel, Norway, South Africa, Sweden, Turkey and Yugoslavia.

de Havilland Mosquito variants

D.H.98: prototype, two 955-kW (1,280-hp) Rolls-Royce Merlin RM.3SM, span 16.00 m (52 ft 6 in), short nacelles
PR.1: Merlin 21, short nacelles, 16.51 m (54 ft 2 in) span, larger tailplane, three vertical and one oblique cameras (total 1 prototype and 10 production)
F.II: Merlin 21, 22 or 23 AI Mk IV radar, four 20-mm and four 7.7-mm (0.303-in) guns, side door, flat windscreen, long nacelles (total 467)
T.III: dual trainer, Merlin 21, 23 or 25, drop tanks (total 343)
B.IV series i: converted PR.I, 907-kg (2,000-lb) bomb load, short nacelles (total 273)
B.IV series ii: first production bomber, Merlin 21 or 23, drop tanks, some with bomb bay for 1814-kg (4,000-lb) bomb; some converted as PR.IV, others for 'Highball' (Wallis skipping bomb) (total 235, including 32 PR.IV)
FB.VI: fighter-bomber, Merlin 21, 23 or 25, F.II guns plus two 227-kg (500-lb) bombs internal plus drop tanks/bombs/rockets (total 2,248)
B.VII: Canadian-built B.IV ii, Merlin 31 (total 25)
PR.VIII: photo version of PR.IV with Merlin 61 (total 5)
B.IX: high-altitude bomber, Merlin 72/73 or 76/77, up to 1814 kg (4,000 lb) of bombs, some H₂S Mk VI radar/Oboe/drop tanks; **PR.IX** photo version of PR.IX, very wide range of electronic fits (total 4 B.IX and 90 PR.IX)
NF.XII: night-fighter, Merlin 21 or 23, AI Mk VIII in thimble nose, four 20-mm only (total 97 conversions from F.NF.II)
NF.XIII: night-fighter, Merlin 21, 23 or 25, Mk VI wings suitable for tanks/bombs/rockets, AI Mk VIII or SCR-720 in universal 'bull' nose (total 270)
NF.XV: high-altitude fighter, long-span (18.03 m/59 ft 2 in) wing, Merlin 73 or 77, four 7.7-mm (0.303-in) guns in ventral pack, reduced fuel, pressure cabin (total 5 conversions from B.IV)
PR.XVI, B.XVI: photo and bomber models with Mk IX engines but pressure cabin, increased fuel as PR.IX, very wide range of electronic fits (total 433 PR.XVI and 1,200 B.XVI)
NF.XVII: Merlin 21 or 23, SCR-720 or 729 (AI

Mk X) radar, some with tail warning (total 100 conversions from F./NF.II)
FB.XVIII: 'Tse Tse Fly', Merlin 25, FB.VI with Molins 57-mm gun with 25 rounds, plus four 7.7-mm (0.303-in) guns and eight rockets (total 25)
NF.XIX: Merlin 25, night-fighter based on Mk XIII (total 220)
B.XX: Canadian B.IV ii, Packard Merlin 31 or 33 (total 145, including 40 **F-8**)
FB.21: Canadian FB.VI (total 3)
T.22: Canadian TIII
B.25: improved B.XX, Merlin 225 (total 400)
FB.26: improved Mk 21, Merlin 225 (total 338)
T.27: improved T.22, Merlin 225
T.29: trainer conversion of Mk 26
NF.XXX: high-altitude night-fighter, Merlin 72 or 76, AI Mk X (total 526)
PR.32: photo aircraft, Merlin 113/114, pressurised (total 5 conversions)
TF. (later TR.) 33: naval torpedo/reconnaissance fighter for carrier use, Merlin 25, four-bladed propellers, oleo legs, folding wings, hook, JATO gear, ASH nose radar, four 20-mm guns, internal bombload or 907-kg (2,000-lb) torpedo or mine
PR.34: long-range photo, Merlin 114 (Mk 34A, Merlin 114A), pressurised, exceptional fuel capacity (total 50)
B.35: long-range bomber, Merlin 113A/114A, pressurised, could carry 2714 litres (597 Imp gal) plus 1814-kg (4,000-lb) bomb; post-war conversions to **PR.35** and **TT.35** (total 122)
NF.36: night-fighter with Merlin 113/114, AI Mk X radar (total 266)
TT.37: variant of TR.33 with ASV Mk XIII radar
NF.38: variant of Mk 36 with Merlin 114A, usually AI Mk IX radar (total 50)
TT.39: conversion of Mk XVI by General Aircraft as Royal Navy target-tug, new forward fuselage, 13.21 m (43 ft 4 in) long
FB.40: Australian Mk VI, Packard Merlin 31 or 33 (total 178)
FB.41: Australian photo aircraft based on Mks XVI and 40, Packard Merlin 69
FB.42: Australian Mk VI with Merlin 69 (total 1 conversion from FB.40)
T.43: Australian T.III, Packard Merlin 33

Bristol Blenheim

The Blenheim light bomber was one of several aircraft which owed their existence to the vision of a few far-sighted individuals in the years leading up to World War II. Sadly it failed to live up to expectations and with the outbreak of war it was meat for the hungry German fighters. However, it survived in various other forms, most notably as a night-fighter, with many air forces till the end of hostilities.

Just as the Supermarine Spitfire could trace its origins to the bene-faction of Lady Houstone in safeguarding the UK's entry in the final Schneider Trophy race, so the Bristol Blenheim owed its acceptance as a military aircraft to the generosity, foresight and patriotism of Lord Rothermere, proprietor of the *Daily Mail* newspaper.

Believing that the UK was likely to be eclipsed in the commercial field of aviation by such promising aircraft as the Douglas DC-2 in 1934, Rothermere ordered from the Bristol Aeroplane Company a six-passenger twin-engine aircraft capable of a speed of around 386 km/h (240 mph). The resulting design by Frank Barnwell was the Bristol Type 142 with two 485-kW (650-hp) Bristol Mercury VIS2 radial engines, a design that was to some extent influenced by a Finnish government requirement for an aircraft that might be adaptable for military use as a light bomber. Early in 1935 the British Air Ministry began to show interest in the new prototype, and when tested at the RAF Martlesham Heath establishment it proved to be 80 km/h (50 mph) faster than the Gladiator fighter prototype. So enthusiastic was the RAF with the new twin-engine monoplane as a potential bomber that, after naming it *Britain First*, Lord Rothermere presented it to the Air Council. In September 1935 Bristol received a contract for 150 light bombers based on the commercial prototype, designated Bristol Type 142M and designed to Specification 28/35.

To permit the fuselage to accommodate a bombload of four 113-kg (250-lb) bombs carried internally, the wing was changed from low to mid position, allowing the bomb bay to be located below the wing spars; a single forward-firing rifle-calibre Browning gun was included, as well as a partly-retractable B.I. Mark I turret amidships with a single Lewis gun. To meet military load factors the airframe was strengthened, and a crew of three (pilot, navigator/bomb-aimer and gunner) was to be carried.

Despite Air Council plans to adopt the new aircraft (named the Blenheim in April 1936) as a replacement for the widely-used Hawker Hind light bomber, Bristol was permitted to negotiate limited export orders with friendly governments, the orders to be fulfilled after the RAF's initial needs had been satisfied. The prototype Blenheim (K7033) was flown on 25 June 1936, and production got under way the following December, an order for 434 further aircraft having been placed in July.

First RAF squadron to take delivery of the Blenheim was No. 114 (Bomber) Squadron at Wyton on 10 March 1937 (the first such aircraft being written off on delivery when the pilot applied the wheel-brakes too harshly, causing the machine to overturn). By the end of the year production at Filton had reached a rate of 24 aircraft a

No 139 Squadron was one of the Blenheim Mk IV units sent to France with the BEF, this trio being seen near the unit's base at Betheniville. Earlier the unit had been the first to enter German airspace in the war, flying a reconnaissance mission over the German fleet on 3 September 1939.

Bristol Blenheim

Painted all black, this is a Blenheim Mk IF night fighter, with AI (airborne interception) radar aerials mounted in the nose and on the port wing. This aircraft wears the 'YX' codes of No 54 OTU, a night fighter training outfit which produced Beaufighter and Mosquito crews.

Shot from the downward-looking camera of a reconnaissance aircraft, this picture shows how effective the dark green/dark earth camouflage was. In the shot is a Blenheim Mk IV.

month, and Nos 44, 90, 139 and 144 (Bomber) Squadrons had also discarded Hinds, Hawker Audaxes and Avro Ansons in favour of the new light bomber. The next year Nos 21, 30, 34, 57, 61, 62, 82, 101, 104, 107, 108 and 110 (Bomber) Squadrons followed.

Early impressions

The Blenheim Mk I proved fairly popular in service, the aircraft being pleasant to fly; the cockpit was roomy and well designed for the pilot, although cramped and awkwardly arranged for the navigator. The field of vision was good, yet the aircraft proved to have many vulnerable areas of defence. In the absence of reliable information about continental light bombers, the Blenheim was thought to be ahead of the world in a balanced assessment of bombload, range and speed, a belief successfully fostered among some foreign governments; exported Blenheims included 18 to Finland (followed eventually by licence production at Tampere), two to Yugoslavia where 16 were subsequently produced under licence, 30 to Turkey and 13 to Romania.

1938 was to prove a year of shattered illusions, however, not least for the RAF. The relatively puny bombload and in-service top speed of 418 km/h (260 mph) of the Blenheim Mk I were seen to be eclipsed

At the outbreak of war in Europe, the Blenheim Mk IV was the mainstay of the light bomber squadrons, and bore the brunt of early cross-Channel raids against German positions. Blenheims were also used by the British Expeditionary Force in France.

by German aircraft, while reports of the new Junkers Ju 88 suggested that the Blenheim would be hopelessly outclassed within a year. Moreoever, even in the UK, where performance comparisons

The Blenheim proved easy to operate in primitive conditions, easily maintainable with rudimentary equipment. Here ground crew work on the Mercury engine and the wing gun.

No 40 Squadron, RAF, was assigned Blenheim Mk IVs in December 1939 to replace Fairey Battles following an unhappy excursion into France. The Blenheims were used for cross-Channel operations until November 1940, when Vickers Wellingtons were received.

of an altogether new design. Subsequent events were to confirm the correctness of this decision, for all the criticism levelled at the Blenheim.

In the meantime, under the auspices of the new Shadow Factory scheme, Blenheim Mk Is were also being built by Rootes Securities Ltd at Speke and by A. V. Roe and Co. Ltd at Chadderton, so that by early 1939 the total production of this version had reached 1,552. And while RAF bomber squadrons continued to convert to Blenheim Mk Is, a new variant of the Mk I had been introduced to Fighter Command. This was the Mk IF night-fighter with four forward-firing Browning guns in a ventral pack (produced by the Ashford works of the Southern Railway), Nos 23, 25, 29 and 64 (Fighter) Squadrons being so equipped in December 1938, and Nos 600, 601 and 604 Squadrons of the Auxiliary Air Force during the next month.

Doubtful improvements

Initial attempts to improve the Blenheim had been confined to increasing its bombload and range, the Mk II featuring additional fuel tanks in the outer wings and provision to carry two additional 113-kg (250-lb) bombs under the wings inboard of the engines; to cater for the increased weight (6,350 kg/14,000 lb) the landing gear was also strengthened. The 627-kW (840-hp) Mercury VIII engines of the Mk I were retained, so that the top speed fell to 380 km/h (236 mph), thereby fuelling further criticism of the aircraft. Not surprisingly this version was shelved after a single aircraft had been modified.

A development of the Blenheim, the Type 149, had been pursued to meet Specification 11/36 and this had been given the name Bolingbroke. To improve the navigator's station the nose of the Blenheim was lengthened by 0.91 m (3 ft), but when the prototype (a converted Blenheim Mk I) was flown, it was criticised on account of the distance of the windscreen from the pilot, resulting in a change to a

with those of fighters had long since been invalidated by the appearance of the Hawker Hurricane and Spitfire, the 1938 Air Exercises proved the bomber to be fatally slow, vulnerable and undergunned. But such was the production momentum associated with the various expansion programmes being undertaken by the British aircraft industry in the pre-war years that it was decided to opt for an improved version of the Blenheim, rather than to attempt a hurried evolution

Bristol Blenheim

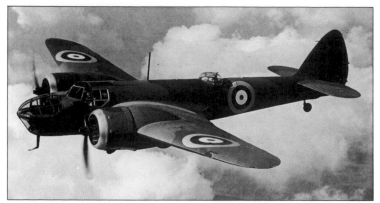

An early production Blenheim Mk IV, seen here prior to delivery to the RAF. Shown to good advantage here is the characteristic 'scalloped' nose, with the pilot's archaic 'ring-and-bead' gunsight.

The introduction into service of the Blenheim Mk V in 1942 was an anachronism, its poor performance resulting in heavy losses to German fighters, and it was hurriedly withdrawn from service in Europe – although it continued to serve in the Far East.

conventional, stepped-down, V-frame screen and a scalloping of the port-side nose decking. To avoid disrupting production, other changes in the design (other than adoption of 686-kW/920-hp Mercury XV engines) were discarded, and the 'long-nose' Blenheim Mk IV entered production early in 1939. With a top speed of 428 km/h (266 mph) and a maximum range increased to 3138 km (1,950 miles) the Blenheim Mk IV joined No. 53 (Bomber) Squadron at Odiham in January 1939, followed by Nos 90, 101, 113 and 114 in the next three months.

By the outbreak of World War II in September 1939, the RAF possessed 13 squadrons of Blenheims Mk IVs, of which one (No. 25) was flying a fighter version, the Mk IVF, modified in the same manner as the Mk IF with ventral gun pack. This squadron had for some months been pioneering the use of the world's first airborne radar interception equipment, albeit with little early success.

The Blenheim at war

The early months of the so-called Phoney War found the Blenheims hard at work, seldom inflicting much damage on the enemy, but nonetheless providing hard-won lessons in the face of a superior Luftwaffe. Flown by Flying Officer A. Macpherson, a Blenheim Mk IV of No. 139 (Bomber) Squadron was the first RAF aircraft to enter German airspace in the war, carrying out a reconnaissance sortie on 3 September. The next day 10 Blenheims (from Nos 107 and 110 Squadrons) and eight Vickers Wellingtons attempted a raid on enemy shipping in Schilling Roads, four Blenheims and two Wellingtons being lost. Provoked by enemy minelaying in the North Sea, an

Blenheim Mk IVs take off for a mission 'somewhere in France'. The type suffered heavy losses at the hands of the Luftwaffe during the time in France, proving to be 'easy meat' for the Messerschmitt Bf 109.

Bristol Blenheim Mk IV cutaway drawing key

1 Starboard navigation light
2 Starboard formation light
3 Wing rib construction
4 Aileron control rod
5 Starboard aileron
6 Aileron tab
7 Starboard outer flap
18 Oil cooler ram air intakes
19 Propeller hub mechanism
20 De Havilland three-bladed propeller
21 Nose compartment glazing
22 Cabin air intake
23 Navigator/bombardier's instrument panel
24 Bomb aiming windows
25 Pitot tube
26 Rearward firing, ventral machine gun cupola
27 Browning 0.303-in (7.7-mm) machine-gun
28 Fireman's axe
29 Nose compartment escape hatch
30 Fire extinguisher
31 Chart table
32 Fixed foresight
33 Back of instrument panel
34 Foot boards

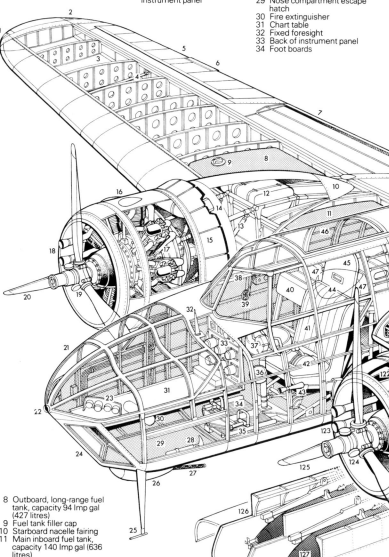

8 Outboard, long-range fuel tank, capacity 94 Imp gal (427 litres)
9 Fuel tank filler cap
10 Starboard nacelle fairing
11 Main inboard fuel tank, capacity 140 Imp gal (636 litres)
12 Oil tank, capacity 11.5 Imp gal (52 litres)
13 Engine bearers
14 Oil cooler exhaust duct
15 Engine cooling flaps
16 Cowling blister fairings
17 Bristol Mercury XV nine-cylinder radial engine

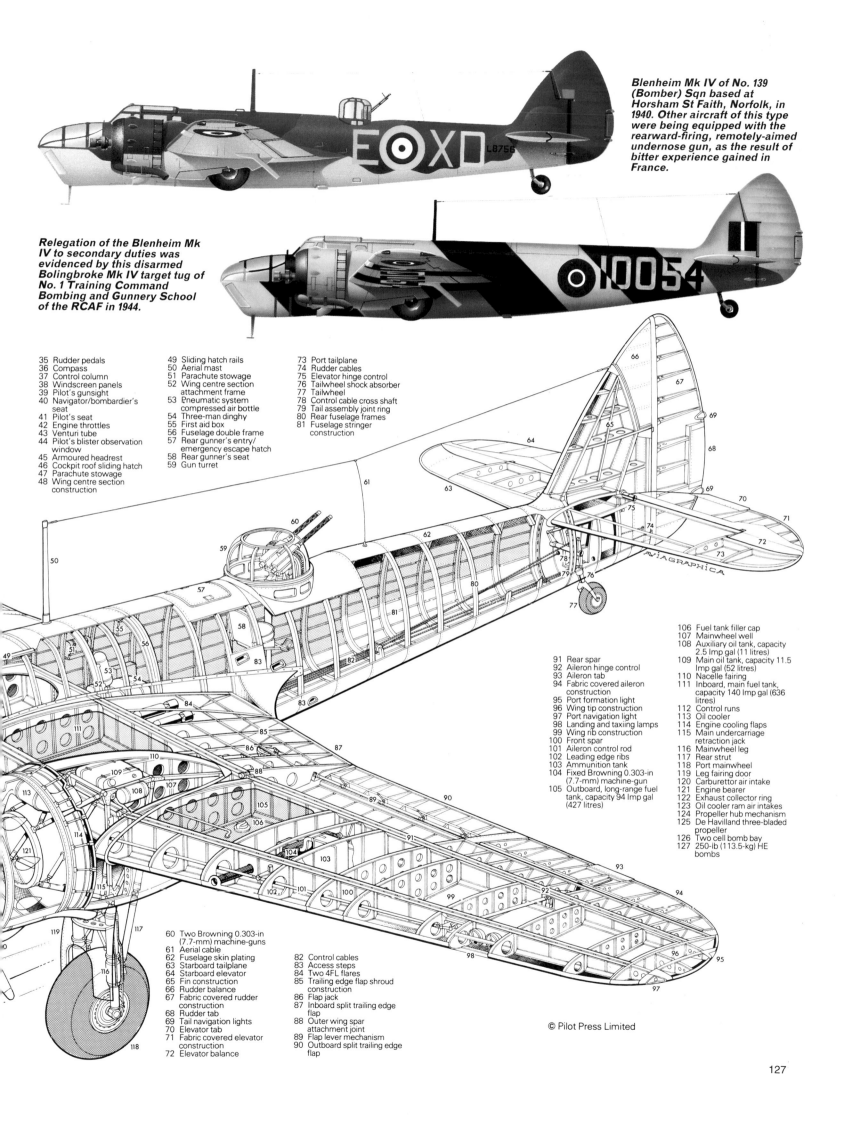

Blenheim Mk IV of No. 139 (Bomber) Sqn based at Horsham St Faith, Norfolk, in 1940. Other aircraft of this type were being equipped with the rearward-firing, remotely-aimed undernose gun, as the result of bitter experience gained in France.

Relegation of the Blenheim Mk IV to secondary duties was evidenced by this disarmed Bolingbroke Mk IV target tug of No. 1 Training Command Bombing and Gunnery School of the RCAF in 1944.

35 Rudder pedals
36 Compass
37 Control column
38 Windscreen panels
39 Pilot's gunsight
40 Navigator/bombardier's seat
41 Pilot's seat
42 Engine throttles
43 Venturi tube
44 Pilot's blister observation window
45 Armoured headrest
46 Cockpit roof sliding hatch
47 Parachute stowage
48 Wing centre section construction

49 Sliding hatch rails
50 Aerial mast
51 Parachute stowage
52 Wing centre section attachment frame
53 Pneumatic system compressed air bottle
54 Three-man dinghy
55 First aid box
56 Fuselage double frame
57 Rear gunner's entry/emergency escape hatch
58 Rear gunner's seat
59 Gun turret

73 Port tailplane
74 Rudder cables
75 Elevator hinge control
76 Tailwheel shock absorber
77 Tailwheel
78 Control cable cross shaft
79 Tail assembly joint ring
80 Rear fuselage frames
81 Fuselage stringer construction

91 Rear spar
92 Aileron hinge control
93 Aileron tab
94 Fabric covered aileron construction
95 Port formation light
96 Wing tip construction
97 Port navigation light
98 Landing and taxiing lamps
99 Wing rib construction
100 Front spar
101 Aileron control rod
102 Leading edge ribs
103 Ammunition tank
104 Fixed Browning 0.303-in (7.7-mm) machine-gun
105 Outboard, long-range fuel tank, capacity 94 Imp gal (427 litres)

106 Fuel tank filler cap
107 Mainwheel well
108 Auxiliary oil tank, capacity 2.5 Imp gal (11 litres)
109 Main oil tank, capacity 11.5 Imp gal (52 litres)
110 Nacelle fairing
111 Inboard, main fuel tank, capacity 140 Imp gal (636 litres)
112 Control runs
113 Oil cooler
114 Engine cooling flaps
115 Main undercarriage retraction jack
116 Mainwheel leg
117 Rear strut
118 Port mainwheel
119 Leg fairing door
120 Carburettor air intake
121 Engine bearer
122 Exhaust collector ring
123 Oil cooler ram air intakes
124 Propeller hub mechanism
125 De Havilland three-bladed propeller
126 Two cell bomb bay
127 250-lb (113.5-kg) HE bombs

60 Two Browning 0.303-in (7.7-mm) machine-guns
61 Aerial cable
62 Fuselage skin plating
63 Starboard tailplane
64 Starboard elevator
65 Fin construction
66 Rudder balance
67 Fabric covered rudder construction
68 Rudder tab
69 Tail navigation lights
70 Elevator tab
71 Fabric covered elevator construction
72 Elevator balance

82 Control cables
83 Access steps
84 Two 4FL flares
85 Trailing edge flap shroud construction
86 Flap jack
87 Inboard split trailing edge flap
88 Outer wing spar attachment joint
89 Flap lever mechanism
90 Outboard split trailing edge flap

© Pilot Press Limited

Bristol Blenheim

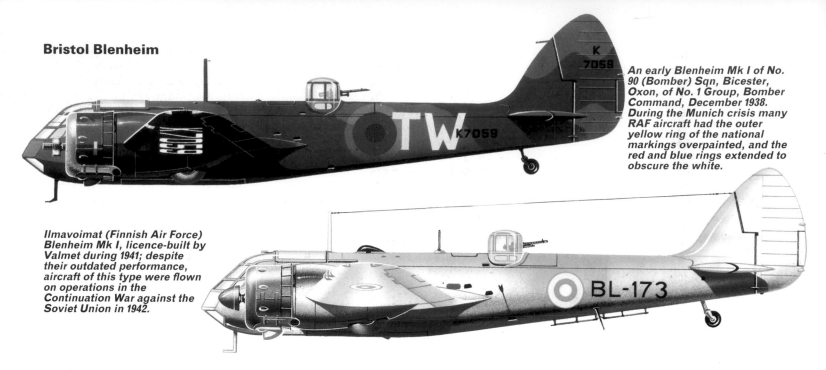

An early Blenheim Mk I of No. 90 (Bomber) Sqn, Bicester, Oxon, of No. 1 Group, Bomber Command, December 1938. During the Munich crisis many RAF aircraft had the outer yellow ring of the national markings overpainted, and the red and blue rings extended to obscure the white.

Ilmavoimat (Finnish Air Force) Blenheim Mk I, licence-built by Valmet during 1941; despite their outdated performance, aircraft of this type were flown on operations in the Continuation War against the Soviet Union in 1942.

attack by 12 Blenheim Mk IFs of Nos 25 and 601 Squadrons on the German seaplane base at Borkum on 25 November also proved a failure as a result of bad navigation.

Meanwhile six Blenheim Mk IV squadrons (Nos 18, 53, 57, 59, 114 and 139) had accompanied the British Expeditionary Force to France, their operations over Germany being first confined to reconnaissance missions because of the British government's reluctance to attack the enemy homeland. By the date (10 May 1940) of the German assault in the West, the number of Blenheim Mk IV squadrons had increased to 22 (including two fighter squadrons), and while the Blenheim Mk I bomber had been declared obsolete at home, the aircraft now equipped Nos 8, 30, 39, 45, 55, 84, 113 and 211 Squadrons in the Middle East, and Nos 11, 34, 60 and 62 Squadrons in the Far East, and No. 203 Squadron (with fighters) at Aden.

As the Battle of France moved inexorably towards defeat for the British and French armies, the Blenheim squadrons of the Air Component and Advanced Air Striking Force were in constant action, suffering heavily from German Flak and fighters. Similarly, home-based Blenheim fighters of No. 600 Squadron attempted raids over the Low Countries, only one of six aircraft returning from an attack on Waalhaven airfield.

Early operations

During the Battle of Britain RAF Fighter Command fielded six Blenheim Mk IF squadrons in the night-fighter role, although such limited success that attended their operations was gained more by day than by night. One notable exception to this was the world's first air victory using airborne radar, achieved by a Blenheim of the Fighter Interception Unit over a Dornier Do 17 during the night of 2/3 July 1940. Three other 'shipping protection' Blenheim squadrons of Coastal Command also came under Fighter Command control from time to time during the Battle of Britain.

Better success was gained by the Blenheim night-fighters as the German night Blitz increased in tempo during the winter of 1940-1, although the number of victories was rapidly overtaken by that of the new Beaufighter, to which the Blenheim gave place at that time.

If the Blenheim Mk I now dropped out of first line service in the UK, the Blenheim Mk IV continued in large-scale production, and by August 1941 there were no fewer than 30 first-line squadrons equipped with the bomber worldwide. This force, of which most was concentrated in Bomber Command's No. 2 Group, had been occupied since the fall of France in constant attacks against the enemy 'invasion ports' on the Channel coast, and later extended their operations further afield to the Norwegian, Danish, Dutch and Belgian coasts, often under heavy cover provided by RAF fighters. In one three-month period the Blenheims sank more than 300,000 tons of enemy shipping for the loss of 68 of their number. By the end of 1941 the Blenheim Mk IV was also beginning its phase-out (although it remained in combat service for another year), giving way to the Douglas Boston, Lockheed Ventura, and soon after these the de Havilland Mosquito. Among the memorable raids carried out by Blenheims was the low-level daylight attack by No. 105 Squadron

Early Blenheim Mk I bombers of an unknown RAF Bomber Command squadron, probably in mid-1938. The aircraft were inferior and vulnerable to the German contemporary aircraft, and when the RAF took their Blenheims to France in 1939-40 they were decimated.

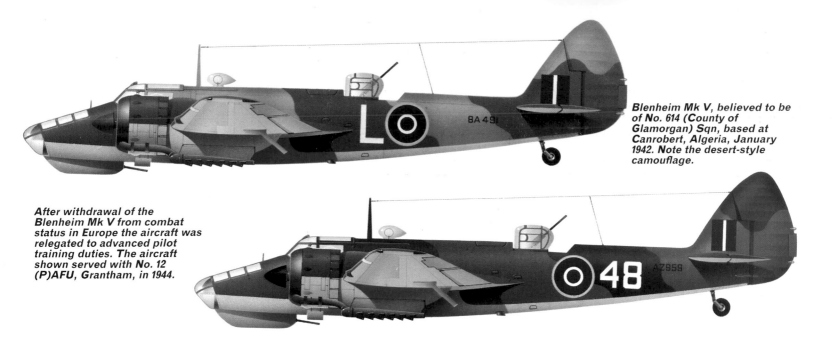

Blenheim Mk V, believed to be of No. 614 (County of Glamorgan) Sqn, based at Canrobert, Algeria, January 1942. Note the desert-style camouflage.

After withdrawal of the Blenheim Mk V from combat status in Europe the aircraft was relegated to advanced pilot training duties. The aircraft shown served with No. 12 (P)AFU, Grantham, in 1944.

against Bremen on 4 July 1941 (for which the leader, Wing Commander H. I. Edwards, was awarded the Victoria Cross), and a raid by 54 Blenheims on power stations near Cologne on 12 August.

A measure of the scale of effort by the Blenheims of Bomber Command during the first 34 months of the war may be gained by consideration of the 11,332 bombing sorties flown (compared with 11,074 by Short Stirlings in the entire war), and the dropping of 3,028 tons of bombs (compared with 1,826 tons by the Avro Manchester heavy bomber). Of course such figures were totally eclipsed later in the war when more than 5,000 tons would be dropped on a single target in a single raid.

Middle East operations

The Blenheim Mk I first appeared in the Middle East with No. 30 Squadron at the RAF base at Habbaniyah, Iraq, in January 1938, these aircraft being moved to Egypt on Italy's entry to the war in June 1940, and converted to fighters for escort duties and defence of the Canal Zone. During the ill-starred campaign in Greece two squadrons of Blenheim bombers and one of Blenheim fighters were sent from Egypt to join the 12 Blenheim Mk IVs of the Greek air force.

A constant flow of reinforcements reached Egypt from the United Kingdom, Blenheim Mk IVs flying direct to Malta (occasionally bombing Milan or Turin en route) and then on to Mersa Matruh. When fuel stocks on Malta began to dwindle, the Blenheims were shipped to Takoradi, whence they flew across Africa to Egypt.

The German victories in Yugoslavia (where the licence-built Blenheim Mk Is had carried out a single, desperate raid on Sofia) and Greece caused the loss of about 70 Blenheims, and it was the Blenheim fighters of Nos 30 and 203 Squadrons (the latter called from

Aden) that were called on to cover the evacuations of Crete.

As in northern Europe, the Blenheim Mk I was almost entirely replaced by the Mk IV during 1941-42, but meanwhile a new version, the Blenheim Mk V, had been undergoing development at Bristol. Evolved to Specification B.6/40, the aircraft was originally intended as a high-altitude bomber with 619-kW (830-hp) Mercury XXX engines; a two-seat close-support version, known as the Bisley, with a four-gun nose and increased armour protection, was developed in parallel. The high-altitude bomber (Type 149HA) was not proceeded with, and from the Bisley were developed the Type 160 Blenheim Mk VA, Type 160CS Blenheim Mk VB, Type 160D Blenheim Mk VD (the Blenheim Mk VC was a dual-control trainer).

The main variant, the tropicalised Blenheim Mk VD (of which 940 were produced), first entered operational service at the time of the 'Torch' landings in North Africa in November 1942, three months after the Blenheim Mk IV had been withdrawn from combat service in Europe. The new version, weighed down with armour, overloaded with tropical equipment and badly underpowered, proved unpopular in service, and its poor performance (maximum speed 386 km/h/240 mph) led to heavy losses. In a raid over Tunisia on 4 December 1942 all 10 Blenheim Mk Vs of No. 18 (Bomber) Squadron were shot down by enemy fighters, the squadron commander, Wing Commander H. G. Malcolm, being awarded a posthumous Victoria Cross.

The Far East and elsewhere

A third Victoria Cross was won by a Blenheim pilot in Malaya during the first hours of the Japanese invasion. Squadron Leader A. S. K. Scarf of No. 62 Squadron was one of a number of pilots ordered off from Butterworth to raid the enemy base at Singora, but a

Initial service evaluation of the Bristol Type 142 was carried out on 'Britain First', and so no prototype as such of the Blenheim Mk I was built. The first production aircraft (K7033), shown here, was flown on 25 June 1936 and served as a test and trials aircraft.

Finland took delivery of 18 Bristol-built Blenheim Mk Is in 1937-38 (BL-104, shown here, was the first to be delivered), some aircraft being flown with fixed ski undercarriage. Finnish Blenheims featured enlarged bomb bays.

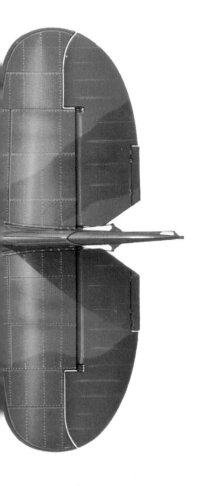

Bristol Blenheim variants

Type 142: *Britain First* commercial prototype, registered G-ADCZ, later K557; Mercury engines
Type 143: enlarged private-venture 8-passenger prototype; Aquila engines; registered G-ADEK
Blenheim Mk 1 (Type 142M): Mercury VIII engines; 700 built by Bristol (including 18 to Finland, 30 to Turkey); 250 built by Avro (including 10 to Finland, 13 to Romania, 20 to Yugoslavia); 422 built by Rootes; 16 built by Ikarus, Yugoslavia; 45 built by Valtion Lentokonetehdas, Finland
Blenheim Mk IF: about 200 Mk Is converted to fighters
Blenheim PR. Mk I: one aircraft (L1348) converted from Mk I for high-speed reconnaissance role; unarmed
Blenheim Mk II: one aircraft (L1222) converted from Mk I with long-range wing tanks and external bombs; Mercury VIII engines
Bolingbroke Mk I: original Bristol project; long-nose prototype (K7072) converted from Blenheim Mk I
Blenheim Mk IV (Type 142L): Mercury XV (100-octane) engines; 312 built by Bristol (including 12 to Greece); 750 built by Avro; 2,060 built by Rootes; 10 built by Valtion Lentokonetehdas, Finland
Blenheim Mk IVF: about 60 Mk IVs converted to fighters
Blenheim Mk V: two prototypes, AD657 (**Bisley**, Type 149CS) and AD661 (Type 149HA); Mercury XXX
Blenheim Mks VA, VB, VC, VD: aircraft built by Rootes
Bolingbroke Mk I (Canadian production): 18 built by Fairchild; Mercury VIII; one converted to **Bolingbroke Mk II** with US equipment, and one to **Bolingbroke Mk III** with floats
Bolingbroke Mk IV: 185 built by Fairchild; Mercury XV engines
Bolingbroke Mk IV-W: 15 built by Fairchild; Pratt & Whitney Twin Wasp Junior engines
Bolingbroke Mk IV-C: one built by Fairchild; Wright Cyclone engines
Bolingbroke Mk IV-T: 457 built by Fairchild; Mercury XX engines; aircrew trainers

Specification
Bristol Blenheim IF

Type: three-seat night fighter
Powerplant: two 627-kW (840-hp) Bristol Mercury VIII nine-cylinder air-cooled radial engines
Performance: maximum speed 459 km/h (285 mph) at 4570 m (15,000 ft); climb to 4570 m (15,000 ft) 11 minutes 30 seconds; service ceiling 8315 m (28,280 ft); range at full load, 1810 km (1,125 miles)
Weights: empty 3674 kg (8,100 lb); maximum take-off 5670 kg (12,500 lb)
Dimensions: span 17.17 m (56 ft 4 in); length 12.12 m (39 ft 9 in); height 3.00 m (9 ft 10 in); wing area 43.57 m^2 (469.0 sq ft)
Armament: one forward-firing 7.7-mm (0.303-in) Browning gun in port wing and four Browning guns in ventral gun pack; one 7.7-mm (0.303-in) gas-operated gun in semi-retractable Bristol dorsal turret.

A Blenheim Mk IF of No. 25 (Fighter) Sqn based at Hawkinge, Kent, immediately before the outbreak of World War II. Points of interest include the black-and-white undersurfaces, the squadron codes RX (changed to ZK in September 1939) and the squadron badge (obliterated when hostilities started) on the fin. The four-gun belly pack was a feature of most Blenheim fighters (including the Mk IVF), but the single gas-operated Lewis gun in the semi-retractable dorsal turret was a relic of inter-war conviction that single dorsal gun armament constituted adequate tail protection for 'fast' aircraft.

Blenheim Mk IVs were built in Canada by Fairchild Aircraft Ltd as the Bolingbroke Mk IV. Most were used for training, this striped example being used for target-towing for gunnery practise.

Japanese raid destroyed all but his aircraft before take-off; nevertheless Scarf took off, completed his attack single-handed and fought his way home to a crash landing, despite being mortally wounded. Blenheim Mk Is and Mk IVs of Nos 22, 27, 45, 89, 176, 177, 211 and 217 Squadrons took part in all the campaigns fought by the RAF against the Japanese during 1941-43, and were joined in the latter year by Blenheim Mk Vs on Nos 11, 42, 113 and 211 Squadrons; their poor

Prior to being incorporated fully into the RAF structure as No 342 Squadron with Douglas Bostons, the Free French 'Lorraine' squadron flew Blenheim Mk IVs in Syria from September 1941 onwards. These aircraft are seen during the successful campaign against the German garrison at Halfaya.

performance prompted their withdrawal after only nine months' service.

In service other than with the RAF, the largest user was the Royal Canadian Air Force, whose special variant retained the name Bolingbroke after the RAF adopted the Blenheim Mk IV. Production was undertaken by Fairchild Aircraft Ltd in Canada, who produced a total of 676 (comprising 18 Mk Is with Mercury VIIIs, and the remainder Mk IVs). The majority was used for navigation and gunnery training.

Finland eventually flew a total of 83 Blenheims, comprising 18 Mk Is exported by Bristol, 10 ex-RAF Mk Is despatched at the time of the Winter War of 1939-40, 45 licence-built Mk Is and 10 licence-built Mk IVs. Production in Finland was undertaken by Valtion Lentokonetehdas at Tampere.

Turkey received a total of 30 Blenheim Mk Is, and Greece 12 Blenheim Mk IVs (already mentioned). The 18 Blenheim Mk Is exported to Yugoslavia were joined by 16 licence-built aircraft, manufactured by Ikarus AD, of Zemun, but 24 others, only partly completed at the time of the German invasion, were destroyed to prevent their falling into enemy hands. Romania's 13 Blenheim Mk Is were part of a deal designed to woo the nation to the Allied cause; the plan failed, and the Blenheims served against the Allies in due course.

Total Blenheim production, excluding the Type 142 and Type 143 prototypes, was 6,185 including 24 Mk Is destroyed before completion in Yugoslavia and five Mk IVs not completed in Finland during 1944.

Believed to be from No 11 Squadron, this is a Blenheim Mk VA, escorted by Hurricane fighters. The type was used to raid Japanese installations in Burma during 1943. The squadron had flown various Blenheims since July 1938, and had been heavily involved in the Middle East campaign before moving back to the Indian theatre.

Petlyakov Pe-2

Petlyakov's Pe-2 was the Soviet Union's Mosquito, though made entirely of metal. Little known outside its homeland, it was built in far larger numbers than its British counterpart and undertook as many different roles. Flying from 1940 and supporting the Soviet offensives soon after that, it contributed greatly to the final victory on the Eastern Front.

On 22 June 1941 the world's most formidable army and air force began to smash their way into the Soviet Union. Outside that country little was known publicly of its modern aircraft; certainly in the first week of the German onslaught it looked as if such knowledge would be academic, because most of the Soviet air force was wiped out. But resistance was dogged, and in the autumn two RAF Hawker Hurricane squadrons, formed into No. 151 Wing, were sent to Murmansk to help bolster the defences and teach the Soviets how to fly the Hurricane.

On No. 151 Wing's first combat mission it was tasked as escort to a regiment equipped with the Pe-2 bomber. This beautiful aircraft was unknown to the RAF, but it made quite an impression, because the Hurricanes had the greatest difficulty in keeping up. It was not then generally known that on combat missions it was common Soviet practice to fly at virtually full throttle all the way. In both climb and speed the twin-finned bombers easily outperformed their escorting fighters, and Wing Commander Ramsbottom-Isherwood's pilots had the agonising choice of pushing their throttles wide open to try to keep up, so risking engine failure and running out of fuel, or of falling behind. To say this was a surprise is an understatement.

The Pe-2 was the one gigantic success of Vladimir M. Petlyakov, who from 1921 (when he was 30) had worked at TsAGI, the national aerodynamic and hydrodynamic research centre. He became the leading expert on metal wing design, and designed the wings for all the early Tupolev heavy bombers, and managed the entire design of the biggest aircraft of all, the ANT-16, ANT-20 and ANT-26. In 1936 he was appointed head of the ZOK experimental brigade to produce a large new bomber, which began life as the ANT-42, entered service as the TB-7 and finally, in World War II, matured as the Pe-8, honouring its designer. But Petlyakov had only 18 months on that programme, because in the Stalinist terror of 1937 he was one of the thousands arrested on trumped-up charges. Incarcerated in the TsKB-29 special prison at GAZ (aircraft factory) No. 156, Petlyakov was told to organise a design bureau called KB-100, and to create the VI-100, VI standing for high-altitude fighter.

At a time when the rest of the world thought all Soviets could do was copy others, the VI-100 was created from the proverbial clean sheet of paper to a higher standard (in aerodynamics, structure, and several aspects of systems and equipment) than anything previously

*Almost certainly operating from a **VVS** front-line base during the summer of 1942, this early production Pe-2 can be distinguished from later models by its engine cowls, glazed sides to the nose, manual upper rear gun and rear-mounted mast. There are pale-coloured bands across the outer wings and vertical tails. **Note the rough airfield.***

existing elsewhere (and Petlyakov's team was not the only one to do this). The stressed-skin structure was superb, being faulted only on the score of complexity. The wing comprised a flat centre-section and tapered outer panels, mounted low in a fuselage of minimum cross section. All control surfaces were fabric-covered. The twin liquid-cooled engines were beautifully cowled, and as on many other Soviet twins of the period the coolant radiators were inside the wings between the lattice spars, fed by ducts from the leading edge and exhausting through flush shutter-controlled apertures in the upper skin, which were intended to give forward thrust. The engines had turbochargers for high-altitude power and drove constant-speed feathering propellers, which were totally unavailable in the UK at the time. It had been planned to fit a pressure cabin, such things having been extensively tested in the Soviet Union, but this was not produced in time, so the pilot and radio operator (who doubled as observer and rear gunner) were in normal cockpits separated by the main fuel tanks. Armament comprised four 20-mm ShVAK cannon in the nose, each with 150 rounds, the backseater having a ShKAS machine-gun firing at 1,800 rounds per minute. Following US practice, the power services were totally electric, some 20 DC motors driving the landing gear, split flaps, radiator shutters, tank booster pumps, trim tabs and many other items.

Bouncy landings

Piotr Stefanovsky and engineer Ivan Markov flew the first of two VI-100 prototypes, possibly on 7 May 1939 (there is confusion about the date), and took part in the 1940 May Day flypast over Red Square. The aircraft's main fault was a tendency to violent bouncing on landing, which for some reason was difficult to cure. There is a persistent report that bomb-aiming was found difficult at high altitude, which conflicts with existing Soviet records which make no mention of any requirement for bombs. Altogether the VI-100 could surely have become an excellent day and night fighter and reconnaissance aircraft, its speed being 630 km/h (391 mph) at 10000 m (32,810 ft). The Soviets were as bad as others at chopping and changing, however, and the decision was taken to expand the KB-100 bureau to handle a mass-production programme, not of the VI-100 but of a three-seat bomber derived from it. Some articles suggest the decision was taken in May 1940, but this is impossible, as the first PB-100 (PB is the abbreviation for dive-bomber) undoubtedly flew not later than 3 June 1940, and it could hardly have been designed and built in a month!

Only a single PB-100 prototype is known, and it differed from the VI-100 in many respects. The outer wings had dive breaks and different taper adjusted to the new centre of gravity position, the fuse-

Representing the start of the next generation after the Pe-2, the pressure-cabin Pe-2VI was a VK-107-engined high-altitude fighter with a speed of 710 km/h (441 mph). It was designed chiefly by Myasishchev, who went on to produce the Pe-21 with VK-108 1342-kW (1,800-hp) engines, DB-108 and VB-16 bombers, and the even more powerful VB-109 of 1945.

Petlyakov Pe-2 variants

VI-100: original high-altitude fighter prototypes

PB-100: prototype(s) of new three-seat bomber

Pe-2: initial production bomber, with three seats, dive brakes and VK-105RA engines

Pe-2M: first of two quite different aircraft with this designation, flown October 1941 with turbocharged engines, slats and larger bomb bay for up to four FAB-500s (no other bombs carried)

Pe-2Sh: *Shturmovik* (armoured attack) version, flown October 1941; prolonged trials with various heavy gun installations including twin-ShVAK ventral pack with guns pivoted down to −40°

Pe-3: initial fighter prototype, early 1941 (believed February), various guns but standardised on two ShVAK plus two UB firing ahead (plus two optional ShKAS as in standard bomber) together with MV-3 dorsal turret; production discontinued after 23rd aircraft

Pe-3bis: hasty modification in summer 1941 to produce night-fighter, identical to Pe-2 but with one ShVAK, one UB and three ShKAS firing ahead (with or without provision for bombs and/or underwing rockets); about 300 delivered, usually as alternate aircraft on GAZ-22 assembly line

Pe-3R: continuing alternate aircraft being different, these were naval reconnaissance aircraft for Northern Fleet with Pe-3 guns and various camera installations; at least one with TK-2 turbochargers

Pe-2L: possibly designated **Pe-3L**, this was a testbed for various retractable ski installations in January 1942

Pe-2MV: possibly designated **Pe-3MV**, a trials aircraft used by MV weapon bureau, fitted with MV-3 turret and photographed with belly tray for two ShVAK plus two UB

Pe-2FT: standard bomber from May 1942 with reduced nose glazing (on underside only), MV-3 turret, extra lower rear guns and, usually, no dive brakes; from early 1943 powered by PF or PF-2 engines

Pe-2FZ: FZ (front-line task) aircraft, a small batch with unglazed nose, no access past pilot in modified cockpit and navigator with twin UBT guns, manually aimed

Pe-2/M-28: at least one aircraft powered by M-82 (ASh-82) radial engines and according to historian V. B. Shavrov fitted with wing of modified profile giving slower landing; heavier but faster than standard aircraft

Pe-2VI: mid-1943 high-altitude fighter with completely revised airframe by Myasishchev (now head of bureau) with VK-107 engines, oil coolers alongside wing radiators and single pilot seat in pressurised cockpit; later developed by Myasishchev into **VM-16** and **DB-108**, and later types

Pe-3M: night-fighter of mid-1943 with 700-kg (1,540-lb) bombload plus two ShVAK, two UB and two DAG-10

Pe-2UT: also known as **Pe-2S, Pe-2T** and

UPe-2, and used by post-war Czech air force as **CB-32**; dual trainer with instructor cockpit amidships and often with full bombload; large numbers built from July 1943

Pe-2 Paravan: test aircraft with long nose probe and wires leading back to balloon-cable cutters on wingtips

Pe-2B: standard 1944 bomber, tested autumn 1943 with many airframe and system improvements, one ShKAS plus three UBT

Pe-2R: limited-production reconnaissance aircraft with PF-2 engines, increased internal fuel, three defensive UB or BS guns, three or four cameras, speed 580 km/h (360 mph) at 7603 kg (16,761 lb)

Pe-2R: same designation applied in 1944 to high-speed reconnaissance prototype with 1230-kW (1,650-hp) VK-107A engines, tankage for 2000 km (1,242 miles) and armed with three ShVAK (plus two UB)

Pe-2I: new standard bomber produced under Myasishchev, new mid-mounting wing with NACA 23012 profile, longer and better streamlined body and nacelles for VK-107A engines, one UB gun at each tip of fuselage, bombload 1000 kg (2,250 lb) internal plus same external; speed on test in May 1944 was 656 km/h (408 mph) despite weight of 8983 kg (19,804 lb), but no production was undertaken

Pe-2K: compromise with regular VK-107PF engines in Pe-2I airframe

Pe-2D: three-seat bomber of September 1944 with VK-107A engines, three BT 20-mm cannon and DAG-10; speed 600 km/h (373 mph) with 4000 kg (8,818 lb) bombload

Pe-2M: second aircraft with this designation, Pe-2I airframe, VK-107 engines, 2000-kg (4,410-lb) internal bombload and three ShVAK; 630 km/h (391.5 mph) at 9400 kg (20,723 lb)

Pe-2RD: achieved 785 km/h (488 mph) with Korolyev/Glushko RD-1 rocket installed in tail, intended to lead to **Pe-3RD** fighter

Pe-2K: second use of this designation for ejection-seat test aircraft in 1946; standard Pe-2 with various test seats installed above trailing edge in radio operator's cockpit

B-32: post-war designation of Pe-2 in Czech air force

Petlyakov Pe-2 cutaway drawing key

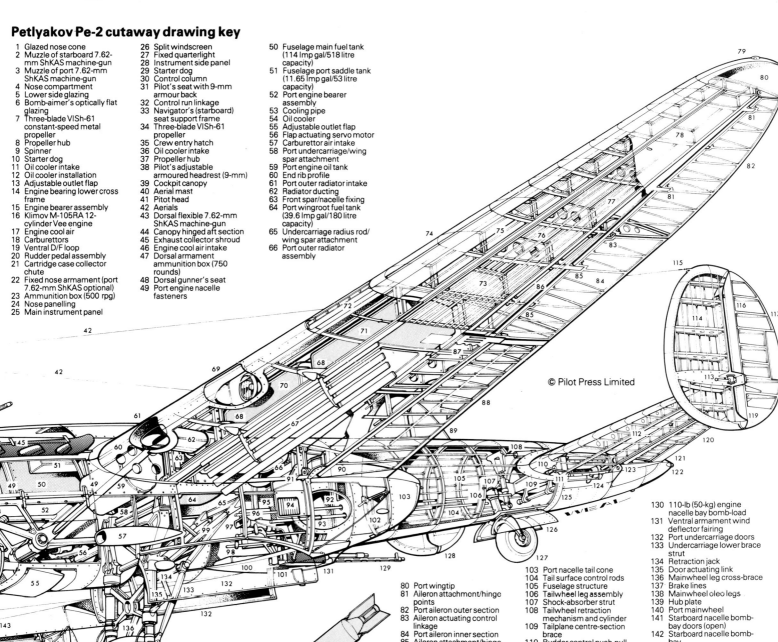

1 Glazed nose cone
2 Muzzle of starboard 7.62-mm ShKAS machine-gun
3 Muzzle of port 7.62-mm ShKAS machine-gun
4 Nose compartment
5 Lower side glazing
6 Bomb-aimer's optically flat glazing
7 Three-blade VISh-61 constant-speed metal propeller
8 Propeller hub
9 Spinner
10 Starter dog
11 Oil cooler intake
12 Oil cooler installation
13 Adjustable outlet flap
14 Engine bearing lower cross frame
15 Engine bearer assembly
16 Klimov M-105RA 12-cylinder Vee engine
17 Engine cool air
18 Carburettors
19 Ventral D/F loop
20 Rudder pedal assembly
21 Cartridge case collector chute
22 Fixed nose armament (port 7.62-mm ShKAS optional)
23 Ammunition box (500 rpg)
24 Nose panelling
25 Main instrument panel
26 Split windscreen
27 Fixed quarterlight
28 Instrument side panel
29 Starter dog
30 Control column
31 Pilot's seat with 9-mm armour back
32 Control run linkage
33 Navigator's (starboard) seat support frame
34 Three-blade VISh-61 propeller
35 Crew entry hatch
36 Oil cooler intake
37 Propeller hub
38 Pilot's adjustable armoured headrest (9-mm)
39 Cockpit canopy
40 Aerial mast
41 Pitot head
42 Aerials
43 Dorsal flexible 7.62-mm ShKAS machine-gun
44 Canopy hinged aft section
45 Exhaust collector shroud
46 Engine cool air intake
47 Dorsal armament ammunition box (750 rounds)
48 Dorsal gunner's seat
49 Port engine nacelle fasteners
50 Fuselage main fuel tank (114 lmp gal/518 litre capacity)
51 Fuselage port saddle tank (11.65 lmp gal/53 litre capacity)
52 Port engine bearer assembly
53 Cooling pipe
54 Oil cooler
55 Adjustable outlet flap
56 Flap actuating servo motor
57 Carburettor air intake
58 Port undercarriage/wing spar attachment
59 Port engine oil tank
60 End rib profile
61 Port outer radiator intake
62 Radiator ducting
63 Front spar/nacelle fixing
64 Port wingroot fuel tank (39.6 lmp gal/180 litre capacity)
65 Undercarriage radius rod/wing spar attachment
66 Port outer radiator assembly

67 Underwing dive-brake (extended)
68 Dive-brake hinge fairings
69 Landing lamp
70 Port outer wing inboard fuel tank (31.5 lmp gal/143 litre capacity)
71 Port outer wing outboard fuel tank (23.5 lmp gal/107 litre capacity)
72 Wing leading-edge strip
73 Wing stiffeners
74 Nose rib stations
75 Wing front spar
76 Wing ribs
77 Wing rear spar
78 Wing skinning
79 Port navigation light
80 Port wingtip
81 Aileron attachment/hinge points
82 Port aileron outer section
83 Aileron actuating control linkage
84 Port aileron inner section
85 Aileron attachment/hinge points
86 Aileron control rod
87 Stiffening plate
88 Port flap outboard section
89 Starboard rudder
90 Flap inboard rib fillet
91 Rear spar/nacelle fixing
92 Fuselage beam window
93 Tail surface control rods
94 Cooling louvres
95 Ventral armament ammunition box (750 rounds)
96 Ventral machine gun mounting/retraction frame
97 Periscopic sight
98 Control grips
99 Undercarriage radius rods
100 Ventral gunner's (prone) pad
101 Ventral retractable 7.62 mm ShKAS machine-gun
102 Port nacelle bomb-bay

103 Port nacelle tail cone
104 Tail surface control rods
105 Fuselage structure
106 Tailwheel leg assembly
107 Shock-absorber strut
108 Tailwheel retraction mechanism and cylinder
109 Tailplane centre-section brace
110 Rudder control push-pull rod link
111 Tailplane attachment fillet
112 Tailplane structure
113 Rudder control linkage
114 Tailfin structure
115 Aerial attachment pick-up
116 Rudder upper hinge
117 Rudder frame
118 Rudder trim tab
119 Rudder lower hinge
120 Port elevator frame
121 Port elevator trim tab
122 Tail navigation light
123 Elevator attachment/hinge bracket
124 Elevator actuating rod and internal counterweight
125 Aft fuselage frame/tailplane front spar join
126 Tailwheel doors
127 Retractable tailwheel
128 Starboard tailfin/rudder
129 Ventral machine gun (deployed)

130 110-lb (50-kg) engine nacelle bay bomb-load
131 Ventral armament wind deflector fairing
132 Port undercarriage doors
133 Undercarriage lower brace strut
134 Retraction jack
135 Door actuating link
136 Mainwheel leg cross-brace
137 Brake lines
138 Mainwheel oleo legs
139 Hub plate
140 Port mainwheel
141 Starboard nacelle bomb-bay doors (open)
142 Starboard nacelle bomb-bay
143 Fuselage bomb-bay doors
144 Starboard engine nacelle mainwheel well
145 Starboard undercarriage doors
146 Telescopic entry step
147 Crew entry hatch door/integral step
148 Carburettor air intake
149 Mainwheel leg cross-brace
150 Brake lines
151 Undercarriage lower brace strut
152 Mainwheel oleo legs
153 Hub assembly
154 Starboard mainwheel
155 551-lb (250-kg) (optional) underwing bomb load
156 441-lb (200-kg) (4×110-lb/50-kg) fuselage internal bomb load
157 882-lb (400-kg) (4×220-lb/100-kg) underwing external bomb load

© Pilot Press Limited

Petlyakov Pe-2

Specification
Petlyakov Pe-2FT

Type: three-seat tactical bomber

Powerplant: two 939-kW (1,260-hp) Klimov VK-105PF vee 12-cylinder piston engines

Performance: maximum speed 449 km/h (279 mph) at sea level and 580 km/h (360 mph) at 4000 m (13,125 ft); service ceiling 8800 m (28,870 ft); range with 1000-kg (2,205-lb) bombload 1315 km (817 miles)

Weights: empty 6200 kg (13,668 lb); maximum 8520 kg (18,783 lb)

Dimensions: span 17.11 m (56 ft 1⅔ in); length 12.78 m (41 ft 11 in); height 3.42 m (11 ft 2⅔ in); wing area 40.5 m² (436 sq ft)

Armament: provision for four FAB-100 (220.5-lb) bombs in internal bomb bay, two FAB-100 bombs in rear of engine nacelles and four FAB-250 (551-lb) bombs on external racks under centre section; two 7.62-mm (0.31-in) ShKAS machine-guns firing ahead aimed by pilot, MV-3 dorsal turret with single 12.7-mm (0.5-in) UBT, one ShKAS aimed by hand from rear ventral position (drawing shows UBS, very unusual) and one ShKAS aimed through left or right rear beam position

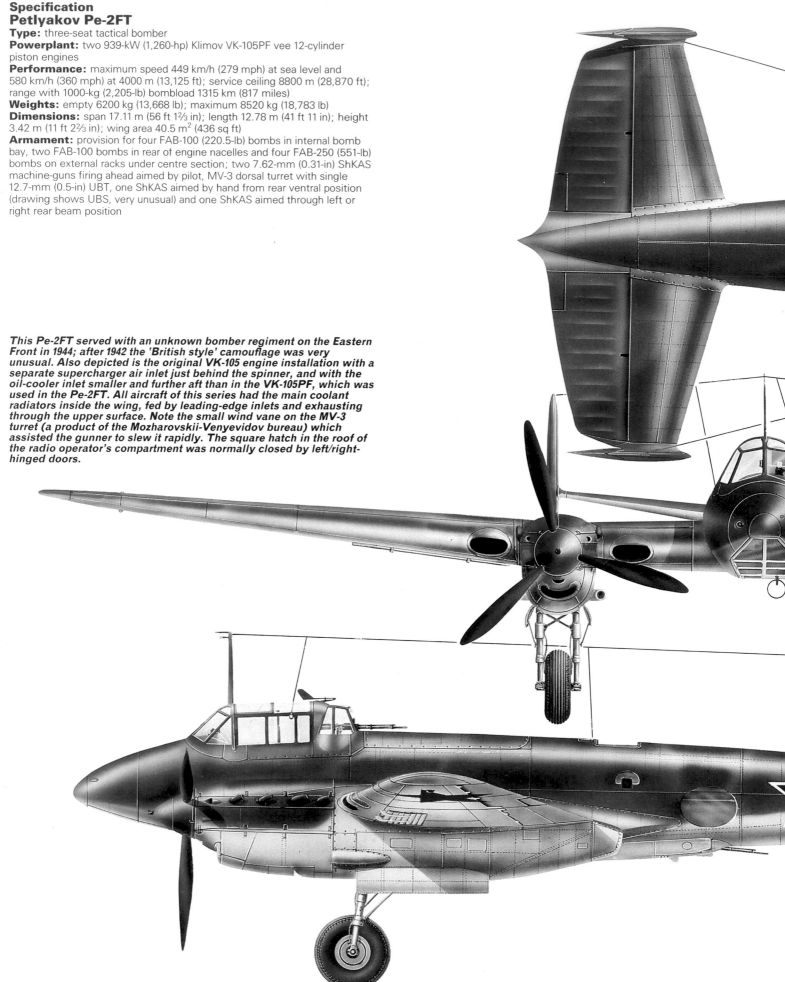

This Pe-2FT served with an unknown bomber regiment on the Eastern Front in 1944; after 1942 the 'British style' camouflage was very unusual. Also depicted is the original VK-105 engine installation with a separate supercharger air inlet just behind the spinner, and with the oil-cooler inlet smaller and further aft than in the VK-105PF, which was used in the Pe-2FT. All aircraft of this series had the main coolant radiators inside the wing, fed by leading-edge inlets and exhausting through the upper surface. Note the small wind vane on the MV-3 turret (a product of the Mozharovskii-Venyevidov bureau) which assisted the gunner to slew it rapidly. The square hatch in the roof of the radio operator's compartment was normally closed by left/right-hinged doors.

PE-211 was one of three early production Pe-2s captured from the Russians and put into service by the Finnish PLeLv 48. Note the required yellow theatre band, as carried by all German-allied aircraft on the Eastern Front. No. 211 had a ventral D/F loop (not visible) and operated on strategic reconnaissance missions from Onttola.

This early production Pe-2 is distinguished by the cowlings for the M-105RA engines, which differ in many details from the final cleaned-up pattern. It is shown in winter garb while serving with the 46th BAP (Bomber Air Regiment), Moscow Military District, in the winter of 1941-42. Note the rear mount of the radio/pitot mast and the glazed nose.

lage was redesigned, the tailplane dihedral was increased, the vertical tails were enlarged and positioned on the tips of the tailplane, and the engine turbochargers were first changed to the smaller TK-2 type and then omitted entirely. The new fuselage provided back-to-back cockpits for the pilot and navigator/bomb-aimer, who near the target could squeeze forward to his prone sighting position in the new glazed nose. A single large multi-pane canopy covered both cockpits. Aft of the fuselage tank was the new third crewman, who entered via a roof hatch and managed the radio and a lower rear gun, sighting not through his side windows (which merely let light in) but with a ventral periscopic sight similar to that used on several Soviet attack bombers, including the Tu-2.

An important engineering change was the installation of an hydraulic system, though this was energised by electrically-driven pumps. Services worked by this system included the twin-strut main and steerable tail landing gears, their twin doors, the split flaps, the Venetian-blind dive brakes and, in some aircraft, the bomb doors. All other services, including armament controls, remained electric. Standard bombload comprised four FAB-250 (250-kg/551-lb) or six FAB-100 (100-kg/220.5-lb) bombs in the main bay; with the latter load, two additional FAB-100 bombs could be carried in small door-enclosed compartments at the rear of the nacelles. As an overload, with six internal FAB-100 bombs it was possible to carry four more FAB-100 bombs externally under the wing roots. Late in the war some aircraft carried four FAB-250 bombs externally, a total load of 1800 kg (3,968 lb). Normal gun armament comprised two 7.62-mm (0.3-in) ShKAS machine-guns firing ahead and aimed by the pilot, plus a single ShKAS aimed by the navigator/bomb-aimer to the upper

rear and another aimed by the radioman to the lower rear, in each case aiming by hand.

Full details of the PB-100 are still lacking. A photograph exists showing ground-attack armament housed in a large ventral bathtub, with two 20-mm ShVAK cannon on the right and two 7.62-mm (0.3-in) ShKAS guns on the left, all pivoted down at a shallow angle for strafing ground targets. A drawing exists showing the normal bomber armament doubled, with four forward-firing ShKAS guns and two pairs at the rear. There is also uncertainty about when the engine turbochargers were removed. Certainly every illustration known of the PB-100 shows long exhaust pipes, and this is also a feature of the initial production version, which in 1941 was redesignated Pe-2 in honour of the lead designer, who with his team was freed from detention in January of that year, and later awarded a Stalin Prize. Use of piped exhausts does not necessarily betoken installation of turbochargers, but it was well into 1942 before the Pe-2 switched to separate ejector stub exhausts.

Speedy progress

There is evidence that preparations for production began long before the completion of NII (state) trials of the PB-100, and the first production drawings (still designated PB-100) were released to GAZ-22 at Fili, north of Moscow, as early as 7 July 1940. Various modifications naturally took place as a result of PB-100 flight trials,

In line with most Soviet combat types (even to this day) the Pe-2 was far better adapted to rough field operations than Western aircraft. Snow and mud were taken in the aircraft's stride easily, and hard grass or concrete could have been considered a luxury for the pilots of combat regiments.

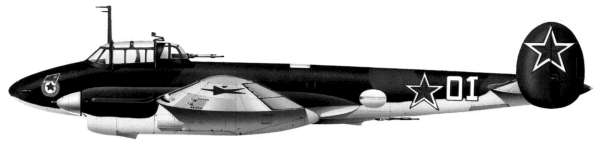

one being to give the pilot simple manual open/shut control of the dive brakes, replacing the complex AP-1 automatic dive control which modulated the brakes according to the dive angle and airspeed. Crew armour was improved, the ruling thickness being increased to 9 mm (0.35 in) throughout, the navigator/bomb-aimer was given a swivelling seat, and all five fuel tanks were made self-sealing and continuously inerted, at first by bottled nitrogen and later by cooled and filtered exhaust gas.

First production aircraft

The first aircraft, possibly by this time known as a Pe-2, came off the line in November 1940, and flew on 18 November. The VI-100 had been flown on skis, and the Pe-2 was also cleared to use skis which, like the normal wheeled gear, retracted backwards. Skis were not always fitted in winter, despite the obvious difficulty of operating such a heavy and fast-landing (200 km/h; 124 mph) aircraft in a Russian winter on wheels.

Very early in production the oil coolers were installed in improved low-drag ducts smoothly faired into the underside of the cowlings. For the remainder of the war the Pe-2 was constantly given small modifications to reduce drag, while the internal fuel capacity was also slightly increased. Production at GAZ-22 built up rapidly, and when Hitler struck on 22 June 1941 about 458 had been completed, of which at least 290 were with operational regiments, including the 24th BAP (bomber regiment) and 5th SBAP (fast bomber regiment). Though the Pe-2 was quite a demanding aircraft, it was immediately very popular and was commonly called 'Peshka', which means 'little Pe' as well as a pawn in chess.

The initial production engine was the VK-105RA, rated at 820 kW (1,100 hp) and driving VISh-61 propellers (which were not electrically driven, as sometimes reported, but were derived from the Hamilton Hydromatic, with hydraulic actuation). By 1943 the 940-kW (1,260-hp) VK-105PF or PF-2 became available, having previously been reserved for Yak fighters, and this powered virtually all the regular Pe-2 production aircraft to the end of the war.

All variants are listed separately. The standard versions, the Pe-2 and Pe-2FT bombers, the Pe-2R reconnaissance aircraft, the Pe-2UT trainer and the Pe-3bis fighter, accounted for a grand total

of 11,427 aircraft when manufacture was stopped in early 1945, just before the end of the war in Europe (though later variants continued as prototypes and development aircraft). This production total was achieved despite the fact that GAZ-22 had to be evacuated to Povolozhye (Kazan) in October 1941, to a factory building which then did not exist. In 1942 GAZ-125, also at Kazan, was completed and doubled the rate of output to 13 aircraft per day.

Significant others

Probably the only variants needing mention in the text are the Pe-2FT and Pe-2UT. The former, with initials meaning 'front-line request', replaced the navigator/bomb-aimer's hand-held ShKAS by a hard-hitting 12.7-mm (0.5-in) UBT in an MV-3 turret, one of the lightweight turrets by the Mozharovsky-Venyevidov team with manual operation facilitated by the use of weathercock fins to balance the drag of the gun when firing abeam. There were naturally many local variations in armament, and despite the increase in weight it was common by 1943 to find that at least one of the front guns as well

Aircraft (Samolyet) No. 100 was the first designation of V. M. Petlyakov's original prototype. Later it was called VI-100, VI meaning high-altitude fighter. It never received its planned pressure cabin, and a great deal of work was needed before this tandem two-seater could emerge as the Pe-2 attack bomber.

as the lower rear gun were also UB versions. A further change, possibly dating from mid-1942, was to make the windows in the rear fuselage hinge open so that one or more extra ShKAS could be fired through them by the radio operator.

The Pe-2UT was the standard dual-control pilot trainer, with the instructor seated in an additional cockpit replacing the mid-fuselage fuel tank, and with a poor forward view. The first flew in July 1943, an unusual case of the trainer lagging far behind initial deliveries of the basic combat aircraft. The Pe-3bis was the only model built in quantity from a sub-family of fighter versions. Some retained the internal bomb bay, and a few even had underwing rails for the RS-82 or RS-132 rockets used in the low-level attack and anti-armour role, but most merely had the bombing equipment and third crew station removed, and instead added heavy gun armament such as one ShVAK, one UB and three ShKAS guns, or two ShVAK plus two UB weapons. There are persistent reports that the Pe-3 had wing slats, though confirmation is elusive. The designation Pe-3 stemmed from the fact that fighter aircraft are designated by odd numbers.

A group of late Pe-2FTs at the moment of release in a level bombing run. Note the opened rear nacelle doors, and the apparent length of the stick dropped from the aircraft at upper left. Fighter escorts were seldom provided after 1942.

Petlyakov's OKB retained several Pe-2s as development aircraft, and also the second production machine which was used as a hack to shuttle between Kazan and Moscow. On 12 January 1942 this aircraft caught fire in the air, and all on board, including Petlyakov, were killed. Stalin personally ordered a wave of arrests and interrogations to see who was responsible for killing 'this great patriot', whom he had only lately released from prison. A. M. Izakson was the unfortunate person picked as successor, closely followed by A. I. Putilov and, finally, V. M. Myasishchev. The OKB was closed in 1946, Myasishchev himself carrying on with his own bureau. By this time, Pe-2s had been passed on to most East European air forces, and three captured aircraft also had useful lives with PLeLv 48 of the Finnish air force. The Pe-2 was even given the NATO name 'Buck'.

This late production Pe-2 is one of the many exhibits outside the Polish army museum in Warsaw. It is quite well preserved but among other changes has had its MV-3 turret replaced by a fixed fairing. Like many Hispano-derived engines the VK-105 had four exhaust pipes on each side, the middle two each serving two cylinders.

One of only three known Pe-2s of any kind, this Czech example was known as a CB-32 in service with the Czech air force immediately after World War II. Soviet designations included Pe-UT, UPe-2 and Pe-2S. It retained full bombload but had no rear defensive guns.

Junkers Ju 87 Stuka

No aircraft in history was ever so deadly effective (when unopposed) as the infamous 'Stuka', nor so vulnerable when it encountered opposition. Its devastating effect in the early months of the war was only equalled by its dismal failure when it met the RAF over England a few weeks later.

Few aircraft have ever caused such terror, to seasoned troops and helpless civilians alike, as the ugly Junkers Ju 87 dive-bomber. Widely known as the Stuka, from the German word for a dive-bomber (*Sturzkampfflugzeug*), the Ju 87 also sank more ships than any other type of aircraft in history, and possibly destroyed more tanks than any other aircraft except the Soviet Ilyushin Il-2. Its stock-in-trade was the accurate placement of heavy bombs on point targets, and this it could do supremely well – provided it was not molested by fighters. Thus, in the first year of World War II, it acquired a reputation that was almost legendary. In the Battle of Britain its bubble of invincibility was burst for ever, and for the rest of the war it went steadily downhill until it was reduced to skulking just above the ground on dark nights, with the conspicuous exception of one Gruppe led by a man who personally flew 2,530 combat missions and continued to fly on the Eastern Front in daylight until the final German collapse.

The technique of dive-bombing was familiar in World War I, but no aircraft designed for the job existed until the 1920s. One of the first was the Junkers K 47, of which two were flown in 1928 with Jupiter engines and 12, with Pratt & Whitney Hornet engines, sold to China. These did extensive research, and demonstrated that a 90° dive is the most accurate. In turn this demands a strong aircraft and a resolute pilot, as well as an indicator of dive angle (60° feels like almost 90°). Many who later were to head Hitler's Luftwaffe became convinced that the dive-bomber had to be a central weapon in an air force dedicated to close support of ground forces. When plans could be made for new combat aircraft for the Luftwaffe, in 1933, the immediate need was ultimately met by a trim biplane, the Henschel Hs 123, while Junkers worked on the definitive Stuka.

The design staff under Hermann Pohlmann adopted the same configuration as that of the K 47: a single-engined low-wing monoplane with prominent fixed landing gear and twin fins and rudders. The Ju 87 differed in having an all-metal stressed-skin structure, without the corrugated skin previously used on Junkers all-metal aircraft, and a cranked wing of so-called inverted-gull form. Like that of the K 47, the entire trailing edge was occupied by patented double-wing flaps and ailerons, and the crew of two sat back-to-back under a large glazed canopy. The prototype flew in the spring of 1935 with a 477-kW (640-hp) Rolls-Royce Kestrel engine. Dive-brakes were then added under the outer wings, but on one of the first pull-outs the tail collapsed and the aircraft crashed.

Full-scale production

After much further development, in the course of which the engine was changed to the intended German unit, the 447-kW (640-hp) Junkers Jumo 210Ca, driving a three-blade variable-pitch propeller, a new single-fin tail was adopted, and the Ju 87A-1 entered full-scale production in early 1937.

About 200 of the A-0, A-1 and A-2 series were built, all with large trouser fairings over the landing gears and the A-2 with the 507-kW (680-hp) Jumo 210Da and an improved VDM propeller. They equipped four Gruppen, of which StG 163 sent three aircraft to see action with the *Legion Cóndor* in Spain, where the type proved outstandingly effective. But in 1939 all A-series aircraft were transferred to training units, and the swelling ranks of Stukageschwäder (dive-bomber wings) were equipped with the much more capable Ju 87B. Visually this differed in having neater spats over the main wheels, but the chief difference was that it had double the power, in the form of the new Jumo 211A, driving a broad-blade constant-speed propeller. The full production sub-type, the B-1, had the 895-kW (1,200-hp) Jumo 211Da with a direct-injection fuel system giving immunity from icing, or engine cuts in inverted flight, or negative-g manoeuvres (the Ju 87 could perform all normal aerobatics). Another important feature was an automatic dive-control, set by the pilot to a chosen pull-out height on a contact altimeter. Having gone through a list of 10 vital actions the pilot opened the underwing dive-brakes, which automatically set up the dive, the pilot adjusting the angle manually by lining up the visual horizon with red lines painted at

One of the surviving colour photographs from World War II, this was taken by the 'backseater' of a Ju 87B-2 flying with StG 77 on a mission over the Balkans – believed to be after dive-bombing British ships during the invasion of Crete.

Junkers Ju 87 Stuka

Use of the Ju 87 by the Italian Regia Aeronautica gave rise to the incorrect belief it was made in Italy as the Breda 201. This Ju 87B-2 was based at Gars el Arid in September 1941 with the 209ª Squadriglia, 101° Gruppo Autonomo (independent group). This unit painted its emblem on the wheel spats.

Seen in temporary white finish for the winter of 1941-2, this Ju 87B-2 also wears the yellow theatre band which by that time was becoming standard on the Eastern Front. It flew with Stab II/StG 1 (originally III/StG 51) whose unit emblem was painted on the cowling. The projection from the main leg is the siren.

various angles on the canopy. The pilot then aimed at the target manually as in a fighter, using aileron alone to achieve the correct bomb line. Often the angle was 90°, the dive being entered in a wing-over from directly above the target. Curiously, the Ju 87 was the one aircraft in which 90° did not feel like an over-the-vertical bunt; indeed, it seemed more at home in its rock-steady dive than in normal cruising flight, when its vulnerability (accentuated by the transparent canopy down to elbow-level) was all too evident. When a signal light on the contact altimeter came on, the pilot pressed a knob on top of the control column for the pull-out at 6 g to happen by itself, with usual terrain clearance of 450 m (1,476 ft). If it did not, the pilot had to haul back with all his strength, assisted by very careful use of elevator trimmer.

The usual load on the Ju 87B series was an SC500 (1,102-lb) bomb on crutches which swung out from the belly to let go of the bomb well away from the propeller. Speed built up to about 550 km/h (342 mph), and it became common practice to fit sirens to the landing gears – they were called 'Trombones of Jericho' – to strike extra terror into those near the target. Over short ranges, four SC50 (110-lb) bombs could also be hung under the wings. The pilot could fire two 7.92-mm (0.31-in) MG 17 guns mounted in the wings outboard of the kink, while the radio operator had an MG 15 of the same calibre to give protection above and behind. Production was transferred from Dessau to Weser Flugzeugbau in the great oval building at Berlin-Tempelhof airport, where it built up to 60 a month by mid-1939. Three B-1s made the first combat mission of World War II when they took off from Elbing at 04.26 on 1 September 1939 and devastated the approaches to the Dirschau bridge over the Vistula at 04.34, some 11 minutes before the Nazis declared war on Poland. Subsequently the Ju 87B-1 played a tremendous part in the Polish campaign, destroying all but two of the Polish surface warships, heavily bombing Polish troops on many occasions within 100 m (330 ft) of advancing German forces, and on one ghastly occasion virtually wiping out an entire Polish infantry division at Piotrkow railway station.

Carrier-borne variant

Alongside the improved Ju 87B-2 variants, which as single-seaters could carry an SC1000 (2,205-lb) bomb, Weser built a batch of Ju 87C-0s with folding wings, hooks and many other changes to suit them for use aboard the carrier *Graf Zeppelin*, which was never completed. Another derived model was the extended-range Ju 87R series, with extra tanks in the outer wings and provision for underwing drop tanks. They entered service in time for the Norwegian

Junkers Ju 87D-3 cutaway drawing key

1 Spinner
2 Pitch-change mechanism housing
3 Blade hub
4 Junkers VS 11 constant-speed airscrew
5 Anti-vibration engine mounting attachments
6 Oil filler point and marker
7 Auxiliary oil tank (5.9 Imp gal/26.8 litre capacity)
8 Junkers Jumo 211J-1 12-cylinder inverted-vee liquid cooled engine
9 Magnesium alloy forged engine mount
10 Coolant (Glysantin-water) header tank
11 Ejector exhaust stubs
12 Fuel injection unit housing
13 Induction air cooler
14 Armoured radiator
15 Inertia starter cranking point
16 Ball joint bulkhead fixing (lower)
17 Tubular steel mount support strut
18 Ventral armour (8 mm)
19 Main oil tank (9.9 Imp gal/45 litre capacity)
20 Oil filling point
21 Transverse support frame
22 Rudder pedals
23 Control column
24 Heating point
25 Auxiliary air intake
26 Ball joint bulkhead fixing (upper)
27 Bulkhead
28 Oil tank (6.8 Imp gal/31 litre capacity)
29 Oil filler point and marker (Intava 100)
30 Fuel filler cap
31 Self-sealing starboard outer fuel tank (33 Imp gal/150 litre capacity)
32 Underwing bombs with *Dienartstab* percussion rods
33 Pitot head
34 Spherical oxygen bottles
35 Wing skinning
36 Starboard navigation light
37 Aileron mass balance
38 'Double wing' aileron and flap (starboard outer)
39 Aileron hinge
40 Corrugated wing rib station
41 Reinforced armoured windscreen
42 Reflector sight
43 Padded crash bar

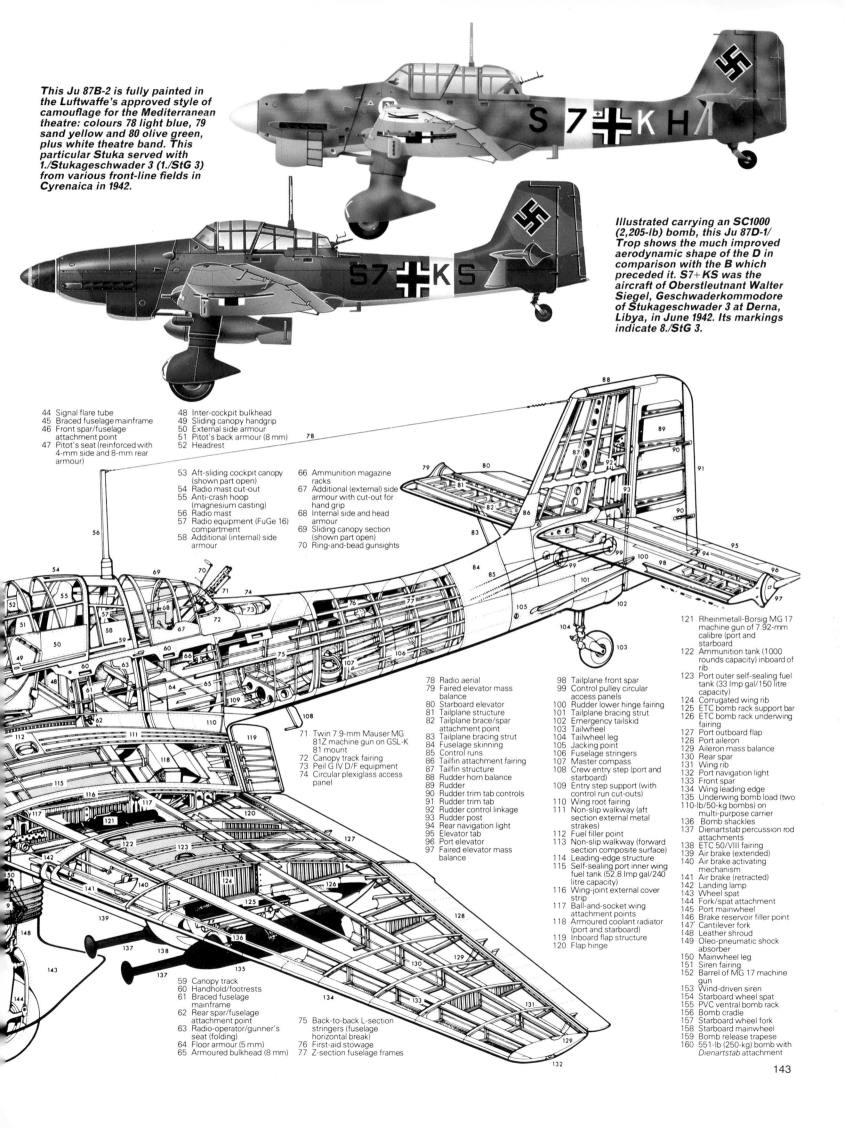

This Ju 87B-2 is fully painted in the Luftwaffe's approved style of camouflage for the Mediterranean theatre: colours 78 light blue, 79 sand yellow and 80 olive green, plus white theatre band. This particular Stuka served with 1./Stukageschwader 3 (1./StG 3) from various front-line fields in Cyrenaica in 1942.

Illustrated carrying an SC1000 (2,205-lb) bomb, this Ju 87D-1/ Trop shows the much improved aerodynamic shape of the D in comparison with the B which preceded it. S7+KS was the aircraft of Oberstleutnant Walter Siegel, Geschwaderkommodore of Stukageschwader 3 at Derna, Libya, in June 1942. Its markings indicate 8./StG 3.

44 Signal flare tube
45 Braced fuselage mainframe
46 Front spar/fuselage attachment point
47 Pilot's seat (reinforced with 4-mm side and 8-mm rear armour)
48 Inter-cockpit bulkhead
49 Sliding canopy handgrip
50 External side armour
51 Pilot's back armour (8 mm)
52 Headrest

53 Aft-sliding cockpit canopy (shown part open)
54 Radio mast cut-out
55 Anti-crash hoop (magnesium casting)
56 Radio mast
57 Radio equipment (FuGe 16) compartment
58 Additional (internal) side armour
66 Ammunition magazine racks
67 Additional (external) side armour with cut-out for hand grip
68 Internal side and head armour
69 Sliding canopy section (shown part open)
70 Ring-and-bead gunsights

71 Twin 7.9-mm Mauser MG 81Z machine gun on GSL-K 81 mount
72 Canopy track fairing
73 Peil G IV D/F equipment
74 Circular plexiglass access panel

78 Radio aerial
79 Faired elevator mass balance
80 Starboard elevator
81 Tailplane structure
82 Tailplane brace/spar attachment point
83 Tailplane bracing strut
84 Fuselage skinning
85 Control runs
86 Tailfin attachment fairing
87 Tailfin structure
88 Rudder horn balance
89 Rudder
90 Rudder trim tab controls
91 Rudder trim tab
92 Rudder control linkage
93 Rudder post
94 Rear navigation light
95 Elevator tab
96 Port elevator
97 Faired elevator mass balance

98 Tailplane front spar
99 Control pulley circular access panels
100 Rudder lower hinge fairing
101 Tailplane bracing strut
102 Emergency tailskid
103 Tailwheel
104 Tailwheel leg
105 Jacking point
106 Fuselage stringers
107 Master compass
108 Crew entry step (port and starboard)
109 Entry step support (with control run cut-outs)
110 Wing root fairing
111 Non-slip walkway (aft section external metal strakes)
112 Fuel filler point
113 Non-slip walkway (forward section composite surface)
114 Leading-edge structure
115 Self-sealing port inner wing fuel tank (52.8 Imp gal/240 litre capacity)
116 Wing-joint external cover strip
117 Ball-and-socket wing attachment points
118 Armoured coolant radiator (port and starboard)
119 Inboard flap structure
120 Flap hinge

59 Canopy track
60 Handhold/footrests
61 Braced fuselage mainframe
62 Rear spar/fuselage attachment point
63 Radio-operator/gunner's seat (folding)
64 Floor armour (5 mm)
65 Armoured bulkhead (8 mm)
75 Back-to-back L-section stringers (fuselage horizontal break)
76 First-aid stowage
77 Z-section fuselage frames

121 Rheinmetall-Borsig MG 17 machine gun of 7.92-mm calibre (port and starboard)
122 Ammunition tank (1000 rounds capacity) inboard of rib
123 Port outer self-sealing fuel tank (33 Imp gal/150 litre capacity)
124 Corrugated wing rib
125 ETC bomb rack support bar
126 ETC bomb rack underwing fairing
127 Port outboard flap
128 Port aileron
129 Aileron mass balance
130 Rear spar
131 Wing rib
132 Port navigation light
133 Front spar
134 Wing leading edge
135 Underwing bomb load (two 110-lb/50-kg bombs) on multi-purpose carrier
136 Bomb shackles
137 Dienartstab percussion rod attachments
138 ETC 50/VIII fairing
139 Air brake (extended)
140 Air brake activating mechanism
141 Air brake (retracted)
142 Landing lamp
143 Wheel spat
144 Fork/spat attachment
145 Port mainwheel
146 Brake reservoir filler point
147 Cantilever fork
148 Leather shroud
149 Oleo-pneumatic shock absorber
150 Mainwheel leg
151 Siren fairing
152 Barrel of MG 17 machine gun
153 Wind-driven siren
154 Starboard wheel spat
155 PVC ventral bomb rack
156 Bomb cradle
157 Starboard wheel fork
158 Starboard mainwheel
159 Bomb release trapese
160 551-lb (250-kg) bomb with *Dienartstab* attachment

Junkers Ju 87 Stuka

campaign – where one put a radio station off the air by ramming the aerials – and then proved useful in the Balkans, Greece and Mediterranean theatres. One Ju 87R tested a large container, hung on the main bomb crutch, intended to carry spares and other cargo.

The Ju 87B and derivatives wrought havoc throughout Europe in the first two years of World War II, meeting only one serious setback. Over England its losses were unacceptably heavy, 41 being shot down in the period 13-18 August 1940, so that from 19 August Stukas were withdrawn from attacks against UK targets. The type had already shown that, with German air supremacy, it could knock out the vital British coastal radars; but it was the same radars that enabled the defending fighters unfailingly to intercept, and the vulnerability of the Ju 87 was suddenly apparent. The aircraft had been designed on the basis of good fighter protection, and in such conditions it had demonstrated such devastating effectiveness that many in the UK – foot-soldiers, journalists and politicians alike – cried 'Where are our dive-bombers?' In fact, the country had dive-bombers, such as the Blackburn Skua and Hawker Henley, but they played little part in the war, and the whole concept of the dive-bomber became a subject of violent argument.

Specification
Junkers Ju 87G-1
Type: anti-tank aircraft
Powerplant: one 1044-kW (1,400-hp) Junkers Jumo 211J-1 inline piston engine
Performance: maximum speed about 314 km/h (195 mph); cruising speed normally about 190 km/h (118 mph); rate of climb and service ceiling not known, but extremely poor; combat radius about 320 km (199 miles)
Weights: empty about 4400 kg (9,700 lb); maximum take-off about 6600 kg (14,550 lb)
Dimensions: span 15.00 m (49 ft 2½ in); length 11.50 m (37 ft 8¾ in); height 3.90 m (12 ft 9¼ in); wing area 33.69 m² (362.6 sq ft)
Armament: two 37-mm BK 3.7 cannon and one flexible 7.92-mm (0.331-in) MG 81 machine-gun, plus a useful bombload when the underwing cannon were not being carried

Variants

Junkers Ju 87 V1: first prototype, with 477-kW (640-hp) Rolls-Royce Kestrel
Junkers Ju 87 V2: second prototype 455-kW (610-hp) Jumo 210Aa, hurriedly fitted single-fin tail unit
Junkers Ju 87 V3: third prototype, properly designed tail, engine lowered to improve pilot view
Junkers Ju 87A: first production series, 477-kW (640-hp) Jumo 210Ca or (A-2) 507-kW (680-hp) Jumo 210Da about 200 built (1937-8)
Junkers Ju 87B: 895-kW (1,200-hp) Jumo 211Da, redesigned canopy and fuselage, larger vertical tail, spatted instead of trousered landing gears, bombloads up to 1000 kg (2,205 lb) (total deliveries in various sub-types about 1,300)
Junkers Ju 87C: navalised version intended for use from aircraft-carrier, folding wings, hook, catapult hooks, jettisonable landing gear, flotation gear and extra tankage; operated from land bases
Junkers Ju 87D: major production version, 1044-kW (1,400-hp) Jumo 211J-1 or 1119-kW (1,500-hp) Jumo 211P-1, redesigned airframe with lower drag, bombload up to 1800 kg (3,968-lb), D-2 glider tug, D-3 increased armour, D-4 for torpedo-carrying, D-5 with extended wingtips, D-7 twin MG 151 cannon and night equipment, D-8 as D-7 without night equipment
Junkers Ju 87G-1: conversion of D-3 to attack armoured vehicles with two 37-mm BK 3.7 (Flak 18) guns
Junkers Ju 87H: dual-control trainers without armament, kinked rear canopy with side blisters
Junkers Ju 87R: derivative of Ju 87B-2 with augmented tankage and provision for drop tanks to increase range, normally with single SC250 (551-lb) bomb

The last variant of the Ju 87 to become operational, apart from the Ju 87H trainer, was the Ju 87G-1 anti-tank model. This was not built as such, but rather converted from Ju 87D-5 airframes. The concept was the brainchild of the extraordinary Hans-Ulrich Rudel, who despite being shot down 30 times flew no fewer than 2,530 combat sorties and destroyed 519 Russian tanks: the basic Ju 87D-5 was adapted to carry a pair of massive Flak 18 (BK 3,7) 37-mm cannon pods under its outer wing panels. The aircraft illustrated was on the strength of II/ Schlachtgeschwader 3, more specifically the unit's 5. Staffel, serving on the Eastern Front in late 1944. The Ju 87G-1 could carry bombs instead of guns, but had no dive-brakes.

No picture could better illustrate the cranked wings of the Stuka than this shot taken through the windscreen by the pilot of an accompanying aircraft. This 1940 Ju 87B is still wearing four-letter factory codes and may be on flight test from Tempelhof. From this angle the dive-brakes are visible, but not the 'double wing'.

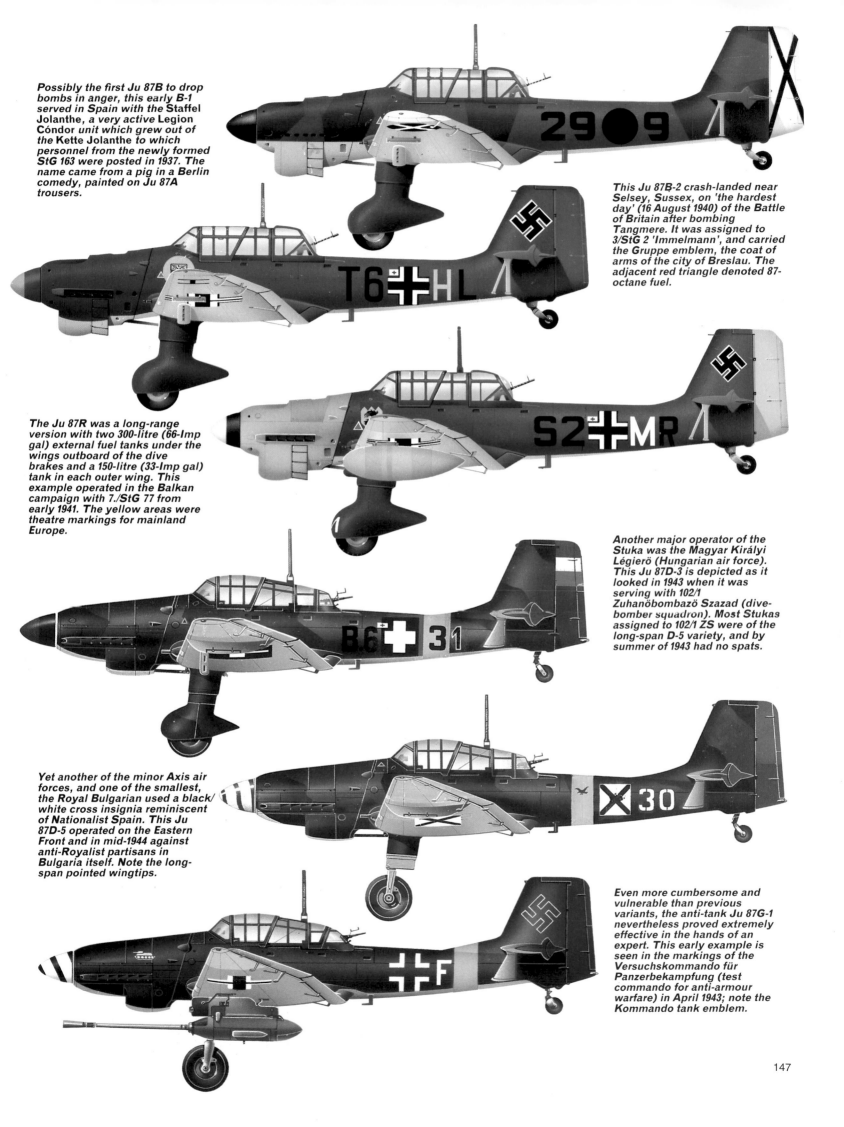

Possibly the first Ju 87B to drop bombs in anger, this early B-1 served in Spain with the Staffel Jolanthe, a very active Legion Cóndor unit which grew out of the Kette Jolanthe to which personnel from the newly formed StG 163 were posted in 1937. The name came from a pig in a Berlin comedy, painted on Ju 87A trousers.

This Ju 87B-2 crash-landed near Selsey, Sussex, on 'the hardest day' (16 August 1940) of the Battle of Britain after bombing Tangmere. It was assigned to 3/StG 2 'Immelmann', and carried the Gruppe emblem, the coat of arms of the city of Breslau. The adjacent red triangle denoted 87-octane fuel.

The Ju 87R was a long-range version with two 300-litre (66-Imp gal) external fuel tanks under the wings outboard of the dive brakes and a 150-litre (33-Imp gal) tank in each outer wing. This example operated in the Balkan campaign with 7./StG 77 from early 1941. The yellow areas were theatre markings for mainland Europe.

Another major operator of the Stuka was the Magyar Királyi Légierö (Hungarian air force). This Ju 87D-3 is depicted as it looked in 1943 when it was serving with 102/1 Zuhanóbombazö Szazad (dive-bomber squadron). Most Stukas assigned to 102/1 ZS were of the long-span D-5 variety, and by summer of 1943 had no spats.

Yet another of the minor Axis air forces, and one of the smallest, the Royal Bulgarian used a black/white cross insignia reminiscent of Nationalist Spain. This Ju 87D-5 operated on the Eastern Front and in mid-1944 against anti-Royalist partisans in Bulgaria itself. Note the long-span pointed wingtips.

Even more cumbersome and vulnerable than previous variants, the anti-tank Ju 87G-1 nevertheless proved extremely effective in the hands of an expert. This early example is seen in the markings of the Versuchskommando für Panzerbekampfung (test commando for anti-armour warfare) in April 1943; note the Kommando tank emblem.

147

Even at the outbreak of war the Ju 87 was recognised as a somewhat dated design, but this was masked by its fantastic successes. As with so many other old Luftwaffe types, lack of a replacement resulted in planned termination of production being countermanded, and like that of the Messerschmitt Bf 110 and He 111, Ju 87 output increased from 1941 to 1944. The standard basic type throughout this period was the Ju 87D, designed in 1940, first flown in early 1941 and in action on the Eastern and North African fronts by the end of 1941. This was powered by the 1044-kW (1,400-hp) Jumo 211J-1 driving a VS 11 propeller with very broad blades, making a major difference to flight performance, which was put to use in carrying much heavier loads. Maximum bomb load rose to 1800 kg (3,968 lb), the main crutch being able to take the PC1400 (3,086-lb) armour-piercing bomb and the wing racks the SC500 (1,102-lb) or a wide range of other stores including gun pods each housing either twin 20-mm cannon or six 7.92-mm (0.31-in) MG 81 machine-guns. Defensive armament at the rear was replaced by a pair of MG 81s, exceptionally light but fast-firing weapons with belt feed instead of 75-round magazines. Additionally, the entire aircraft was refined to reduce drag, the most noticeable improvement being to the cowling and canopy. The landing gear was cleaned up, but from 1942 the spats and leg fairings were increasingly discarded.

The most numerous variant was the Ju 87D-3, which embodied better protection for the crew and vital parts of the aircraft, reflecting the Ju 87's increasing use as a *Schlachtflugzeug* (close-support aircraft). From 1942 all versions were often called upon to fly missions other than dive-bombing, such as glider-towing, anti-partisan attacks and general utility transport with a great diversity of loads. A few Ju 87D-4s were equipped as torpedo-bombers, but the next main variant was the Ju 87D-5 with extended wingtips to help counter the considerably increased weight of Ju 87D versions. Reflecting the increasing peril of day operations, the Ju 87D-7 was a night variant with the more powerful Jumo 211P engine and long exhaust pipes extending back across the wing. Together with the day-flying Ju 87D-8 it replaced the wing guns by the far more powerful 20-mm MG 151, and dive-brakes were at last omitted. The Ju 87D-8 was the last version in production, the total number built by late September 1944 – when almost all aircraft production other than fighters was terminated – being generally accepted as 5,709.

Anti-armour

There were several schemes for successors, including the Ju 87F and Ju 187, but the only other Stuka variants were built by conversions of the ubiquitous D models. The most important sub-type was the Ju 87G series, of which only the Ju 87G-1 became operational. The Ju 87G was a specialised anti-armour version, fitted with two BK 3,7 (Flak 18) guns hung under the wings just outboard of the landing gears. This 37-mm gun was a formidable weapon weighing over 363 kg (800 lb) and in wide service as ground-based Flak (anti-aircraft artillery) equipment. In 1942 a trial installation was tested in a converted Ju 87D-5 and found more effective than the many other Luftwaffe anti-tank aircraft such as the Henschel Hs 129 and Junkers Ju 88P. Fed by clips of six rounds, the BK 3,7 had a muzzle velocity with armour-piercing ammunition exceeding 850 m (2,790 ft) per second, and the greatest exponent of the Ju 87G-1, Hans-Ulrich Rudel, was ultimately credited with the personal destruction of 519 Russian armoured vehicles. It was he who flew 2,530 combat missions and continued to lead Stuka formations in daylight long after the other Stukagruppen had replaced their vulnerable aircraft with the Focke-Wulf Fw 190.

Another variant produced by converting aircraft of the Ju 87D series was the Ju 87H dual-control trainer. No trainer had been considered necessary in the early days of Ju 87 service, but by 1943 the art of surviving in the type had become so specialised and important on the Eastern Front that even experienced bomber and fighter pilots had to go out with a Ju 87 instructor before taking up their places in the decimated ranks of the Stukagruppen. Almost all versions of Ju 87D were converted into H models, retaining the same suffix numbers. Outwardly the differences included removal of armament and the addition of bulged side panels in the rear cockpit to give the instructor a measure of forward vision.

Sand and snow

All versions could fly with tropical equipment and sand/dust filters, and many aircraft on the Eastern Front operated on skis in winter. There were several experimental variants, mainly concerned with tests of weapons intended for later aircraft. One of the most striking test programmes concerned one Ju 87D-3 fitted with large streamlined overwing passenger cabins. The idea was that the Ju 87, an aircraft well used to front-line operations, should become a vehicle for putting down agents behind enemy front lines. The trials programme got under way in early 1944 at the Graf Zeppelin Research Institute at Ruit, and the final design of cabin seated two men in tandem, both facing forward, with ample side windows which gave the pilot some lateral vision. In a shallow dive the two pods were to be pulled off the wing by streaming large parachutes, but there is no record of this actually being done, though the pods were flown with passengers.

The Ju 87 was widely used by all the Axis air forces, including those of Italy, Hungary, Slovakia, Romania and Bulgaria. When Ju 87s were discovered in Italian markings the totally fictitious belief arose among the British that the type was being made in Italy, even the invented type-designation of Breda 201 Picchiatelli was widely published! In fact, from 1939 every Ju 87 was made by Weser in the same Tempelhof building.

Weatherbeaten Ju 87B-2s of II/StG 1 on the Eastern Front, probably in autumn 1941. Nine more Ju 87s are in the distance at lower level. These aircraft are probably returning from a combat mission, with bomb racks empty. Spats were still in use at this time, and opposition to the Stuka was still generally feeble.

The Ju 87D-5 introduced a wing of greater span to allow the heavy weapon loads to be carried with a better margin of safety. This D-5 was photographed on final landing approach, with full flap, on return from a mission with 8./StG 2 in the Kursk area in the summer of 1943. Its code was T6+AS, T6 being that of StG 2 itself.

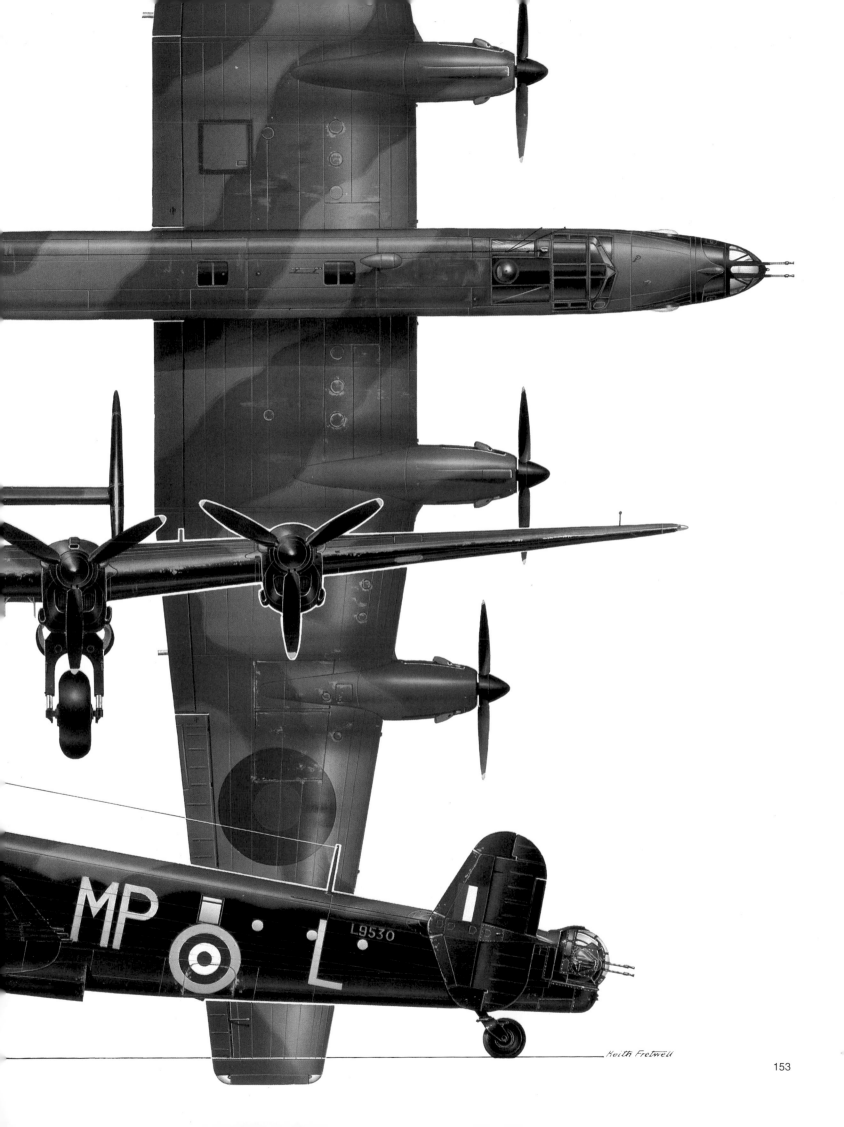

Keith Fretwell

Handley-Page Halifax

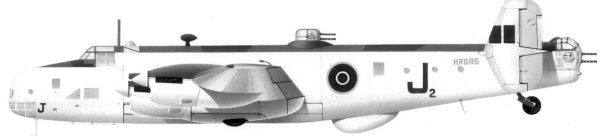

Various Halifaxes scored major successes against U-boats in the grey/white livery of RAF Coastal Command. This GR.Mk II Series 1 (Special) has plain ejector exhausts, H₂S radar and the original wing and tail, but has the Defiant-type top turret with a surrounding fairing, the latter removed from the subsequent marks.

No. 76 Sqn was the second to fly the Halifax operationally. Aircraft 'L', a Halifax Mk I, flew with that unit until August 1941 when it went missing. When this picture was taken it had flown four missions.

further swelled by the LAPG (London Aircraft Production Group), the key organisation in which was the London Passenger Transport Board whose great works at Chiswick and Aldenham were part-nered by such motor firms as Chrysler, Duple Bodies, Park Royal Coachworks and Express Motor and Body of Enfield, all the parts coming together at a vast shadow factory at Leavesden, outside Watford.

Few aircraft of such size and complexity have ever been cleared for service more quickly or rushed into production on such a scale with so few delays. By November 1940 No. 35 Squadron was form-ing at Boscombe Down, moving to Leeming and finally to Linton-on-Ouse as the first of 36 Halifax squadrons of Bomber Command, mainly as part of No. 4 Group in north-east England. The first night mission was to be Le Havre on 11/12 March 1941, and a day attack on *Scharnhorst* led to a series of missions against German warships, the only serious loss being the fifth production machine, which was shot down by an RAF night fighter.

Vibration problems

As often happens, the major problems emerged only when large numbers of aircraft were in service. By the end of 1941 No. 4 Group had 11 squadrons converted, and the otherwise superb and popular bomber was marred by problems with landing gear and reduction gears. In one period of six months there were 95 failures of reduction gears, in many cases resulting in the propeller parting company with the aircraft, and over 75 per cent were on the no. 1 (port outer) engine. It was difficult to establish the precise cause, but it was clearly due to aerodynamically induced vibration. The problem was greatly eased (but not cured) by fitting four-bladed propellers, and crews became used to flying with four-bladers on all engines, or on just the outers or even on no. 1 engine alone (because such propell-ers were in short supply). The hydraulic problems with both the main and tail wheels were severe, taking the form chiefly of the main gears refusing to stay up in flight and the tail gear refusing to extend

for landing. The main gears had enormous welded bridge-pieces carrying the twin legs, giving a feeling of strength that was con-spicuously absent from the towering units of the Short Stirling. Once the up-locks and hydraulics had been redesigned the units stayed up, but the simplest thing to do with the tailwheels was to lock them down.

The crew of seven entered via an upward- and inward-hinged door low on the left side behind the wing. Unobstructed movement was possible from nose to tail, it being easy to step over the two massive wing spars on the dural floor above the 6.7-m (22-ft) bomb bay. The latter had no fewer than eight doors which overlapped laterally when open. There were a further 24 doors covering six bomb cells in the inner wing. All doors were driven hydraulically, as were the large slotted flaps, but the two Boulton Paul turrets were electro-hydraul-ically actuated. A prominent feature was the triplet of fuel jettison pipes under each wing, with flexible joints under the flap hinges. As for the leading edges, these lost their slats, despite progressive in-creases in gross weight, because of the problems of de-icing and fit-

The second prototype, L7245, was the first Halifax to carry armament (two nose 7.7-mm/0.303-in Brownings, four in the tail, and two Vickers 'K' guns fired through beam hatches). It differed from L7244 in other respects, such as the omission of slats (which interfered with de-icing and cable-cutters). Note the day-bomber camouflage.

L9601 is seen here immediately before being delivered from Radlett airfield in August 1941. It was followed by only seven further Mk I Halifaxes before, from L9609, the Hudson-type dorsal turret became standard on the Mk II. This large turret was tested from 3 July 1941 on L9515 and significantly reduced speed.

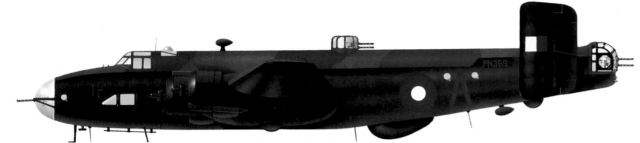

The two large masts identify this long-span B.Mk III as a special aircraft used by No. 462 RAAF Sqn to carry out high-power jamming of German radio and radar transmissions using the Airborne Cigar transmitters. No. 462 Sqn operated in 1944-45 from Foulsham, Norfolk, mainly as a unit of No. 100 (Bomber Support) Group.

Electronic warfare was pioneered by an alert RAF in World War II, even the Indian theatre being equipped with such advanced listening and recording platforms as this Halifax B.Mk III (Special). Some of the added HF and VHF whip aerials can be seen along the underside of the fuselage. PN369 flew with No. 1341 Flight based at Digri.

ting balloon-cable cutters. The rather lumpy engine installations had twin drum radiators, with a smaller lower drum for the oil cooling, and carb-air inlets being low on each side. Above the inboard cowlings were ram inlets for the heated cabin air. Exhaust was led forward and discharged aft in a single stack which from late 1941 was hidden under a cool shroud.

Merlin for the Mk II

After 100 Halifax Mk I Series 1 aircraft had been built, production switched to the successive versions listed in the variants panel. The Halifax Mk II Series 1 introduced the Merlin XX which, thanks to 'Doc' Hooker's brilliant supercharger, gave much great power to help counter increases in weight. The new mid-upper turret, however, substantially reduced the speed at all power settings (it was the same turret as used on the Lockheed Hudson) and the Halifax Mk II Series 1 Special eliminated all turrets except the one that mattered, at the tail. Most also left off the flame-damped exhausts, it being felt that speed and height were better than a few flames visible from a few hundred metres. The Halifax Mk II Series 1A introduced a much more pleasing moulded Perspex nose with a hand-aimed gun (7.7-mm/0.303-in Vickers 'K' or Browning, or on the Halifax GR.Mk II for Coastal Command a 12.7-mm/0.5-in Browning). One Halifax Mk II Series 1A had extended inner nacelles and there were several other trial modifications, but the most important ones were large rectangular fins to improve directional stability (there had been landing accidents due to coarse rudder demands, and in any case bomb-

ing accuracy was previously poor), and the compact, low-drag Boulton Paul Defiant-type mid-upper turret with four guns. The cowlings were also refined with single Morris-block radiators, and as a result cruising speed increased by over 32 km/h (20 mph).

One of the most famous Halifaxes was V9977, the second Preston-built Halifax Mk II, which was the first aircraft in the world fitted with mapping radar. Codenamed H$_2$S, the new device gave a picture of the terrain below, but it relied on the wonderful magnetron valve which was not known to the enemy. Sadly V9977 crashed during trials by flying into a Welsh mountain, killing the radar team, in June 1942. Subsequently hundreds of Halifaxes (and other 'heavies') had H$_2$S, but many Halifaxes displayed a smaller and more symmetrical bulge in this location and these were the lucky ones with a hand-aimed 12.7-mm (0.5-in) gun. Alone among the great armadas of Bomber Command, these Halifaxes could both see and hit the Luftwaffe night-fighters which formated on them from below, with upward-firing cannon.

Shortage of Messier landing gears and hydraulics led to the Halifax Mk V, with a complete Dowty hydraulical system and landing gears, the latter looking less massive. Landing weight was restricted to 18144 kg (40,000 lb), and most Halifax Mk Vs had four-bladed propellers throughout and served mainly in tug, maritime and transport roles. All were built by Rootes and Fairey.

Biggest improvement of all was the switch to the Bristol Hercules sleeve-valve air-cooled engine, first fitted to Radlett hack R9534 in October 1942. The snag was that the 38-litre (2,320-cu in) radial

Powered by a quartet of Hercules XVI engines, almost 100 Halifax C.Mk IIIs were built. Unarmed and fitted with 11 passenger seats, it served as a wartime transport but after 1945 the bulk of those produced were converted for civilian duties (as the Halifax C.Mk 8) like many other British bomber 'heavies'.

One of the last production marks was the Halifax C.Mk VIII (post-war C.Mk 8) freighter, seen with its 3629-kg (8,000-lb) cargo pannier installed. The airframe was that of the B.Mk VI, but without armament, and the portholes served an 11-seat passenger cabin. This version led directly to the civil HP.70 Halton used by BOAC.

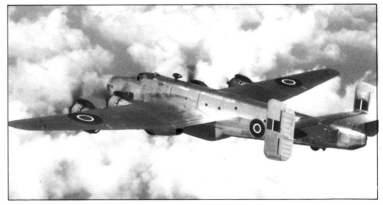

Halifaxes of Burn-based No. 578 Squadron flew from their Yorkshire home to support the D-Day landings on 6 June 1944. This aircraft is seen over Hazebrouck, its target for the day.

burned more fuel than the 27-litre (1,650-cu in) Merlin, but its greater power at last removed the crippling limitations on altitude and speed, and made the Halifax a tractable and totally respected aircraft. The first radial-engined Halifax B.Mk III flew in July 1943, and swiftly supplanted the Merlin versions. DH Hydromatic propellers without spinners were fitted, together with long flame-damped exhausts. The tailwheel was at last made to retract and extend reliably, and a further improvement in ceiling resulted from extending the span to 31.75 m (104 ft 2 in) with rounded tips. From February 1944 the performance of the Halifax B.Mk III was such that previous restrictions on bombing hazardous targets were lifted, while Merlin-engined Halifaxes were withdrawn from German skies altogether.

In Bomber Command Halifaxes served with Australian, Canadian, New Zealand, Free French and Polish squadrons, together with the Pathfinder Force from its inception. The Halifax was also the chief

heavy electronic-warfare aircraft of No. 100 Group, and the only long-range transport for the special-duty squadrons (Nos 138 and 161) which flew numerous breathtaking missions to pinpoint drop areas as far away as Norway, eastern Poland and southern Czechoslovakia. Halifaxes were by far the most important heavy bombers in the North African theatres, from Palestine in 1942 westward to Tunisia and northern Italy by 1945. Many Halifaxes towed Airspeed Horsa gliders non-stop from the UK to North Africa for the invasion of Sicily, and over 1,000 Halifax Mk IIIs and Mk Vs towed gliders in northern Europe, including the attack on the Norwegian heavy-water plant on 19 November 1942. Both marks were the only aircraft cleared to tow the tank-carrying General Aircraft Hamilcars.

Sole example of Mk IV

Only one Halifax Mk IV was built, to test a modified form of engine mounting. On 10 October 1944 the first Halifax B.Mk VI introduced the 1342-kW (1,800-hp) Hercules 100, together with an extended pressurised fuel system and injection carburettors for long-range tropical missions against Japan. Shortage of the Mk 100 engine led to the Halifax B.Mk VII which was a Mk VI with the old Hercules XVI, used mainly by Canadian and French units. The Halifax C.Mk VIII served with Nos 301 and 304 (Polish) Squadrons, both unarmed and with a twin-12.7-mm (0.5-in) tail turret. The Halifax A.Mk IX was a post-war airborne model which replaced the converted Halifax A.Mk III, A.Mk V and A.Mk VII, and had very full equipment for 16 paratroops and heavy loads of dropped stores.

The last subcontracted 'Halibag' was a Fairey-built Halifax A.Mk VII delivered on 5 October 1945, and the last by the parent firm a Halifax A.Mk IX delivered on 11 November 1946 (it later went to the Egyptian air force). Production by marks is listed separately. Handley Page built 1,590 Halifaxes, English Electric 2,145, the LAPG 710, Rootes 1,070 and Fairey 661. At least four Halifax Mk IIIs completed 100 missions over Germany, the nose art of *Friday the 13th* (128 missions with No. 158 Squadron from Lissett) being displayed in the RAF Museum. In the post-war RAF the number of Halifax A.Mk 9 and GR.Mk 6 aircraft (post-war designations) dwindled until one of the latter species flew the final sortie from Gibraltar on 17 March 1952, though Henlow's Halifax A.Mk 9 was still on parachute testing in January 1955. The Armée de l'Air used many Halifax B.Mk 6s as bombers and in many research and trials roles, and also as 32-seat airliners on routes to West Africa and even Brazil.

With 9,600 horsepower visible in this photograph, Halifax B.Mk IIIs of No. 462 Squadron (RAAF) cross the sea on their way to bomb synthetic oil plants in the Ruhr during September 1944.

Handley Page Halifax variants

H.P.57: two prototypes, no. 1 without armament, with slatted wings
Halifax B.Mk I: Merlin X engines, **Halifax Mk I Series 2** stressed to 27216 kg (60,000 lb) (total 84)
Halifax B.Mk II: Merlin XX engines, mid-upper turret; **Halifax Mk II Srs 1 (Special)** no nose or mid-upper turret; **Halifax Mk II Srs 1A** new moulded nose, four-gun mid-upper turret, Merlin XXII engines and larger fins progressively introduced (total 1,966; conversions to **Halifax GR.Mk II Srs 1** and **Halifax GR.Mk II Srs 1A**)
Halifax B.Mk III (H.P.61): Hercules XVI engines and all B.Mk II improvements, plus H₂S or ventral gun, later with extended span (total 2,081; conversions to **Halifax GT.Mk III** and **Halifax R.Mk III**, and two post-war civil) **Halifax Mk.IV:** one-off trials of engine mounts
Halifax Mk V (H.P.57): Merlin XXII engines, hydraulics and main gears by Dowty instead of British Messier; built as **Halifax B.Mk V Srs 1** and **Halifax B.Mk V Srs 1A, Halifax GR.Mk V, Halifax A.Mk V, Halifax Met.Mk V** and (designation unconfirmed) **Halifax GT.Mk V** (total 916)
Halifax B.Mk VI: Hercules 100 engines in improved installations, tropical long-range fuel

system (total 557; conversions to **Halifax GR.Mk VI** (later **GR.MK 6**) and **Halifax Met.Mk VI (Met.Mk 6)**, and at least 41 post-war civil)
Halifax B.Mk VII: as B.Mk VI but Hercules XVI (total 193)
Halifax A.Mk VII: airborne forces variant, unarmed except twin 12.7-mm (0.5-in) tail turret special transport/paradrop provisions (total 234-HP 45, Rootes 120 and Fairey 69)
Halifax C.Mk VIII (H.P.70): Hercules XVI; unarmed transport normally with 11 passenger seats plus detachable pannier (pre-loaded) for 3628-kg (8,000-lb) cargo (new production believed 96, of which over 81 registered post-war as civil **Halifax C.Mk 8** conversions)
Halifax A.Mk IX (H.P.71A): Hercules XVI; airborne forces definitive multi-role aircraft with 16 paratroop seats, provision for 3628-kg (8,000-lb) supply containers or other stores and glider-tow cleat; developed by Boulton Paul but production (140) by H.P.; post-war 68 civil
Halifax A.Mk 9 conversions, including 38 UK; served as RAF Halifax A.Mk 9 and with Egyptian air force
H.P.70 Halton: rebuilds by H.P. in 1946 of Halifax C.Mk 8 as transports for BOAC, with 10-passenger cabin and 3628-kg (8,000-lb) pannier (total 13)

Avro Anson

In 1928 A. V. Roe & Co. Ltd had taken up a licence to build the Fokker F.VII three-engined transport. This version, the Avro Ten, led Avro into a new way of thinking about its production and design methods. The experience led to a modified version, the Avro Eighteen (Avro 642), and later to the Avro 652, better known as the famous Anson.

In 1934 Imperial Airways issued a requirement for a light monoplane to be used as a fast four-passenger charter type. Avro scaled down the Avro Eighteen and developed a low-wing design which was powered by a pair of 216.3-kW (290-hp) Armstrong Siddeley Cheetah V engines and fitted with retractable landing gear. The prototype Avro 652 (G-ACRM) made its first flight on 7 January 1935 and, with its sister ship (G-ACRN), was delivered to Imperial Airways two months later. These two machines were fairly streamlined and they could cruise at 266 km/h (165 mph), which was quite outstanding by comparison with other light transport aircraft of the day.

At about this time the Air Ministry issued its specification G.18/35 for a new coastal reconnaissance and patrol aircraft for the Royal Air Force. The two principal contenders were de Havilland with a modified version of the D.H.89A Dragon Rapide and Avro with the model 652A, which was virtually the same as the two earlier Imperial Airways machines. The prototype Avro 652A (K4771) was first flown from Woodford on 24 March 1935, and the main change from the Avro 652 was the installation of two Cheetah VI engines and the adoption of a heavily-framed Armstrong Whitworth gun turret in the upper fuselage behind the wings. It also had an observation panel in the underside of the nose and three square cabin windows on each side in place of the oval transparencies of the civil aircraft.

The prototype Avro 652A was delivered to Martlesham Heath in April 1935 for initial evaluation, following which some alterations were made to the area of the horizontal tail surfaces. K4771 was then sent to the Coastal Defence Development unit at Gosport where it met up with the Rapide for comparative tests. It showed itself to be superior in terms of speed and range with the result that, in July, an initial contract for 174 examples (carrying the name Anson) was issued by the Air Ministry. A good number of minor modifications were demanded on the production version and these were laid down in the manufacturing specification which was issued at that time. Many of the changes were internal and related to systems and controls.

Equipping 11 RAF squadrons at the beginning of World War II, the Avro Anson was destined to play a major part in the crew training programme, as well as in a relatively short-lived role as a general reconnaissance aircraft with RAF Coastal Command. Illustrated is an Anson Mk 1 fitted with the Armstrong Whitworth dorsal turret.

Ansons were built with a welded steel-tube fuselage structure (with internal wire bracing in the rear section) and fabric covering. The production version had excellent visibility for the crew through the continuous strip of windows that ran the full length of the cabin from the cockpit to a point parallel with the wing trailing edge. The prominent turret was fitted with a single Lewis gun for manual operation by the air gunner, who had access to the turret from the rear cabin. Coastal reconnaissance Ansons also had provision for a fixed gun set into the nose on the port side for operation by the pilot. The wings were built from spruce and plywood with a formed plywood covering. Initial production Ansons (delivered in 1936, 1937 and 1938) were painted silver overall with pre-war 'A'-type roundels and black serial numbers but, in early 1939, all aircraft received the standard RAF temperate land camouflage of dark green and light earth with the new wartime roundels and grey or white unit codes on the fuselage sides. Those machines used for training tasks were painted with yellow undersides, and the coastal patrol Ansons had their lower surfaces painted light grey. These early Ansons were also notable for the contoured engine cowlings which were shaped for the seven individual cylinder heads. Controls on the Anson took a little getting used to: the Schrenck split flaps were worked by a hydraulic hand pump and the landing gear had to be retracted by a hand-winding mechanism which could make the raising of the gear a protracted exercise. Nevertheless, the Anson was a strong and reliable machine and aircrews soon forgave it for these minor shortcomings.

The first Anson deliveries were made to No. 48 Squadron at Manston in March 1936. Rather than going straight into the primary reconnaissance role, these aircraft were pressed into service as navigation trainers as part of the RAF Expansion Scheme, which was then moving into high gear. Thousands of new airmen were being rapidly trained to meet the threat of war

Anson Mk 1s were initially employed in the maritime patrol role with Coastal Command. This aircraft is seen flying with No. 48 Sqn, from Hooton Park in 1940/41. During this period the squadron's main role was to cover the Irish Sea and to shepherd convoys into Liverpool and the Clyde.

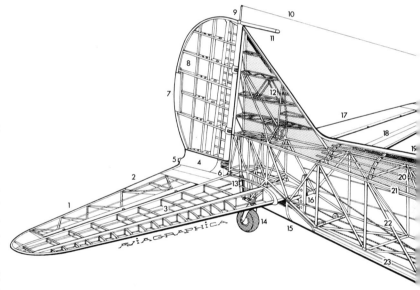

In the post-war years, Ansons were to be found serving in a variety of roles, with many swopping their military identities for civil markings. With a bulbous nose housing radar and avionics equipment, G-ALIH was used by Ekco Electronics Ltd. The aircraft was withdrawn in 1967.

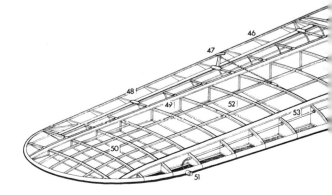

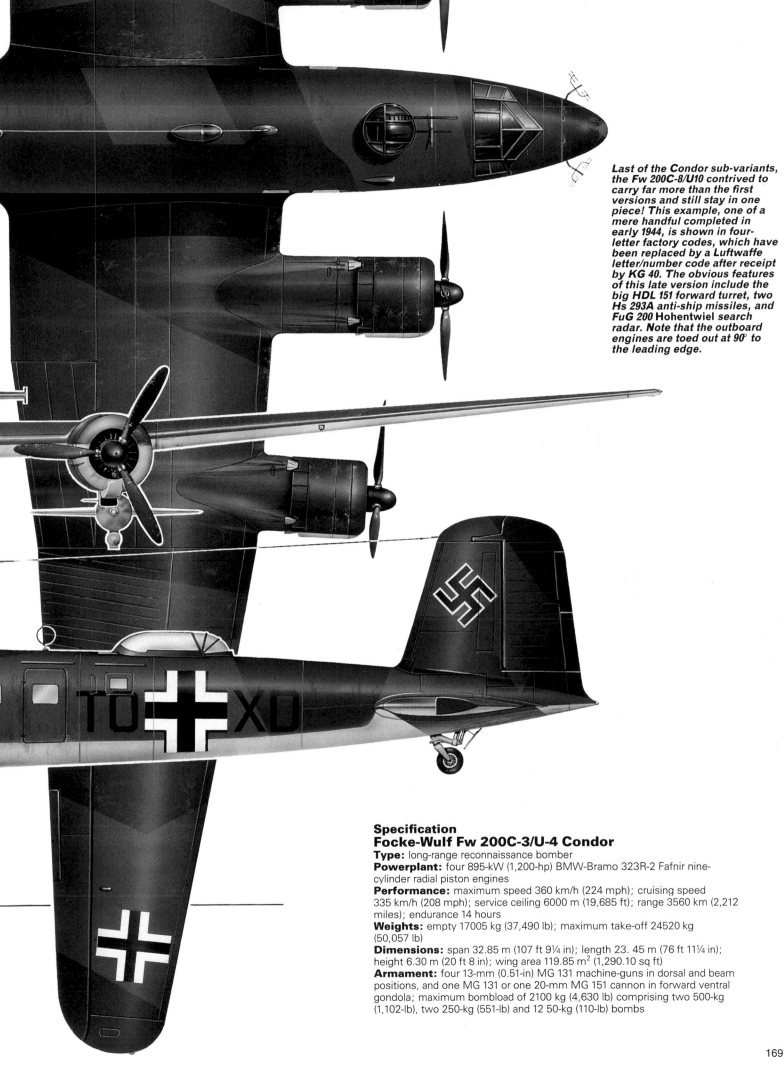

Last of the Condor sub-variants, the Fw 200C-8/U10 contrived to carry far more than the first versions and still stay in one piece! This example, one of a mere handful completed in early 1944, is shown in four-letter factory codes, which have been replaced by a Luftwaffe letter/number code after receipt by KG 40. The obvious features of this late version include the big HDL 151 forward turret, two Hs 293A anti-ship missiles, and FuG 200 Hohentwiel search radar. Note that the outboard engines are toed out at 90° to the leading edge.

Specification
Focke-Wulf Fw 200C-3/U-4 Condor
Type: long-range reconnaissance bomber
Powerplant: four 895-kW (1,200-hp) BMW-Bramo 323R-2 Fafnir nine-cylinder radial piston engines
Performance: maximum speed 360 km/h (224 mph); cruising speed 335 km/h (208 mph); service ceiling 6000 m (19,685 ft); range 3560 km (2,212 miles); endurance 14 hours
Weights: empty 17005 kg (37,490 lb); maximum take-off 24520 kg (50,057 lb)
Dimensions: span 32.85 m (107 ft 9¼ in); length 23. 45 m (76 ft 11¼ in); height 6.30 m (20 ft 8 in); wing area 119.85 m² (1,290.10 sq ft)
Armament: four 13-mm (0.51-in) MG 131 machine-guns in dorsal and beam positions, and one MG 131 or one 20-mm MG 151 cannon in forward ventral gondola; maximum bombload of 2100 kg (4,630 lb) comprising two 500-kg (1,102-lb), two 250-kg (551-lb) and 12 50-kg (110-lb) bombs

Posed in front of 'their' Condor, which already has its engines turning, this KG 40 crew reviews their map details before leaving Bordeaux-Mérignac on another long mission.

very experienced pilot, to form a squadron which could sink ships out in the Atlantic, on which the obvious enemies, France and especially the UK, would depend during a war. The problem was that there was no suitable aircraft. The intended machine, the Heinkel He 177, was years from combat duty. The only answer seemed to be the 'Japanese' Fw 200 V10.

As in the case of the Ju 52/3m, Dornier Do 17 and several other types, the RLM was faced with botching up a combat aircraft from a commercial transport, which is ironic, because British observers thought at the time the Luftwaffe was busily developing bombers in the false guise of civil aircraft. The Fw 200 was fundamentally un-suited to its new role because it had been designed to operate at lighter weights and at civil load factors. The airframe would hence-forth have to operate from rough front-line airstrips with heavy loads of fuel and weapons, and in combat would certainly have to 'pull g' in tight turns or dive pull-outs, and all at low level in dense air. The Bre-men stressmen did what they could to beef up the structure, but this consisted of a few local reinforcements which added just 29 kg (63.9 lb) to the airframe weight. Ideally they should have started again, but the proposed Fw 200C-series was almost immediately accepted when it was offered in August 1939. A pre-production batch of 10 Fw 200C-0 aircraft was ordered just after the start of the war, and by agreement as many as possible were modified from B-series transports already on the line. The first four had to be delivered as Fw 200C-0 transports. Their only modifications were to introduce twin-wheel main gears, long-chord cowlings with gills and various in-ternal equipment items. All four were delivered just in time for the invasion of Norway in April 1940.

The remaining six Fw 200C-0s were given the locally reinforced structure and simple armament comprising three MG15s, one in a small (almost hemispherical) turret behind the flight deck, one in a

rear dorsal cockpit with a fold-over hood and the third fired from a rear ventral hatch. An offensive load of four 250-kg (551-lb) bombs could be carried, two hung under the enlarged outer nacelles and the others on racks immediately outboard under the roots of the outer wings. Production continued immediately with the Fw 200C-1, which was planned as the definitive version though it still had a weak structure, very vulnerable fuel system (especially from below), no armour except behind the captain's seat and many inconvenient features. The main addition to the Fw 200C-1 was a ventral gondola, offset as in the Japanese Fw 200 V10 but longer in order to provide room for a weapon bay (which was normally used to carry a cement bomb with 250-kg/551-lb ballistics dropped as a check on bomb-sight settings). At the front of the gondola was a 20-mm MG FF aimed with a ring-and-bead sight mainly to deter any AA gunners aboard the enemy ships. At the rear was an MG15 replacing the previous ventral gun. The only other change was to replace the forward turret by a raised cockpit canopy with a hand-aimed MG15 firing ahead.

Operational experience

Normal crew numbered five: pilot, co-pilot and three gunners, one of the last being the engineer and another the overworked radio-operator/navigator. There was plenty of room inside the airframe, and all crew stations had provision for heating and electric light, but from the start the crews of Petersen's new maritime unit, Kampf-geschwader (KG) 40, were unhappy with the Condor's structural in-tegrity and lack of armament. There is no evidence any Condors were delivered to any prior combat unit, as sometimes stated, but only to the transport *Gruppe* already mentioned. KG 40 was hence-forth to be virtually the sole Fw 200C operating unit. There were never to be enough Condors to go round. Focke-Wulf was well aware of the demand, and organised dispersed manufacture at five plants with final assembly at Bremen and Cottbus, and also by Blohm und Voss at Finkenwerder. It is thus a reflection on the frustrations of the programme, which did not enjoy top priority, that by the ter-mination in February 1944 only 252 Fw 200C Condors had been built. Moreover, because of high attrition, KG 40 never had full wing strength and seldom had more than 12 aircraft available. Indeed, more than half the aircraft delivered in the first year suffered major structural failure, at least eight breaking their backs on the airfield.

The first missions by 1/KG 40 were flown from Danish bases from 8 April 1940 against British ships. In late June the *Geschwader* was transferred to Bordeaux-Mérignac, which was to be the main base until it had to be evacuated in autumn 1944. Initially, from July 1940, the Condors simply added their small offensive weight to the Luft-waffe's assault on the UK, usually flying a wide sweep west of Corn-wall and normally west of Ireland, dropping four bombs and heading

The sole Focke-Wulf Condor to wear British civilian markings, this aircraft was previously OY-DAM of Danish Air Lines. It subsequently served for a short time with the Royal Air Force in 1941 before being written off. Note the increased size of the fin and rudder compared with the prototype.

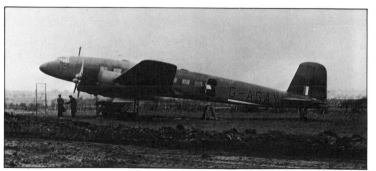

CE+IB, seen here with the yellow theatre band of the Eastern Front, was one of two transport Condors – FW 200C-4/U1 (illustrated) and U2 – built in 1942. These had all regular C-4 improvements but only had four 7.92-mm (0.31-in) MG15 guns, two in small dorsal turrets and two in a short gondola. There were 11 passenger seats.

The Focke-Wulf Fw 200C-3/U2 was readily identified by the bulge in the gondola for the Lofte 7D bombsight. Fitting this accurate device necessitated a reorganisation of the ventral armament.

was a major redesign with a real attempt to cure the structural problems despite even higher weights; the attempt did not quite succeed. Engines were BMW-Bramo Fafnir 323R-2s, with water-injection rating of 894.8 kW (1,200 hp). The bombload was increased by clearing the nacelles to 500 kg (1,102 lb) each and adding 12 SC50 bombs of 50 kg (110 lb) each in the gondola. The forward dorsal blister was replaced by an Fw 19 turret (one MG15) and two more MG15s were aimed through sliding panels in each side of the rear fuselage, crew rising to six. The Fw 200C-3/U1 at last gave real defensive firepower with an MG151/15 in an HDL151 forward turret, and the MG FF was replaced by an MG151/20, but the big turret reduced top speed at sea level from some 305 km/h (190 mph) to little over 275 km/h (171 mph).

In 1941 only 58 Condors were built, these including the Fw 200C-3/U2 with the complex but extremely accurate Lotfe 7D bombsight, which caused a prominent bulge under the front of the gondola and necessited replacement of the cannon by a 13-mm (0.51-in) MG131. Most Fw 200C-3/U2s also reverted to the small Fw 19 turret. Next came the Fw 200C-3/U3 whose dorsal armament comprised two MG131s, one in an EDL131 forward turret and the other in the manually aimed rear position. The Fw 200C-3/U4 had increased internal fuel, bringing maximum weight to 22700 kg (50,045 lb), which the reinforced airframe could just manage. The beam guns were changed for MG131s, giving much greater firepower, but the forward turret went back to the Fw 19.

Standard and special versions

If any sub-type can be considered 'standard' it was the Fw 200C-4, from February 1942, which added search radar, initially the pre-production Rostock and then the standard FuG 200 Hohentwiel, the latter giving blind-bombing capability. Oddly, the Fw 200C-4 went back to the HDL151 turret and MG15s elsewhere except for the front of the gondola, which had the MG131 or MG151/20 depending on whether or not the Lotfe 7D was fitted. Two 'specials' in 1942 included the Fw 200C-4/U1 and Fw 200C-4/U2 transports, with VIP interiors and just four MG15s. The former, flown in 1945 at Farnborough, was Himmler's personal transport, the Gestapo chief having a vast leather chair with heavy armour and a personal escape hatch.

In early 1943 some Fw 200C-3s were modified to launch and guide the Hs 293A anti-ship missile, which was hung under the outer nacelles. The associated Kehl/Strassburg radio guidance installation was in the nose and front of the gondola. These missile carriers were designated Fw 200C-6, and the last few Condors to be built, in the winter of 1943-44, were Fw 200C-8s specially designed to carry the Hs 293 and with deeper outboard nacelles and a longer forward section to the gondola.

for Norway, making the return trip a day or two later. At least two were shot down, though a pilot of No. 87 Sqn, who unusually caught a Condor on the direct run to Plymouth, ran out of ammunition so continued to intercept on camera-gun film only. From August the Condors got on with their real task and within two months had been credited with 90,000 tonnes of British shipping. On 26 October they made headlines for the first time when Oberleutnant Bernhard Jope and crew found the 42,348-ton *Empress of Britain* south west of Donegal. Their bombs crippled the liner, which was then torpedoed by a U-boat. By 9 February 1941 1/KG 40's claim had reached 363,000 tonnes. By this time it had been joined by two further *Staffeln*, totalling a nominal 36 aircraft.

Tackling the problems

In the winter of 1940-41 Cottbus delivered a few interim Fw 200C-2 Condors whose main improvement was scalloped outer nacelle racks and low-drag wing racks, the former also being plumbed for small (300-litre/66-Imp gal) external tanks. The big advance came with the Fw 200C-3, first flown in February 1941. This

The initial production reconnaissance model of the Condor for Luftwaffe service was the Fw 200C-1. This picture clearly shows the ventral gondola and forward dorsal blister toting MG15 machine-guns, and similar armament in the rear dorsal position. Bombs could be hung beneath the enlarged outer nacelles.

This Condor, F8+GH, was photographed serving with I/KG 40 in Greece in 1942. It does not carry the white Mediterranean theatre band and was probably on temporary detachment. It is apparently an Fw 200C-3, for it has large wing stores attachments, an MG 151/20 in the front of the gondola and Fw 19 turret.

Focke-Wulf Condor

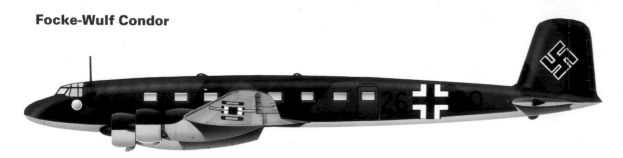

Differing from the Fw 200 V1 in having BMW engines (though basically a licensed Hornet) and enlarged vertical tail, the Fw 200 V3 was taken on Luftwaffe strength as D2600, the Führermaschine for the use of Hitler and other top Nazis. It went through three changes of livery before receiving wartime camouflage. Its base was Berlin-Tempelhof.

In 1940 the Bremen factory delivered four Fw 200C-0 transports. These were not only the first batch of Condors for the Luftwaffe but also the first with long-chord cowls, three-bladed propellers and twin-wheel main gear. X8+BH is shown on Stalingrad supply duties from Zaporozhye with KGrzbV 200 in January 1943.

Had such aircraft been available in 1940, the 'Scourge of the Atlantic' would have been much more deadly even than it was. Fortunately, while the weak early Condors were almost unopposed, the improved models had a very hard time, from ship AA guns, from Grumman Martlets (Wildcats) based on escort carriers and, not least, from the CAM (catapult-armed merchantman) Hawker Hurricanes, which scored their first kill on 3 August 1941. Even a Short Sutherland could catch a Condor and shoot it down, and from 1942 Condors tried never to come within the radius of Coastal Command

Bristol Beaufighters and de Havilland Mosquitoes. In addition, their effectiveness was hampered not only by poor serviceability, but also by repeated urgent calls to undertake transport duties in various theatres, including Stalingrad. KG 40 was disbanded in autumn 1944, its Biscay bases having been captured, and the few surviving Condors finished the war as rarely used transports.

The Fw 200C-4 was once again fitted with a HDL 151 turret behind the cockpit, and this aircraft carries a 20-mm MG151 cannon in the gondola, signifying that it is not fitted with a Lofte 7D bomb-sight.

B-24 Liberator

Just as the Handley Page Halifax was overshadowed in the UK by its partner, the Avro Lancaster, so the B-24 never gained the popular appeal of its USAAF partner, the Boeing B-17. In fact the B-24 was newer, more efficient, built in far greater numbers and, unlike the B-17, served on every front in World War II.

More effort, more aluminium and more aircrew went into the Liberator than into any other flying machine ever built. Nothing better underlines American industrial might than the fact that the prototype Liberator did not even fly until after the beginning of World War II, and the last (except for the PB4Y-2 model) came off the assembly line before the end of the war; yet, in between, deliveries of some 15 major variants totalled 18,188, or 19,203 including spares. This compares with 12,731 B-17s and 7,366 Lancasters.

The accomplishments of the Liberator were in proportion to its astronomic quantities; and, particularly in the matter of range, which to some degree stemmed from its having an unusually efficient wing, the Liberator gave the Allies capabilities they would not otherwise have possessed. Early in the war the first Liberators, in RAF markings, were the first aircraft in history to make North Atlantic crossings a matter of everyday routine. In 1942 a more developed version at last closed the gap in the Western North Atlantic where U-boats had been able to operate beyond the range of other RAF aircraft. On countless occasions Liberator formations made attacks on targets that could be reached by no other Allied bomber until the advent of the B-29. Though primarily a heavy bomber, the Liberator was also a most effective fighter (in that it shot down something like 2,600 enemy aircraft), the leading Allied oceanic patrol and anti-submarine aircraft, and the leading Allied long-range cargo transport.

A demanding aircraft

At the same time it was a most complicated and advanced machine, leading to prolonged pilot training programmes and on occasion to severe attrition. Not only was it demanding to fly, even to a pilot fully qualified on the type, but it was eventually cleared to operate at such high weights that take-offs became marginal even with full power on all engines. Flight stability was also marginal, and escape from a stricken machine was extremely difficult once the pilot or pilots had let go of the controls. Moreover, though more modern and in most ways more efficient than the B-17, the overloaded late-model B-24s were hardly any improvement over their more primitive partners, and several commanders, including 'Jimmy' Doolittle, famed commanding general of the 8th Air Force, preferred the old B-17.

The most famous of all the B-24's many missions were those aimed against the great oil refineries at Ploesti in Romania. Here B-24Js of the US 15th Air Force drone through heavy flak defences above the Concrida Vega refinery during the raid of 31 May 1944.

B-24 Liberator

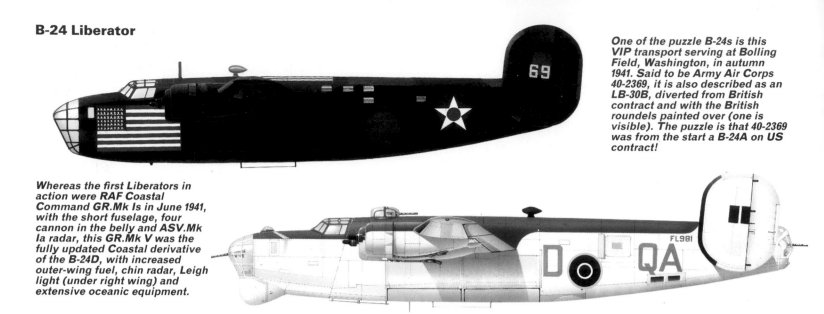

One of the puzzle B-24s is this VIP transport serving at Bolling Field, Washington, in autumn 1941. Said to be Army Air Corps 40-2369, it is also described as an LB-30B, diverted from British contract and with the British roundels painted over (one is visible). The puzzle is that 40-2369 was from the start a B-24A on US contract!

Whereas the first Liberators in action were RAF Coastal Command GR.Mk Is in June 1941, with the short fuselage, four cannon in the belly and ASV.Mk Ia radar, this GR.Mk V was the fully updated Coastal derivative of the B-24D, with increased outer-wing fuel, chin radar, Leigh light (under right wing) and extensive oceanic equipment.

In fact the B-24s might have been B-17s, because in October 1938 Consolidated Aircraft Corporation was asked if it would set up a second-source production line of the Boeing bomber. Consolidated had moved just three years earlier from icy Buffalo in New York state to sunny San Diego in California, and was well placed to expand its large new plant. But chief engineer Isaac M. 'Mac' Laddon had already made studies for long-range bombers and was confident of producing a superior design. Part of this confidence rested on the wing patented by David R. Davis: this had a particularly deep section, with sharp camber and a reflex curve on the underside, and was almost as slender as the wing of a sailplane. Tunnel tests confirmed Davis's claim that this wing offered from 10 to 25 per cent less drag than ordinary wings, but no full-scale wing had flown. Laddon had designed a giant flying-boat, the Model 31, and this was to fly in spring 1939 with a Davis wing. Pending its measured drag figures he quickly drew a heavy bomber with the same wing and tail but a new fuselage with a futuristic smooth nose and tricycle landing gear. Under the mid/high-mounted wing were two bomb-bays, each as large as that of a B-17.

The commanding general of the US Army Air Corps, H. H. 'Hap' Arnold, studied the plans of the Model 32 in January 1939 and told Laddon to go ahead, and "build a bomber that will fly the skin off any rivals." Consolidated received a contract for the Model 32, designated XB-24, on 30 March 1939. It was to be able to reach 483 km/h (300 mph), 10670 m (35,000 ft) and 4828 km (3,000 miles). The Model 31 flying-boat flew on 5 May 1939, and met the promised drag figures. Design of the Model 32 went ahead quickly though it was drastically altered to have a conventional nose with the

A beautiful portrait of the Consolidated Model 32 (XB-24) prototype taken from an accompanying chase aircraft on 29 January 1940, just a month after the first flight. This aircraft, USAAC 39-680, had no turbos on its Twin Wasp engines and had an armament of six manually-aimed 7.62-mm (0.3-in) calibre machine-guns, all in single mounts.

navigator and bombardier in the front and a side-by-side cockpit further back with a stepped windscreen. The first XB-32 (US Army serial 39-680) made a successful flight from Lindbergh Field on 29 December 1939.

In through the bomb-bay

This prototype was modern and impressive rather than beautiful, with a deep and stumpy fuselage and very large oval fins and rudders contrasting with the graceful wing. The engines were 821-kW (1,100-hp) Pratt & Whitney R-1830-33 Twin Wasps with geared superchargers, though it was planned to fit turbosuperchargers later to increase the speed from the achieved 439 km/h (273 mph) to beyond the contractual figure. Each of the bomb-bays could carry 1814 kg (4,000 lb) of bombs, with a catwalk down the centre to provide structural strength and crew access to the rear fuselage. To enter the aircraft the usual drill was to flick a small hydraulic lever on the right side of the bay. This opened the bomb doors, which rolled up the outside of the fuselage like a roll-top desk, the moving sections driven by large sprockets working directly on the corrugated inner stiffening skins. Then the crew of seven climbed onto the catwalk, the pilots, navigator, bombardier and radio operator going forwards and three gunners aft. Armament comprised five hand-held machine-guns. Apart from the general complexity of the systems, and the extremely advanced Minneapolis-Honeywell autopilot, features included 12 flexible fuel cells in the wing, Fowler flaps and unusual main gears comprising single legs curved round the outside of single very large wheels which retracted hydraulically outwards to lie flat in the wing, where the wheel projected below the undersurface and needed a fairing.

In March 1939 the US Army Air Corps ordered seven YB-24s, and these were delivered in 1940 with additional fuel and equipment and pneumatic de-icer boots, but without fixed outer-wing slots. Only a month later, in April 1939, the French ordered 175 Model 32s in a version designated 32B7, but that country collapsed before delivery and the UK took on this contract, whilst ordering 165 on its own account. Of the 165, 25 were retained by the US Army and eventually 139 were delivered to the RAF as the LB-30 (Liberator British type 30), with the British designation Liberator Mk II. These were developed to British requirements and had self-sealing tanks, ample armour, R-1830-S3C4G engines driving Curtiss instead of Hamilton propellers, a lengthened nose, and completely re-thought equipment including 11 7.7-mm (0.303-in) Browning guns, eight of them in mid-upper and tail Boulton Paul electric turrets. Serial numbers began at AL503. The second LB-30 was completed as the unique VIP personal transport of Prime Minister Churchill, with the name Commando, unpainted bright finish and (in 1943) the tall single fin also used on the US Navy RY-3 transport and PB4Y-2 (its designation was Liberator C.Mk IX).

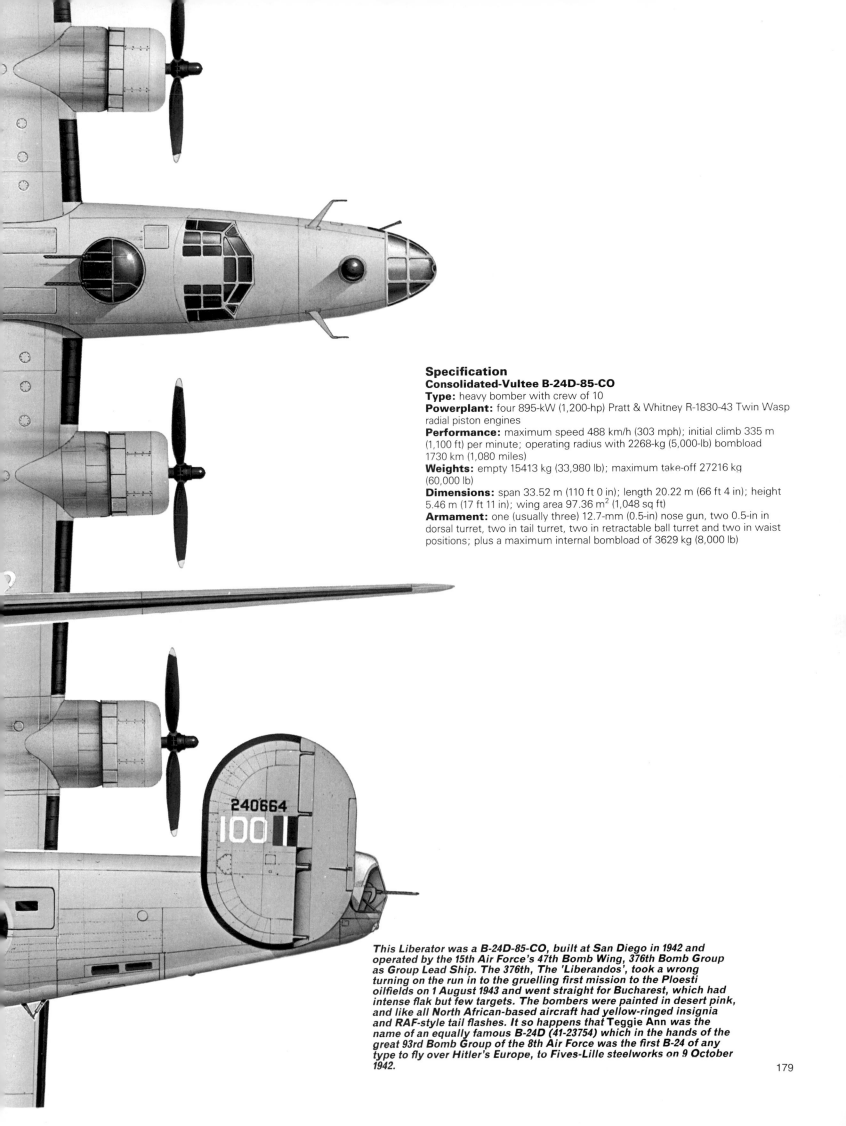

Specification
Consolidated-Vultee B-24D-85-CO
Type: heavy bomber with crew of 10
Powerplant: four 895-kW (1,200-hp) Pratt & Whitney R-1830-43 Twin Wasp radial piston engines
Performance: maximum speed 488 km/h (303 mph); initial climb 335 m (1,100 ft) per minute; operating radius with 2268-kg (5,000-lb) bombload 1730 km (1,080 miles)
Weights: empty 15413 kg (33,980 lb); maximum take-off 27216 kg (60,000 lb)
Dimensions: span 33.52 m (110 ft 0 in); length 20.22 m (66 ft 4 in); height 5.46 m (17 ft 11 in); wing area 97.36 m^2 (1,048 sq ft)
Armament: one (usually three) 12.7-mm (0.5-in) nose gun, two 0.5-in in dorsal turret, two in tail turret, two in retractable ball turret and two in waist positions; plus a maximum internal bombload of 3629 kg (8,000 lb)

This Liberator was a B-24D-85-CO, built at San Diego in 1942 and operated by the 15th Air Force's 47th Bomb Wing, 376th Bomb Group as Group Lead Ship. The 376th, The 'Liberandos', took a wrong turning on the run in to the gruelling first mission to the Ploesti oilfields on 1 August 1943 and went straight for Bucharest, which had intense flak but few targets. The bombers were painted in desert pink, and like all North African-based aircraft had yellow-ringed insignia and RAF-style tail flashes. It so happens that Teggie Ann was the name of an equally famous B-24D (41-23754) which in the hands of the great 93rd Bomb Group of the 8th Air Force was the first B-24 of any type to fly over Hitler's Europe, to Fives-Lille steelworks on 9 October 1942.

This B-24J was fitted with the bluff-fronted Emerson nose turret in place of the much more common Consolidated (which resembled the tail turret). After Lend-Lease RAF service in India it was passed to the Indian air force, the tail number being Indian (many also retained previous RAF numbers).

The B-24D was developed through block numbers up to 170, bringing in the Dash-65 engine and the Briggs-Sperry retractable ball turret (in place of the tunnel gun), which were to remain standard on subsequent bomber versions. Gross weight climbed to 32296 kg (71,200 lb), much heavier than any other Allied bomber except the B-29 and quite unanticipated when the B-24 was designed. Even the most gentle turns were best made on the autopilot; the controls were both very heavy and very sluggish, and at weights much in excess of 27216 kg (60,000 lb) any rapid manoeuvre (even to avoid a collision) was impossible.

Over the Hump

The B-24E (RAF Liberator Mk IV) had Curtiss propellers and was the first model built at Willow Run; later some B-24Es were made at Fort Worth and Tulsa. The C-109 was a gasoline tanker conversion of the B-24E (later of the B-24D also) able to carry 10978 litres/2,900 US gal (2,415 Imp gal) of fuel in metal tanks in the fuselage, linked to a single socket in the side of the fuselage and with an inert-gas safety system. Later models had Mareng bag tanks, and their main use was to ferry fuel 'over the Hump' from Burma into China, especially to support B-29 missions. The XF-7 was a rebuilt B-24D with extra tankage and a large installation of reconnaissance cameras, from which the later F-7 reconnaissance versions were derived, and two one-off experimental prototypes were the XB-24F and XB-41. The XB-24F was fitted with thermal de-icing, and it is surprising it was not adopted because the rubber-boot de-icers were useless if punctured by shell splinters and thousands of man-hours were wasted carefully inspecting them after combat missions. The XB-41 was a 'destroyer' (escort fighter) carrying 14 guns in twin dorsal, chin and tail turrets and duplicated waist positions, and extra ammunition.

One of the definite shortcomings of the B-24 in combat proved to be its vulnerability to head-on attack. At best there were only three hand-held guns in the nose, and despite progressive modification to the armour the internal protection was so poor that, both in Europe and over the Pacific Ocean, numerous waist gunners were killed by shells entering at the nose and often killing the pilots *en route*. Some pilots took to carrying slabs of sheet armour held in front of their bodies by hand during crucial periods. One B-24E (42-7127) was fitted with a nose turret and powered lateral barbettes low on the fuselage sides, flying in this form on 30 June 1943. By the time it flew the decision had been taken to make nose turrets standard, and the vast floods of orders for B-24D and B-24G models were switched to have turrets. North American's B-24G line had the turret from the start, the selected type being the Emerson A-15; 430 of the B-24G model were built. A new optical bombing station was built in under the turret, and to give the navigator sufficient room and house the 1,200 rounds of nose-turret ammunition the nose was extended by 0.254 m (10 in).

Fitting the nose turret to an extended nose was the last major modification, and from mid-1943 the gigantic production machine poured out aircraft superficially almost identical. Those bought under 1941 and early 1942 contracts were designated B-24H, and the 738 built at Forth Worth retained the flat-fronted Emerson electric nose turret as used on the B-24G. The 1,780 built at Willow Run and 582 from Tulsa had the sloping-front Consolidated hydraulic turret, the first Tulsa block being the last B-24s not to have the Dash-65 engine. Called Liberator Mk VI, the RAF and Commonwealth versions usually had the Boulton Paul tail turret, so that all four turrets were of different makes. Made in much larger numbers than any other variant, the B-24J was initially merely a rationalised B-24G or B-24H, with the new C-1 autopilot and M-9 bombsight and, usually, the A-6A (Consolidated) or A-6B (Motor Products) nose turret. From spring 1944 all five plants delivered aircraft to USAAF service depots where any of a wide range of tail armament and equipment schemes could be installed according to the destination theatre. Those for the US Navy, the PB4Y-1, which originally had a B-24D-type nose, switched to the A-6A turret and then, for the main run in 1944, to the near-spherical Erco nose turret. From April 1944 B-24s were unpainted, and the only significant modifications after that month were the introduction of the improved General Electric (B-22 type) turbocharger, giving higher performance at altitude, and a lightweight Consolidated M-6A twin-gun tail 'stinger' (basically manual, with hydraulic assistance, and with a wider field of fire than a turret) which resulted in the designation B-24L. San Diego built 417 of these, and Willow Run 1,250. Some were again rebuilt as B-29 gunner trainers with that aircraft's complex remote sighting and barbette armament, with designation RB-24L; later they received additional radar as the post-war TB-24L. The many British variants were designated Liberator Mk VI, Coastal Command models being the GR.Mk VI and GR.Mk VIII (the C.Mk VII was a Liberator Express transport series and the C.Mk IX was similar to the US Navy RY-3 with the tall single fin).

New tail — new generations

In March 1943 Consolidated had merged with Vultee to form Convair, and the last major wartime variant was the B-24M with a lightweight Motor Products tail turret, Convair building 916 and Willow Run 1,677. Among the experimental versions were the XB-24P and the Ford-built XB-24Q with a radar-controlled remotely sighted tail stinger, which led to that fitted to the B-47. These were the last of the familiar models with the original tail.

*Ship 42-107263 (the 107,263rd aircraft funded for the **US Army Air Force** in 1942) was a **C-87-CF**, one of the numerous unarmed long-range transport derivatives of the B-24. The basic airframe was that of the B-24D but the fuselage was redesigned for 25 passengers and there was a cargo door on the left side. Finish was olive-drab.*

AL504, Commando, was the personal transport of Prime Minister Winston Churchill. Built as the second Mk II in early 1941, it was converted to VIP use and in late 1943 returned to Convair for modification close to the standard of the US Navy RY-3, with longer fuselage and tall fin (but retaining non-elliptical non-turbocharged engine cowls).

As far back as 1942 it had been clear that a single fin would be better, and on 6 March 1943 a converted B-24D flew with the fin and rudder of a Douglas B-23. After refinement the whole tail end of this machine was grafted onto another aircraft (42-40234, originally a B-24D but with a nose turret) to become the XB-24K. Ford also fitted 1007-kW (1,350-hp) Dash-75 engines, and the result was a bomber that was considerably faster, had more than double the full-load rate of climb and much better power of manoeuvre.

Convair were busy with further major improvements including longer nacelles housing larger oil tanks, an Emerson ball nose turret and lightweight ball turret in the tail, a completely new cockpit window arrangement giving better pilot view, and a further refined tail, and this became the next standard model after the B-24J, the B-24N. Thousands were ordered, the XB-24N flying in November 1944, but only seven YB-24Ns had flown when production stopped on 31 May 1945, 5,168 being cancelled.

Independently, the US Navy had been developing an optimised patrol version with the even taller single fin of the RY-3, low-rated engines without turbochargers and a further lengthened and completely re-arranged fuselage. Work began on 3 May 1943, and the first of the prototype PB4Y-2 Privateers flew on 20 September that year. Absence of turbochargers resulted in the engine cowls being made oval vertically instead of horizontally, but the main differences lay in the capacious fuselage which resulted in an overall length of 22.73 m (74 ft 7 in) with accommodation for a crew of 11. Armament comprised 12 guns in a Consolidated tail turret, fore and aft Martin dorsal turrets, an Erco nose turret and Erco twin-gun waist blisters. The internal bomb-bay was basically that of the B-24, but ASM-N-2 Bat radar-homing anti-ship missiles could be carried on underwing

attachments, and there were extensive maritime sensors. A total of 736 production Privateers was delivered by October 1945, some being converted into other versions including the PB4Y-1G for the Coast Guard, with no guns but more extensive glazing and a mass of special avionics. One variant, the P4Y-2K target, even survived to become the QP-4B under the 1962 unified designation system.

Consolidated B-24 Liberator variants

(all versions powered by four Pratt & Whitney R-1830 Twin Wasp 14-cylinder radials)
XB-24: Model 32 prototype
YB-24: seven pre-production with many small changes
LB-30A: British transport versions similar to YB-24 but unarmed
Liberator Mk I: various RAF models mainly converted in UK for Coastal Command with ASV radar and ventral cannon installation
Liberator Mk II: improved RAF bomber, longer nose, two Boulton Paul four-gun turrets, first operationally ready variant
LB-30: transport derivative of Liberator Mk II
B-24A: first US Army version, with six 12.7-mm (0.5-in) guns but otherwise similar to Liberator Mk I, used mainly as transports
XB-24B: Model 32 rebuilt with turbocharged engines in flattened elliptical cowlings used on most subsequent versions
B-24C: production B-24B with new 12.7-mm (0.5-in) twin-gun turrets behind cockpit and in tail
B-24D Liberator Mk III: first mass-produced version, progressively greater bomb load and armament, final blocks having three nose guns, two (rarely four) waist guns and twin guns in retractable ventral ball turret in addition to dorsal and tail turrets
C-87 Liberator Express: major rebuild of B-24D as transport; RAF **Liberator C.Mk VII**, US Navy **RY-2**
XF-7: reconnaissance rebuild of B-24D
B-24E: Ford-built variant with minor changes
XB-24F: prototype with thermal instead of pneumatic de-icers
B-24G: lengthened fuselage with nose turret
B-24H: mass-produced variant of B-24G with minor changes; RAF designation **Liberator IV**
Liberator GR.Mk V: RAF modification of Liberator Mk III with extra fuel, radar, Leigh light, ASW rockets and other additions
C-109: various bombers (mainly D and E) rebuilt as fuel tankers
B-24J: mass-produced bomber, standard production 1943-44; RAF **Liberator Mk VI**; RAF rebuilds included **C.Mk VI** and **C.Mk VIII** transports and Coastal **GR.Mk VIII**
PB4Y-1: wide range of US Navy models; initially equivalent to B-24D and later based on B-24J but with spherical Erco nose turret and major equipment changes
AT-22: advanced trainers, mostly rebuilt C-87s; later redesignated **TB-24**
C-87A: VIP sleeper passenger transport; US Navy **RY-1**
F-7: production strategic reconnaissance rebuild of B-24H; **F-7A** rebuild of B-24J with nose and bomb-bay cameras; **F-7B** rebuild of B-24J with all cameras in bomb-bay
XB-24K: with experimental single-fin tail
B-24L: production B-24J with twin manually-controlled tail guns
B-24M: production B-24J with lightweight tail turret
B-24N: new-standard production bomber with single fin, new nose and cockpit, and many other improvements
PB4Y-2 Privateer: redesigned US Navy patrol aircraft with longer fuselage, very tall single fin, vertical-ellipse cowlings and new armament; transport relatives were **C-87**, **RY-3** and **Liberator C.Mk IX**

Last of all the Liberator-type aircraft, the PB4Y-2 Privateer was a redesigned aircraft which flew long maritime patrol missions for the US Navy. Features included engine cowls elliptical vertically instead of horizontally, the tall single fin, Erco nose turret, waist blisters and a fuselage lengthened by 2.1 m (7 ft).

Heinkel He 177 Greif

The Luftwaffe failed to appreciate the value of strategic bombing, and began work on suitable designs too late to save the war. One of the few aircraft that did get off the ground was Heinkel's remarkable Greif. Not the most reliable of aircraft, it still managed some noteworthy missions, including pioneering air-to-surface missile work.

In the final three years of World War II Hitler's Germany was steadily reduced to rubble by the greatest fleets of heavy bombers the world will ever see. In reply the mighty Luftwaffe fielded just one type of heavy bomber, which achieved very little except to frighten its crews to death (often literally). Not to put too fine a point on it, it suffered from problems.

To be frank, while the RAF and US Army Air Force was deeply imbued with the urge to deploy strategic airpower, the Luftwaffe was primarily a tactical force dedicated to support the Wehrmacht in its land battles. Moreover, when in 1936 Goering was asked to back the launch of a heavy bomber, he explained the Führer was only interested in how many bombers there were, not how big they were. At that time, the Berlin air ministry was supporting the development of a 'Ural-bomber' programme with two rival types, the Do 19 and Ju 89. Had these continued, they would have been obsolescent by World War II. This programme was cancelled in 1937, and replaced by a requirement called 'Bomber A' which it was hoped would lead to a better aircraft. This requirement demanded a maximum speed of 540 km/h (335 mph) and the ability to carry a 2000 kg (4,410 lb) bombload over a radius of 1600 km (995 miles) at a cruising speed of 500 km/h (310 mph) – challenging figures. To make matters much more difficult it also required the capability of making medium-angle diving attacks.

Ernst Heinkel AG was given the job, without competition, and Projekt 1041 was actually started in late 1936. Under Technical Director Hertel, the gifted Günter twin brothers planned a bomber incorporating many radical new features, intended to give it the highest possible performance. Later designated He 177, the new bomber was marvellously clean aerodynamically. The fuselage was like a tube, with a glazed nose and a gun position in the glazed tailcone. The mid-mounted wing had high aspect ratio, for maximum efficiency, and under it was room for a large bomb bay. Clearly, power had to come from four engines of about 895.2 kW (1,200 hp) or two of 1790.4 kW (2,400 hp), but there were no 1790.4 kW (2,400 hp) engines. Boldly, in partnership with Daimler-Benz, Heinkel had designed a dive bomber, the He 119, powered by a DB 606 double engine comprising two DB 601 inverted-V12 engines side-by-side joined through a common gearbox to a single propeller. Two of these were to power the new heavy bomber, clearly offering lower drag and better manoeuvrability than four separate engines. To reduce drag further it was planned to augment the engine cooling by using surface condensation of steam in sandwich panels forming part of the wing skin. There were to be four main landing gears, one retracting inwards and another outwards under each engine to lie in the wing ahead of the main spar. Defensive guns were to be in remotely controlled turrets above the forward fuselage in the front and rear of a ventral gondola, as well as in the manned tail position. Altogether the 177 promised to have lower drag than any previous aircraft (even an unarmed civil one) of its size.

Things began to go wrong from the outset. By early 1939, when the V1 first prototype was taking shape, it was reluctantly concluded that steam cooling was impractical. Much larger radiators had to be used (they were made circular, round the front of each double

The He 177 had a checkered career in Luftwaffe service, its advantages negated by a plague of troubles mostly concerning the propulsion system. Worst of these problems was a tendency for the engines to catch fire without warning, leading to the uncomplimentary nickname 'Luftwaffenfeuerzeug'.

Heinkel He 177 Greif

The He 177 V1 first flew on 19 November 1939, but was only aloft for 12 minutes before engine temperatures soared, heralding a long saga of such problems. Another problem to surface was the inadequacy of the tail surfaces, which were increased on the second prototype, and again on production machines.

Aside from the engine problems, the He 177 exhibited a nasty swing on take-off, resulting in several accidents. The A-1 version introduced larger tail surfaces and stronger damping on the tailwheel. This is the A-03 pre-production aircraft, showing the unique mainwheel arrangement.

engine). In turn this meant greater drag, which demanded extra fuel which meant increased weight, in a vicious circle. The ministry officials then decreed that this big bomber had to be able to make steep 60° dive attacks, which resulted in a considerable increase in structure weight, further reducing performance and also requiring addition of large dive brakes under the wings. To slow the landing of the overweight aircraft full-span Fowler flaps were adopted, the outer portions coming out from under the ailerons. Again there were problems because the wing had not been stressed for the large lift and drag loads of the flaps.

The V1 made its maiden flight on 19 November 1939. Despite being unarmed it failed to come anywhere near the Bomber A requirement, maximum speed being 460 km/h (285 mph) and range being inadequate. On the other hand it handled reasonably well, and the few snags recorded gave no indication of the years of toil and disaster that were to follow.

Seven further prototypes followed, each heavier than its predecessor. Vertical tail area was increased, triple bomb bays were incorporated, various types of defensive armament fitted (low-drag remotely controlled guns were replaced by conventional turrets or hand-aimed guns) and ceaseless efforts made to try to eliminate the most serious problem, which was the frequency of engine fires. V2 suffered flutter and disintegrated, V4 crashed into the sea and V5's engines caught fire at low level, the aircraft flying into the ground and exploding.

In 1939 a total of 30 He 177A-0 pre-production aircraft were ordered, plus five from Arado. These had many changes including a redesigned nose for a crew of five, armament comprising a 7.92-mm MG81 in the multi-pane hemispherical nose, a 20-mm MG FF in the front of the gondola, a twin MG81Z at the rear of the gondola, a

This He 177A-5 was captured by British forces and allocated the serial TS439. Painted with large black and white stripes, it returned to England for evaluation. A high-altitude He 177A-7 was also obtained.

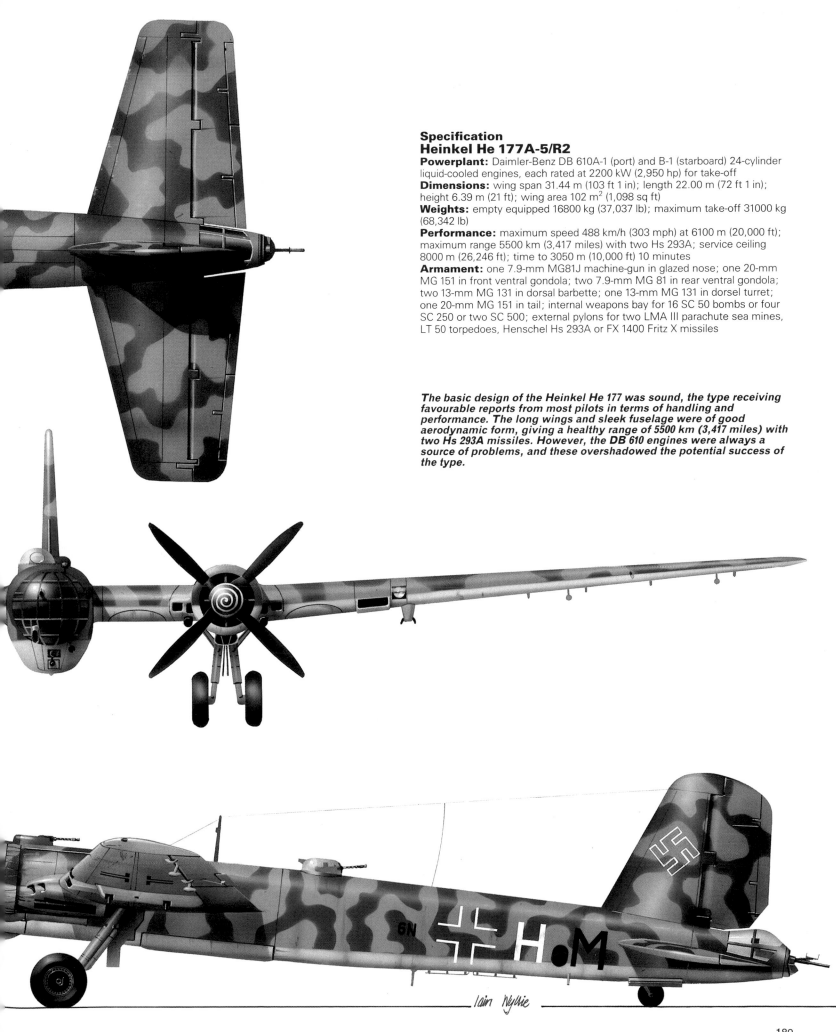

Specification
Heinkel He 177A-5/R2
Powerplant: Daimler-Benz DB 610A-1 (port) and B-1 (starboard) 24-cylinder liquid-cooled engines, each rated at 2200 kW (2,950 hp) for take-off
Dimensions: wing span 31.44 m (103 ft 1 in); length 22.00 m (72 ft 1 in); height 6.39 m (21 ft); wing area 102 m² (1,098 sq ft)
Weights: empty equipped 16800 kg (37,037 lb); maximum take-off 31000 kg (68,342 lb)
Performance: maximum speed 488 km/h (303 mph) at 6100 m (20,000 ft); maximum range 5500 km (3,417 miles) with two Hs 293A; service ceiling 8000 m (26,246 ft); time to 3050 m (10,000 ft) 10 minutes
Armament: one 7.9-mm MG81J machine-gun in glazed nose; one 20-mm MG 151 in front ventral gondola; two 7.9-mm MG 81 in rear ventral gondola; two 13-mm MG 131 in dorsal barbette; one 13-mm MG 131 in dorsel turret; one 20-mm MG 151 in tail; internal weapons bay for 16 SC 50 bombs or four SC 250 or two SC 500; external pylons for two LMA III parachute sea mines, LT 50 torpedoes, Henschel Hs 293A or FX 1400 Fritz X missiles

The basic design of the Heinkel He 177 was sound, the type receiving favourable reports from most pilots in terms of handling and performance. The long wings and sleek fuselage were of good aerodynamic form, giving a healthy range of 5500 km (3,417 miles) with two Hs 293A missiles. However, the DB 610 engines were always a source of problems, and these overshadowed the potential success of the type.

Heinkel He 177 Greif

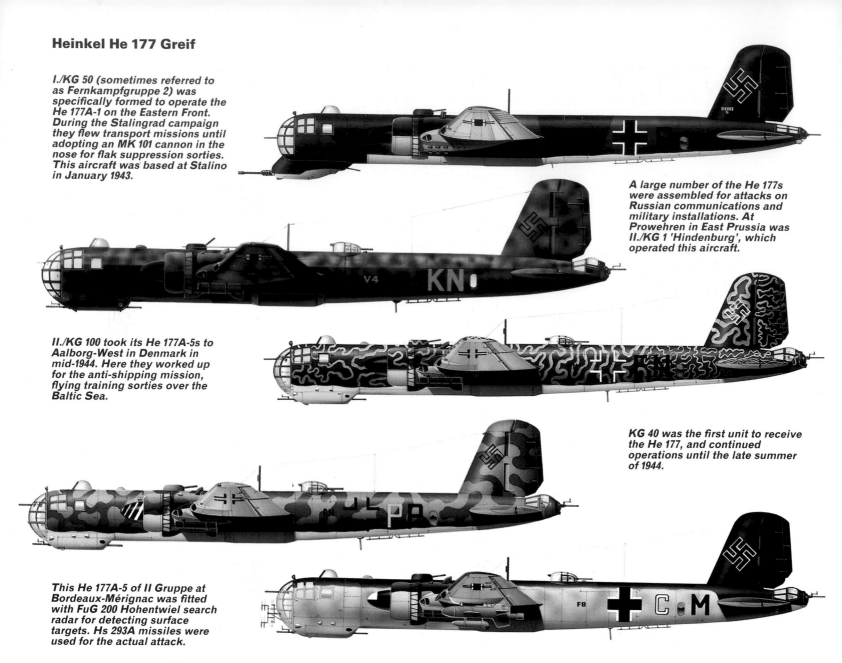

I./KG 50 (sometimes referred to as Fernkampfgruppe 2) was specifically formed to operate the He 177A-1 on the Eastern Front. During the Stalingrad campaign they flew transport missions until adopting an MK 101 cannon in the nose for flak suppression sorties. This aircraft was based at Stalino in January 1943.

A large number of the He 177s were assembled for attacks on Russian communications and military installations. At Prowehren in East Prussia was II./KG 1 'Hindenburg', which operated this aircraft.

II./KG 100 took its He 177A-5s to Aalborg-West in Denmark in mid-1944. Here they worked up for the anti-shipping mission, flying training sorties over the Baltic Sea.

KG 40 was the first unit to receive the He 177, and continued operations until the late summer of 1944.

This He 177A-5 of II Gruppe at Bordeaux-Mérignac was fitted with FuG 200 Hohentwiel search radar for detecting surface targets. Hs 293A missiles were used for the actual attack.

There were many sub-variants made in small numbers. Front-line armourers near Stalingrad – which was resupplied at great cost by a handful of He 177s used as transports – fitted 50-mm BK5 anti-tank guns under the nose. Later the He 177A-3/R5 was fited with the 75-mm gun, but this strained the structure and was altogether too powerful and only five were built. Several were flown with an electrically powered tail turret with two MG 151/20 guns, and the planned He 177A-6 was to have either this turret or one with four MG81s. The A-6, of which six were built, had a pressurised cabin, as did the A-5/R8, the latter being a single aircraft with remotely controlled barbettes in the chin and tail locations. One of the last of the numerous development protoytypes, the V38 (basically an A-5), was stripped down at the Letov factory at Prague and (it was said) prepared to carry 'the German atomic bomb'. This may have been a mere rumour, but unlike several of the later variants which deleted the front and middle bomb bays, the V38 was to have had a single gigantic bomb bay. Another unusual version was intended for destroying formations of heavy bombers. The 177 Zerstörer, three of which were produced in 1944 by conversion of bombers (believed to be A-3s), were fitted with a battery of 33 large rocket launch tubes aimed upwards, slightly ahead and slightly to the right. The idea was

that the He 177 should formate below, behind and to the left of the bombers, but Allied fighters made the idea impractical.

Last version to get into limited production, and then only in an interim form, the A-7 had a wing extended in span from 31.46 m (103 ft 2 in) to 36.6 m (120 ft). It was intended to have 2685.6-kW (3,600-hp) DB613 engines, but these were not ready. It carried extra fuel, and intensely interested the Japanese who considered building it under licence. They planned to fit four separate engines, but Heinkel's own He 277 with four separate engines never had official approval and only a string of prototypes were built mainly with DB603A engines.

The weapon most associated with Heinkel He 177 in the anti-shipping role is the Henschel Hs 293A missile. These could be carried under the wings or, as here, on a special pylon fitted to the blanked-off forward bomb bay. Releases were usually made between 10 and 14 km (6.2 and 8.7 miles) from the target.

INDEX

Note: page numbers in italics refer to illustrations